M000277938

IKTO'MI BRINGS ABOUT THE DEATH OF AN IYA

■ ■ ■ ■ ■ ■

A traditional Lakota story retold by
the Thunder Valley Lakota Language Initiative

Illustrated by Christine Nih'shaw

Ink & watercolor paint/pencils were used for the illustrations.
The text type is Times New Roman. Display type is Phosphate. Book design
copyright (c) by Riversong Studio. All rights reserved. No part of this publication may be
reproduced, stored in a retrieval system, or transmitted in any form or by any means, electronic,
mechanical, photocopying, recording, or otherwise, without written permission of the publisher.
For information regarding permission, write to:
Riversong Studio
Attn: Permissions Department,
P. O. Box 118, Grantham, NH 03753
or contact: riversongstudio@hotmail.com
(include: Permissions Department in subject line)

Distributed by Riversong Studio (c) through IngramSpark Independent Publishing.
Riversong Studio and associated logos are trademarks and/or registered
trademarks of Riversong Studio.

Riversong Studio

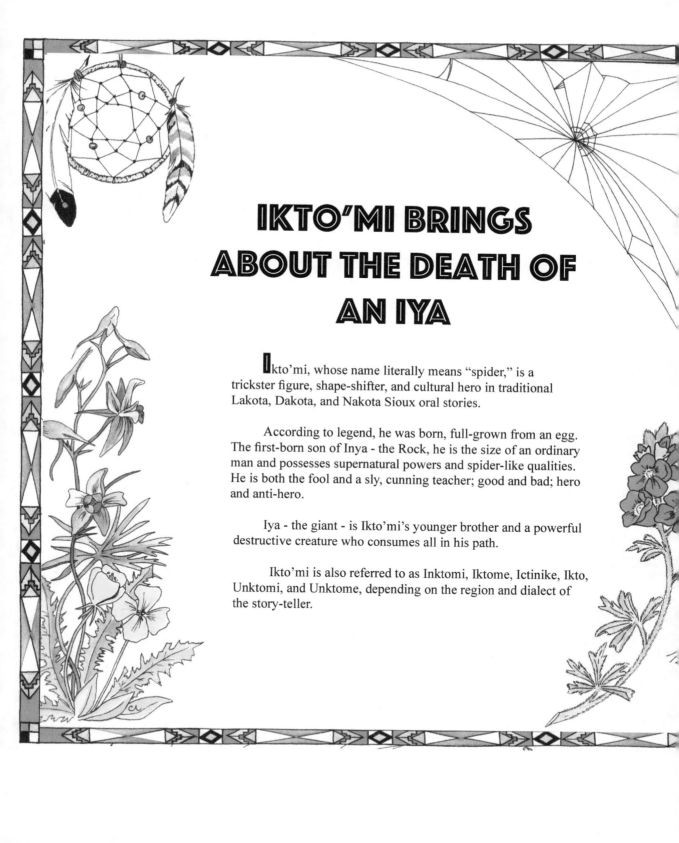

IKTO'MI BRINGS ABOUT THE DEATH OF AN IYA

Ikto'mi, whose name literally means "spider," is a trickster figure, shape-shifter, and cultural hero in traditional Lakota, Dakota, and Nakota Sioux oral stories.

According to legend, he was born, full-grown from an egg. The first-born son of Inya - the Rock, he is the size of an ordinary man and possesses supernatural powers and spider-like qualities. He is both the fool and a sly, cunning teacher; good and bad; hero and anti-hero.

Iya - the giant - is Ikto'mi's younger brother and a powerful destructive creature who consumes all in his path.

Ikto'mi is also referred to as Inktomi, Iktome, Ictinike, Ikto, Unktomi, and Unktome, depending on the region and dialect of the story-teller.

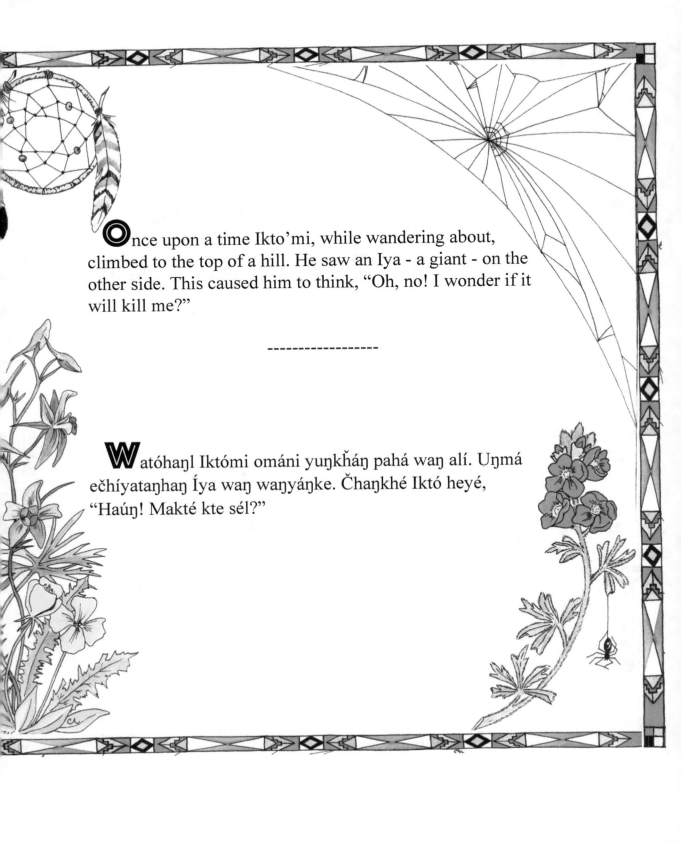

Once upon a time Ikto'mi, while wandering about, climbed to the top of a hill. He saw an Iya - a giant - on the other side. This caused him to think, "Oh, no! I wonder if it will kill me?"

Watóhaŋl Iktómi ománi yuŋkȟáŋ pahá waŋ alí. Uŋmá ečhíyataŋhaŋ Íya waŋ waŋyáŋke. Čhaŋkhé Iktó heyé, "Haúŋ! Makté kte sél?"

Despite his nervousness, Ikto'mi went up to the Iya and said, "Hey, Little Brother or Older Brother, where are you going?"

Nihíŋčiye éyaš Íya kiŋ ektá yíŋ na heyé, "Hó misúŋ, naíŋš čhiyé, tókhiya lá hwo?"

The Iya did not answer, so Ikto'mi then said, "Little Brother, or Older Brother, when were you born?"

Íya kiŋ ayúpte šni, čha Iktó heháŋl heyé, "Misúŋ, naíŋš čhiyé, tóhaŋ nitȟúŋpi hwo?" eyé.

The Iya then said, "I was born back when the heavens and Earth were made."

Yuŋkȟáŋ Íya, "Maȟpíya na makȟá kiŋ kágapi k'uŋ héhaŋ matȟúŋpe ló," eyé.

Ikto'mi answered, "Geez, you kook! It was I who created the heavens and Earth! So I am your older brother."

Čha Iktó léčhel ayúpte, "Wáŋ, witkóla! Maȟpíya na makȟá kiŋ miyé wakáǧe ló! Čha čhiyémayaye ló," eyé.

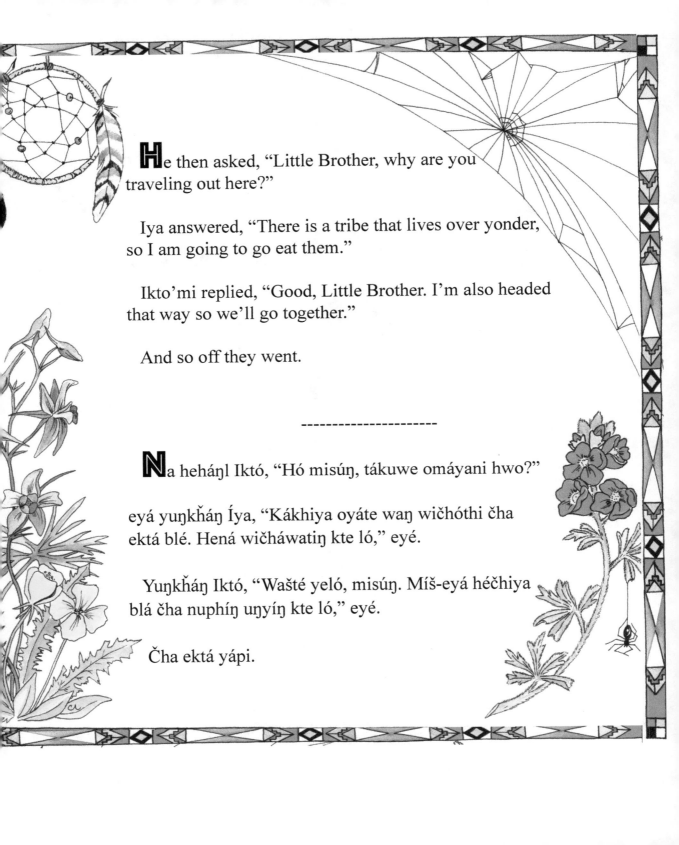

He then asked, "Little Brother, why are you traveling out here?"

Iya answered, "There is a tribe that lives over yonder, so I am going to go eat them."

Ikto'mi replied, "Good, Little Brother. I'm also headed that way so we'll go together."

And so off they went.

Na hehán̄l Iktó, "Hó misún̄, tákuwe omáyani hwo?"

eyá yuŋkȟáŋ Íya, "Kákhiya oyáte waŋ wičhóthi čha ektá blé. Hená wičháwatiŋ kte ló," eyé.

Yuŋkȟáŋ Iktó, "Wašté yeló, misún̄. Míš-eyá héčhiya blá čha nuphíŋ uŋyíŋ kte ló," eyé.

Čha ektá yápi.

As they neared the camp, Iya said he was very tired and he lay down to sleep. While he slept, Ikto peered into his open mouth and here he saw many nations of people - whom Iya had devoured - living in his belly.

Wičhóthi kiŋ khiyéla ihúŋnipi yuŋkȟáŋ Íya líla yuǧó kéyiŋ na ištíŋme. Čha Iktó í kiŋ él waŋyáŋka yuŋkȟáŋ thezí mahél oyáte óta waŋwíčhayaŋke, hená Íya tȟeb wíčhaya čha.

ere happily playing and dancing and singing, and seemed unaware of the fact that they
le Iya.

Iyókiphiya škátapi na wačhípi na lowáŋpi, na Íya thezí kiŋ imáhel úŋpi kiŋ slolyá s'eléčheča.

Now Ikto was really scared. Just then Iya awoke. Ikto'mi said to him, "Little Brother, a question. What all are you afraid of?"

Iya answered, "I am afraid of the ringing of bells, the beating of drums, the hooting of owls, and war whoops!"

Waná Iktó líla nihíŋčiye, yuŋkȟáŋ uŋgnáhela Íya kiktá. Na Iktó hekíye, "Misúŋ, takúku kȟoyákipȟ hwo?"

eyá yuŋkȟáŋ, "Ȟláȟla kaȟlápi na čháŋčheǧa apȟápi na hiŋháŋ hotȟúŋpi naháŋ akíš'api kiŋ kȟowákipȟe ló,"

eyé.

Ikto'mi replied, "Gee, Little Brother, I'm afraid of all those things too!"

Then he said, "Okay, Little Brother, stay here. I'll walk to the camp and go as far as the center tipi and then I will return here. After that we can both go and eat up all the people."

Yuŋkȟáŋ Iktó, "Wáŋ misúŋ, hená iyúha míš-eyá kȟowákipȟe ló," eyé.

"Oháŋ, misúŋ, lél yaŋká yo. Wičhóthi ekta mníŋ na thípi waŋ čhokáta hé kiŋ hé ektá waí na waglíhuŋni kte ló.
Na heháŋl nuphíŋ ektá uŋyíŋ na oyáte kiŋ iyúha wičhúŋyutiŋ kte ló," eyé. Čha Íya "Oháŋ!" eyíŋ na akhé ištíŋme.

At that point, Ikto'mi ran to the camp and began to call out, "People, listen up! Hear what I have to say! A big, scary Iya is coming! And he told me what he is afraid of: bells and drums, owls hooting and war whooping. So hurry up and get ready!"

Ikto then told them, "And while he was sleeping, I looked into his mouth and here there was a great number of people inside him!"

Čha hetáŋhaŋ Iktó íŋyaŋkiŋ na wičhóthi ektá ihúŋni yuŋkȟáŋ líla páŋ: "Oyáte, anáǧoptaŋ po! Namáȟ'uŋ po! Íya waŋ wókȟokpȟeka čha ú weló! Na takúku kȟokípȟe kiŋ omákiyake: Ȟláȟla na čháŋčheǧa na hiŋháŋ hotȟúŋpi na akíš'api kȟokípȟa kéye ló. Čha ináȟni iglúwiŋyeya po!" eyé.

Yuŋkȟáŋ heyé: "Na ištíŋma čha í kiŋ mahél waŋbláka yuŋkȟáŋ imáhel oyáte tȟáŋka úŋpe ló," eyá čha líla ináȟni iglúwiŋyeyapi.

With this, the people really hurried with their preparations. So Ikto'mi left and returned to the place where Iya was sleeping. He woke him up to go. Then the people came ringing bells, beating drums, hooting like owls, and shouting war whoops.

Iya sat up but by then the people were charging at him. They set upon him and beat him until he died.

Hehánl Iktó iyáyiŋ na tuktél Íya kiŋ ištíŋma ȟpáye kiŋ ektá khihúŋni, na yukíkta. Uŋgnáhelaka oyáte kiŋ ȟláȟla kaȟlápi na hiŋháŋ hotȟúŋpi na čháŋčheǧa apȟápi na akíš'api.

Íya kiŋ woslá íyotake éyaš oyáte kiŋ natáŋ úpi na kat'ápi na ečhél ktépi.

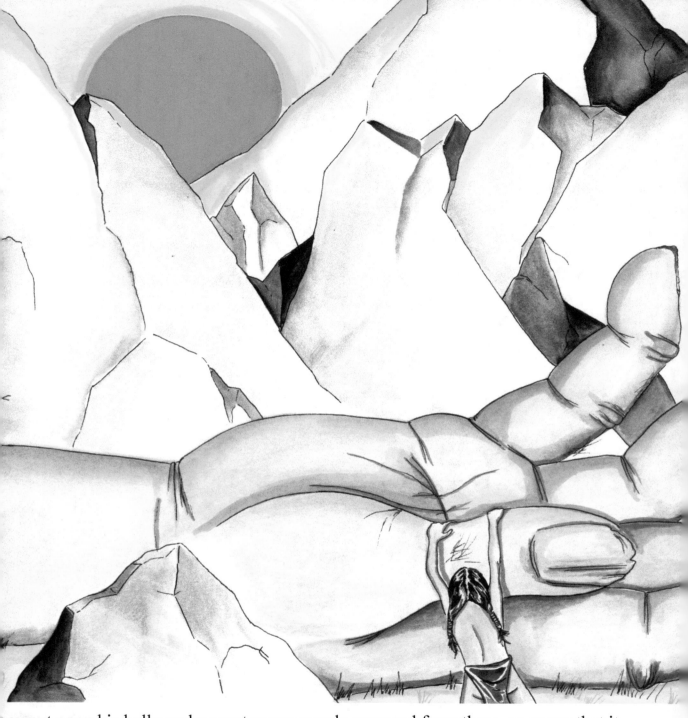

hey cut open his belly and a great many people emerged from there, so many that it
ole day for all of them to come out.

Hehánl thezí kiŋ waȟléčapi na yuǧáŋpi na oyáte líla óta Íya thezí etáŋhaŋ glináp
Aŋpétu waŋ átaya héčhuŋpi.

Then there was great rejoicing among the people and since that time, there has always been a multitude of people in the world.

Yuŋkȟáŋ líla oíyokiphi tȟáŋka, na hetáŋhaŋ oyáte líla óta yukȟáŋpi.

THUNDER VALLEY LAKOTA LANGUAGE INITIATIVE

Less than 3% of our community speak Lakota fluently. We are working to create fluent speakers of all ages, build confidence around the language, and increase Lakota educational opportunities in the community by building an all-embracing movement that incorporates our traditional language into daily life, with the high status it once occupied.

"Lakota isn't just a language we use to talk about the distant past...we can use [it] to discuss everything from biology to plate tectonics, everyday life to astrophysics. It has just as much relevance today as it did a hundred years ago."

-- Peter Hill, Director of Interpretation and Engagement

To learn more, please visit them at: www.thundervalley.org.

ABOUT THE ILLUSTRATOR

Christine Nih'shaw (Blackfeet/Onondaga Iroquois) lives in New Hampshire where she is either busy working on her next book, wandering the woods with camera-in hand, or finding any excuse to heed the call of the sea. This is her second collaboration with the Thunder Valley Lakota Language Initiative.

To learn more about Christine, her work, and upcoming events, please visit her at: www.christinenihshaw.com

inted in the USA
PSIA information can be obtained
www.ICGtesting.com
VHW010232101123
53580LV00004B/14

EARLY PRAISE FOR
Development & Deployment of Multiplayer Online Games

"By far the most comprehensive book on specifics of multiplayer games."

— **Dmitri Dain,** Managing Director @*Amaya Software*

"Finally!"

— **Boris Taratine,** Cyber Security Programme Chief Architect @*Lloyds Bank Group*

"Looking forward to read the book when it is finished."

— **Nuno Leiria,** Senior Software Engineer @*Polystream,*
formerly Core Tech Programmer @*Lionhead Studios*

*"Looking forward to read the final book. The promise is great.
Finally a book on the subject that isn't outdated or vague."*

— **Özkan Can,** formerly Backend Technical Director @*Blue Byte, A Ubisoft Studio*

"TCP is a complex beast and you know much more about it than I do. Thank God!"

— **Glenn Fiedler,** GDC speaker,
veteran of AAA multiplayer development, and UDP fanboy for life

"The colossal book you are writing… looks very promising and exciting."

— **Alessandro Alinone,** Co-Founder and CEO @*Lightstreamer*

*"The really useful and highly practical book. This book will be a
valuable addition to the library of anyone game developer."*

— **Michael Morgovsky,** Co-Founder and CTO @*Plarium*

*"I've been looking for a book like this for a decade. This will be invaluable
for teaching game devs the ins and outs of multiplayer development."*

— **Robert Zubek,** GDC speaker, Founder @*SomaSim,*
formerly Principal Software Engineer @*Zynga*

*"Even unfinished, it already is the most comprehensive reference for networking
and multiplayer game development that I have ever seen, and it is constantly
teaching me new things. An absolute must-have for the serious developer."*

— **Matt Pritchard,** AAA veteran, author, and CTO @*Forgotten Empires,*
former RTS/FPS/IoT developer @*Ensemble Studios / Valve / Disney*

'NO BUGS' HARE

Sarcastic Developer
Co-Architect of a G20 Stock Exchange
Sole Architect of a Game with 400'000 Simultaneous Players
Author of Articles in CUJ, C++ Report, and Overload

DEVELOPMENT AND DEPLOYMENT OF
MULTIPLAYER ONLINE GAMES

From Social Games to MMOFPS, with Stock Exchanges In Between

ARCHITECTURE AND PRE-DEVELOPMENT

Victorious warriors win first and then go to war,
while defeated warriors go to war first and then seek to win.

—Sun Tzu, *The Art of War*, circa 500 BC

In Part ARCH, we will discuss activities that need to be performed even before the coding can be started. It includes many things that need to be done, from formulating business requirements to setting up your source control and issue tracking systems, with lots of critical architectural decisions in between.

GDD, AUTHORITATIVE SERVERS, COMMUNICATIONS

The man who moves a mountain begins by carrying away small stones.

—Confucius (5th century BC), *Civilization IV* (21st century AD)

Copyright © ITHare.com Website GmbH, 2015-2017

All Rights Reserved. No part of this book may be reproduced or utilized in any form or by any means, electronic or mechanical, including photocopying, recording, or by any information storage and retrieval system, without permission in writing from the publisher.

Translated from Lapine by Sergey Ignatchenko (ITHare.com Website GmbH, ithare.com)
Cover and Interior Illustrations by Sergey Gordeev (Gordeev Animation Graphics, gagltd.eu)
Editing by Erin McKnight (Kevin Anderson & Associates, ka-writing.com)
Interior and Cover Design by A. Kate Reynolds (Kevin Anderson & Associates, ka-writing.com)

978-3-903213-05-0 – (Paperback)
978-3-903213-06-7 – (Hardcover)
978-3-903213-07-4 – (PDF)
978-3-903213-08-1 – (ePub)
978-3-903213-09-8 – (Kindle)

Published by ITHare.com Website GmbH
Hormayrgasse 7A/19
1170 Wien
Austria

CONTENTS

Chapter 3. Communications   **139**

Game-World States and Reducing Traffic

ACKNOWLEDGMENTS

Family

It is customary for authors to say thanks to the family members who have supported them during the endeavor of book writing. However, while I am infinitely grateful to my family (especially to my wife Natalia), I strongly prefer to thank them in person. To the best of my knowledge, they prefer it this way too.

Comments That Helped Shape the Book

From the beginning, this book was intended as a "crowd publishing" project. Beta chapters were published on my blog, ithare.com, as soon as they were ready (and even *before* they were ready), with an aim of receiving as many comments as possible. Overall, beta chapters from Volumes I-III got over 400 comments made by over a hundred different people. And while not all these comments were exactly useful, there were quite a few people who pointed out important not-too-clearly-explained things, forgotten-at-the-moment but good-to-mention technologies and use cases, and some have also taught me certain things (yes, I have to admit that if you're looking for a book written by a divine-inspired knowing-everything oracle, you've got the wrong one).

Here goes an alphabetical list of people who have made important comments during beta testing of the book and who were also kind enough to provide their details to be included:

B

Michael Bartnett from New York, United States
Robert Basler from Vancouver, Canada
Marcos Bracco from La Plata, Argentina

C

Jean-Michaël Celerier from Bordeaux, France

Oded Coster from London, United Kingdom

D

Przemysław Danieluk from Poland

Bill Dieter from Portland, United States

Matt P. Dziubinski from Warsaw, Poland

F

Nir Friedman from New York, United States

Timothy Fries from Spring Hill, United States

I

Dmytro Ivanchykhin from Kiev, Ukraine

J

Nathan Jervis from Hamilton, Canada

Luciano José Firmino Júnior from Recife, Brazil

K

Chris Kingsley from Longmont, United States

Mario Konrad from Zurich, Switzerland

L

Ivan Lapshov from Moscow, Russia

Nuno Leiria from Lisbon, Portugal

Dmitry Ligoum from Toronto, Canada

N

Jesper Nielsen from Gråsten, Denmark

R

Nathan Robinson from Stuttgart, Germany

S

David Schroeder from Spokane, United States

Alessandro Stamatto from Porto Alegre, Brazil

Jon Stevens from Seattle, United States

T

David Turner from Leeds, United Kingdom

W

Jon "hplus" Watte

Z

Vadim Zabrodin from Novosibirsk, Russia

Robert Zubek from Chicago, United States

...and everybody else who made important comments but declined to be included in this list.

Thanks a lot, friends; your feedback was really important to make the book better.

Special Thanks to Kickstarter Backers

This book was Kickstarted and the money raised was used for professional editing and design. There aren't enough bits in the RAM of my computer to express all my gratitude to each and every one of you. The book certainly wouldn't be the same without you (and your patience has certainly been saintly). You've been a wonderful [funding] crowd—THANKS A LOT!

Here goes the "Kickstarter backers' Hall of Fame":

0-9

10tons.com

A

ABeardOnFire
Aled
ALEJOLP
Ander Amo
Andrew
AustinK
Dan Avram
David Antúnez
 (eipporko)
Guillaume A
Islam Aliev
Jonathan Adams
Jorge Moreno Aguilera
Kylie Au
Luis Armendariz
Nacho Abril
Rafael "GeekFox"
 Araujo
Scott Anderson
Sergey Annenkov
Sharad Cornejo Altuzar
Tomáš Andrle
Victor da Cruz Amaro
Wali Akande

B

Alicia Boya García
Asher Baker
Babyjeans
bmac & ingrid
botiq
Bumek
busho
Christian Bryan
ck @ bsg
Cory Bloor
D Barnard
Dan Brewer
David G. Brewington II
Emeric Barthélemy
Frank Lyder Bredland
Georg Begerow
Heiko Behrens
Hrvoje Bandov
Jasmine Bulin
Kirill Belov
Leandro Barreto
Luke Beard
Marcos Bracco
Mateus Borges
Maxim Biro
Michael Brüning
Nicholas "LB" Braden
Patrick B
Patty Beauregard
Richard Baister
Robert Brackenridge
Stephen Bentley
Tomas Bilek
Vincent Bilodeau
Vincent Blansaer
Vladan Bato

C

Ben Carruthers
Bulent Coskun
caj
camfurt
Catprog
Charlie
Chris Cox
Christian Corsano
ChuangTseu
Dmitry Chuev
Edward Carmack
Ian Compton
Javier Calvo
Laurent CETIN
Liam Costello
Milo Casagrande
Morrison Cole
Neil Coles
Ozkan Can
P. Chaintreuil
Paul Caristino
Sam Coleman
Shawn Cassar
Stuart Cassidy

D

Andreas Drewke
Andy Dunn
Chris Downs
Ciaran Deasy

Cristián Donoso

dajomu

Dan Dudley

Daniel Dimitroff

Daniele Dionisi
  (Danguru)

dd33

Digital Confectioners

Dooks Dizzo

Jamie Dexter

Jean-Michel Deruty

Julien Dumétier

Justin Drury

Ken Drycksback

Kyle Dean

Matthew DeLucas

Matthew Douglass

Michael Dwan

Niclas Darville

Oliver Daff

Pat Duquette

Petar Dobrev

Tim Drury

E

Craig Edwards

David Erosa Garcia

Egon

empty2fill

Eric Espie

Ethereal World

Geoff Evans

Jon Edwards

Matthew Erickson

Michael Ellwood

Ryan Evans

Sebastian Eggers

Semih Energin

Vlad Engelgardt

E

Антон Евангелатов

F

Andrew Fox

Bruno V. Fernandes

Bryce Fite

Eric Faehnrich

Glenn Fiedler

Mad William Flint

Matthew Fritz

Rosco Farrell

Rui Ferreira

Rui Figueira

Steve "Tech-Imp"
  Fernandez

Thomas Frase

Zach Fetters

G

Arvid Gerstmann

Bart Grantham

Bernardo A. Gonzalez
  (Jasnis)

David Garcia
  (le-dragon-dev)

Dorian George

Evan M. and Nathan G.

Gerardo

Gero Gerber

giant_teapot

Jason Gassel

Jonathan Gough

Maxime Guillem

Philip Gurevich

Risnoddlas Grytarbiff

Stu 'BloodyCactus'
  George

Szymon Gatner

Tadej Gregorcic

Tim Goshinski

H

Adam Hill

Alex Holzinger

Alun Hickery

Andrew Handley

Andrew Holmes

Carlos Hernando

David Hontecillas

Dermot Hannan

Garry Hornbuckle

Johannes Hartenstein

Jez Higgins, JezUK Ltd

Jurie Horneman

Lars Hamre

Martin S. Hehl

Michael Hoyt

P. Halonen

Remko van Haften

Sean Hernandez

Shawn H.

Tom Hawtin
Tom Haygarth
Wolfgang Haupt

I

Christopher Igoe
Dmytro Ivanchykhin
Ikrima
Improbable
Martin Ivanov
Ray Ion

J

Corinna Jaschek
Greg Jandl
JackyWongCW
Jaewon Jung
Jerry Jonsson
Jesper Geertsen Jonsson
Jonathan Johnson
JOS
Karl Jensen
Kenneth Jørgensen
Luciano Jose Firmino
  Junior
Rainer Jenning
Rajnesh Jindel
Randolpho de Santana
  Juliao
Robert Janeczek
Thomas Sebastian
  Jensen
Wilmot-Albertini
  Jordan

K

Allan Kelly
Andrew Koenen
Andreas Koenig
Bernhard Kaufmann
Bronek Kozicki
Chris Kingsley
Daniel Kirchen
DM Klein
Dongseob Kim
Ivan Kravets
Joona-Pekka Kokko
Kristofer Knoll
Kwaki3
Lars-Göran Karlstedt
Malte Krüger
Marko Kevac
Matej Kormuth
Mike Kasprzak
Patrick Kulling
Pawel Kurdybacha
Pit Kleyersburg
Roope Kangas
Shay Krainer
Vladimir "ai_enabled"
  Kozlov
Wesley Kerr

L

Andrew Lee
Andrew Lombardi
Antony Lloyd
Callum Lawson
César Laso

Damien Lebreuilly
Daniel Ludwig
David Latham
Evgenii Loikov
Game L10N,
  localizedirect.com
Jamie Law
Jan-Christoph
  Lohmann
Javi Lavandeira
Jeffrey Lim
Johan Lohmander
Justin LeFebvre
Justin Liew
KC Lee
LordHog
Mikola Lysenko
Mun Kew Leong
Richard Locsin
Wilhansen Li

M

Adam Mikolaj
Altay Murat
Andrew McVeigh
Angel Leigh McCoy
Benoit Maillot
Bradley Macomber
Brett Morgan
Brian Marshall
Chris Murphy
Dan "DMac"
  MacDonald
Fernando Matarrubia

Gordon Moyes
Heather Martin
Hervé MATYSIAK
Jeroen Meulemeester
Johan Munkestam
John McDole
Kevin McCabe
Marcus Milne
Martin Moene
Mārtiņš Možeiko
Matthew Ma
Matthew Mckenzie
MaxHouYeah
Maximilian Mellhage
Michael Mayr
Michal
Michal Mach
Mike
mp3tobi
Oddur Magnusson
Richard Matthias
Richard Maxwell
Ronald McCormick
Rory Marquis
Seamus Moffat
Seth J. Morabito
Shawn MacFarland
Stefan Moschinski
Thijs Miedema
Tobi Müller
Troy McAnally
Umar Mustafa
Vlad Micu

N

André Pacheco Neves
Andrey Naumenko
Dan Nolan
Ivan Nikitin
J. Djamahl Nolen
Marek Niepiekło
Nischo
NOM
Simon Nicholass
Tivadar György Nagy
Tran Dang Nguyen

O

Albert Olivera
Andreas Oehlke
Bradley O'Hearne
Carsten Orthbandt
David Osborne
Jason Olsan
Jonathan Ogle-
 Barrington
Lukas Obermann
Magnus Osterlind
OakFusion.pl
Ryan Olds

Ø

Knut Ørland

P

Alex Price
Alexander Popov
Alexandru Pana
Andreas Pfau
Behrouz Poustchi
Ben Perez
David Pong
Donald Plummer
Eric Pederson
 (sourcedelica)
James Pelster
Jamie Plenderleith
Jason Pecho
Lloyd Pearson
Matt Pritchard
Maxxx Power
Michael Powers
Pablo Díaz Pumariño
paste0x78
Patrick Palmer
Penda
Peter Petermann
Phil Peron
Pindwin
PragTob
Rafael Pasquay
Scott Posch
Sylvain P.
Tim Plummer
Tomaso Pye
Tony P
Wayne Pearson
Yevgeniy Pinskiy

Q

Andrew Quinn

R

Agata Ratz

Anton Rogov

Chris Rice

Clay Ravin

Darren Ranalli

Denis Reviakin

Francois Rouaix

Guillermo Gijon Robas

James Rowbotham

Juan Rufes

Juanma Reyes

Maxime Raoust

Michael A. Ryan

Pasha Riger

Peter Richards

RagManX

Ralph Reichart

Rdslw

Really Good TV

reopucino

Reuben R

Ron Roff

RyanH

Scout Rigney

Valentinas Rimeika

Zeno Rawling

S

Albert Smith II

Brian Sheriff

Christian Funder
  Sommerlund

Christopher Sierra

Dan Sosnowski

David Salz

David Sena

David Sheldon

Deovandski Skibinski

Dylan "PoundCat" Spry

Enrico Speranza

Eric Schwarzkopf

Erik Sixt

Ewan Stanley

Fabian Schaffert

Fredrik Stromberg

Geoff Schemmel

Håkan Ståby

Harvinder Sawhney

http://sava.ninja

Jeff Slutter

Joey "TML" Smith

Jonathan Soryu

Kevin Salvesen

Kishimoto Studios

Kostiantyn
  Shchepanovskyi

Kurt "Thunderheart"
  Stangl

Lennart Steinke

Marcin Slezak

Mario Sangiorgio

Michael Savage

Michael Schuler

Michel Simatic

Morgan Shockey

Moriel Schottlender

Nathanael See

Philip Stein

Raphael Salomon

René Schmidt

Richard Searle

Robert Singletary

Rory Starks

Ross Smith

sassembla

SemanticSiv

Sergio Santana Ceballos

SleepyRabbit-David

Spielraum Tirol

Sproing Interactive
  Media

Stef

Tania Samsonova

Tengiz Sharafiev

Tero Särkkä

Todd Showalter

Victor Savkov

Wilson Silva

Winston Joseph Smith

Zsolt Somogyi

Ś

Grzegorz Świt

T

Barrie Tingle

Chris Threlfo

Daniel Espino Timón

Diogo Teixeira

Garai Tamás, Gerendás
  András

James Tatum
Julian Tith
Matt Toegel
Nicolas Tittley
Rajan Tande
Rodney J. Thomas
Ryszard Tarajkowski
Steven Turek
Test_nuke
Theo
Tim Tillotson
Troxbanv
tuntematon
Wei Tchao

U

uonyx
Urs

V

Alex Vaillancourt
Carson V
Felton Vaughn
Sam Velasquez
Silvo Vaisanen

Thomas Viktil
Yoann Le Verger

W

Andre Weissflog
Andres Weber
Ashley Williams
Bret Wright
Chris Wine
Christian Weiss
Daniel Wippermann
David Wyand
Dominik Wit
Garrick Joshua
   Williams
James Wright
Jate Wittayabundit
Jonathan Watson
Jorik van der Werf
Kevin Waldock
Lee Wasilenko
Mike Watkins
Nicholas Wymyczak
Nick Waanders
Peter Wolf

Richard Williams
Simon Withington
Wanderer
wcampos
WeirdBeard Games
Windbringer

X

Xenide
Xlxla
Xywzel

Y

Jason Young
Kyungho Yun
Rouzbeh Youssefi
Tim Yates
Weikie Yeh

Z

George Zakharov
Maxim Zaks
Mike Zbleka
Z-Software
Zara

*...and all those backers who decided
to remain anonymous.*

P.S. This is not the last book I'm going to launch on Kickstarter, so...stay tuned!

THE STORY BEHIND THIS BOOK

- Once upon a time…
- boy, how do they come up with these catchy openings?
   —Garfield the cat

Once upon a time, in the rabbit warren of Bunnylore, there lived a young software developer bunny.

And he was *that much* obsessed with writing bug-free software[1] that pretty soon he got the nickname of No Bugs.

He quickly got into an architect's shoes,[2] and in this capacity he took part in quite a few projects, including seemingly different ones such as:

    a.   A stock exchange for a G20 country, and

    b.   A game handling hundreds of thousands of simultaneous players (and making hundreds of millions of dollars in the process).

At some point in his career, he started to write articles for industry journals, and then started a software development blog. Everything was going his way until on a {sunny|rainy|gloomy|pick your poison} day, he opened a book on multiplayer game development and found as many as sixteen different mistakes (and thirty-nine instances of these mistakes) on just two leaves [Hare].

From this point on, he started to research other books about multiplayer game development, and found that there are only two related books that are worth opening.[3]

That was when No Bugs started to think about writing his own book about development and deployment of multiplayer online games.

But he'll do a better job describing it himself.

---

1   No Bugs: Obsessive-Compulsive Wannabe-Perfectionist. Guilty as charged.

2   No Bugs: More like "chief cook and bottle washer," if you ask me.

3   No Bugs: since that time, the third such book has been published (see *Recommended Reading* section below for all three). TBH, with the field to be covered being *that* large, it didn't change the landscape much.

THE HARE AND THE PEOPLE BEHIND...

 **About the Author:** The author of this book is a No Bugs Hare from the warren of Bunnylore. He is known for being a columnist for *Overload Journal* (ISSN 1354-3172) and for his significant contributions to the software development blog ithare.com. As No Bugs is a rabbit with a mother tongue of Lapine, he needed somebody to translate the book into human language. And of course, as the book is highly technical, to translate technical details with the highest possible fidelity, he needed a translator with substantial software development experience.

 **About the Translator:** This book has been translated from Lapine by Sergey Ignatchenko, a software architect since 1996. He is known for writing for industry journals since 1998, with his articles appearing in *CUJ*, *Overload*, *C++ Report*, and *(IN)SECURE Magazine*. His knowledge of Lapine is quite extensive, and he routinely translates the column No Bugs writes for *Overload*. During Sergey's software architecting career, he has led quite a few projects, including as a co-architect of a stock exchange for a G20 country (the same software has been used by stock exchanges of several other countries), and as a sole original architect of a major gaming site (with hundreds of thousands of simultaneous players, billions of database transactions per year, and that processes hundreds of millions of dollars per year). As a kind of paid hobby, he also invents things: he's an author and co-author of about a dozen of patents (unfortunately, owned by his respective employers).

 **About the Illustrator:** Illustrations for this book are by Sergey Gordeev, currently from gagltd.eu. He is a professional animator with a dozen awards from various animation festivals, and is best known for directing a few animated Mr. Bean episodes.

About the Editor: Erin McKnight is an internationally award-winning independent publisher and the editor of multiple books of fiction and non-fiction from both emerging and eminent writers. She was born in Scotland, raised in South Africa, and now resides in Dallas—though this is her first time working with the Lapine language.

ON REAL-WORLD EXPERIENCES

All happy families are alike; each unhappy family is unhappy in its own way.

—Leo Tolstoy, *Anna Karenina*

As mentioned above, the trigger for writing this book was realizing the pitiful state of MOG-related books. However, there was another experience that served as additional motivation to write this book.

Quite a few times, when speaking to a senior dev/architect/CTO of some gamedev company (or more generally, any company that develops highly interactive distributed systems), I've been included in a dialogue along the following lines:

- How are you guys doing this?
- Psssst! I am ashamed to admit that we're doing it against each and every book out there, and doing this, this, and this...
<pause>
- Well, we're doing it exactly the same way.

This basically means two things:

► There *are* MOG practices out there that *do* work for more than one game.

   ▪ Probably, there are even practices that can be seen as "best practices" for *many* games out there (stopping short of saying that all successful projects are alike).

► OTOH, *lots* of these practices are not described anywhere (never mind "described in one single place"), so each team of multiplayer gamedevs needs to re-invent them themselves. <ouch! />

This is where *Development and Deployment of Multiplayer Online Games* tries to come in. Overall,

> this book is an attempt to summarize a body of knowledge that is known in the industry, but is rarely published, let alone published together.

In other words, this book (taken as a complete nine volumes) intends to cover most of the issues related to architecting, developing, and deploying an MOG (with a few exceptions as outlined below).

Of course, given the scale of this (probably overambitious) task, I will almost certainly forget quite a few things. Still, I will try to do my best.

WHAT IS THIS BOOK ABOUT?

Whenever you look at a book for the first time, you naturally have two questions: "What is this book about?" and "Is this book for me?" Let's start with answering the first one.

Genres: From Social Games to MMOFPS, with Stock Exchanges In Between

First, let's consider the spectrum of the game genres where experiences and techniques shared within this book may be relevant. And surprisingly, all the multiplayer games, from social ones on one side of the spectrum to MMOFPS on the other, have a lot in common and, as a result, this book aims to cover *all of them*.[4]

---

4   Exactly as it says on the tin.

ISO/OSI Model

The Open Systems Interconnection model (OSI model) is a conceptual model that characterizes and standardizes the communication functions of a telecommunication or computing system without regard to their underlying internal structure and technology.

—Wikipedia

Looking at it from 30,000 feet, all MOGs use the Internet, and the Internet is all about packets being exchanged (with each of the packets at risk of being lost). Even if we consider higher-level abstractions (moving from considering IP packets, which correspond to L3 in ISO/OSI network model, to L4), we'll see that there are basically only two L4 protocols we can realistically use for gaming purposes and these are UDP and TCP. Moreover, as we'll see in Volume IV's chapter on Network Programming, even when using TCP for interactive purposes, there is a need to keep in mind those underlying IP packets and their potential loss.

Server-Side also has quite a few similarities across the genres. As we'll see in Volume III's chapter on Server-Side Architecture, even web-based architectures (which are typical for social games) are not *that* drastically different from "classical" simulation-oriented servers as it might seem on first glance. And when speaking about persistence (as discussed in Volume III and in more detail in Vol. VI's chapter on Databases), well, all the MOGs need their DBs,[5] and these DBs (once again) tend to be quite similar across the board. And I didn't even start to mention such common-for-most-of-the-games topics as authoritative servers, payments, random number generation, CRM (as in Customer Relation Management), organizing your Servers within the data-center, DDoS protection, and so on.

Of course, there will be variations between different genres. In particular, Clients are going to be rather different, though even with Clients certain concepts will apply more or less consistently; and, of course, latency requirements will also be very different, causing quite a few complications-necessary-for-MMOFPS to be pointless for social games. Of course, I'll try to pinpoint these differences wherever I can spot them; however, be sure to Bring Your Own Salt when applying advice from this book to your specific game (see the *BYOS As in, "Bring Your Own Salt"* section below). Using advice that is generally-good-but-inapplicable-to-your-specific-case is a Big Fat Problem™ in software development in general (and, unfortunately, games are no exception).

---

5   Or a reasonable facsimile.

Stock Exchanges Are Games.
Even Worse, They're Betting Games

> Anybody who plays the stock market not as an insider
> is like a man buying cows in the moonlight.
> —Daniel Drew

By this point, I have hopefully managed to convince you that all multiplayer games have a lot in common. However, you may still wonder how come stock exchanges also qualify as games.

Games (especially those that have any association with betting something and receiving a reward) tend to have a significant social stigma attached to them. In other words, if you tell somebody that you're playing poker (or betting on an outcome of sports) as a way of paying your bills, chances are you won't be invited to that all-important BBQ held by your neighbors (especially those with well-respected jobs as office clerks and used-car salesmen; uni professors are usually much more accommodating in this regard). If you tell them that you're getting your income from eSports you may be fine, but only so long as they don't realize that this means playing *video games* ("You're making your living doing *what*?").

Chances are you won't be invited anymore to that all-important BBQ held by your neighbors (especially those with well-respected jobs as receptionists and used-car salesmen; uni professors are usually much more accommodating in this regard).

On the other hand, playing the stock exchange is traditionally viewed differently: it is a Very Respectable Occupation™. However, let me tell you—

> *There is no substantial difference between the stock exchange and games. Even worse, there is no substantial difference between the stock exchange and betting.*

Of course, people who are playing the stock market (and especially those who are making money from it in other ways), will tell you lots of interesting stories explaining why the stock market is so different.

Still, the sad truth is that gambling, (sports) betting, and the stock exchange all include the following:

▶ You wager some money (or the equivalent), expecting to win

▶ There is *something* pretty much beyond your control happening (ranging from the cards dealt to the company issuing a profit warning to "Team A beats Team B" in between)

■ There *may* be some skill involved that affects the outcome, from estimating odds in a poker hand to predicting how the horses will run or teams will play or stocks will perform; however, luck is still a very significant contributor to the end result

▶ You either win or lose[6] depending on that something-beyond-your-control

After writing it down, I hope it is obvious that all of the {blackjack|poker| betting|stock exchanges} fit firmly in this description. If you still have doubts, you can take a look at [31 U.S. Code § 5362 – Definitions], which is as official as it gets; we can easily see that *they needed to exclude stock exchanges (as "any activity governed by the securities laws") explicitly(!) from the definition of "bet or wager."*

If not for this explicit exclusion, any stock exchange would qualify as a "bet or wager." I rest my case.[7]

From a technical standpoint (and this is what's important for the purposes of this book),

If not for this explicit exclusion, any stock exchange would qualify as a "bet or wager."

> *There are very few differences between stock exchanges and other types of games.[8]*
> *As I've worked both on a stock exchange and a not-so-small game platform, I can personally attest to this similarity.*

---

6 Usually, lose.

7 BTW, I do agree that investment is different from gaming, but playing and investing are two different things; moreover, making a living out of *investment* is not feasible unless you happen to be the only heir of a really rich uncle.

8 Except for certain security considerations.

In turn, it means that a good book covering MOGs will cover most of the technicalities that apply to stock exchanges purely as a side effect. And as I hope this book is going to be good, well, it should also achieve it.

On Interactive Distributed Systems in General

If going beyond games and stock exchanges—given the number and scope of the systems I've seen and heard of—I am prepared to be audacious and generalize my experience beyond those fields that I've tried myself, saying that—

> Pretty much **any** interactive distributed system, at least one that uses in-memory states, is similar to a game.

In other words: if your system can live with its state being DB-only, it can be built using usual stateless middleware; however, at the very moment when you need an in-memory state that goes beyond the cache, you're very much in the realm covered by this book.

Moreover, even for some of those interactive distributed systems that are currently storing their state within DB only, some of the techniques described in this book (in particular, Vol. III's chapter on Server-Side Architecture and Vol. VI's chapter on Databases) have been seen to perform and scale much better than the traditional approach of throw-everything-at-DB-and-hope-it-will-cope; as we'll see, it is perfectly feasible to handle 100 billion real-world OLTP transactions per year (writing ~1 trillion rows per year) from a single pretty standard 4-Socket/4-rack-Units (4S/4U) Server box (!).

First, in this book, we won't try to answer questions such as "What should your game be about?" or "How should your game look?" or "What should be your game mechanics?" or "How to make money out of your game?"; these are all-important business questions that you need to answer yourself.

Topics: All But Gameplay/ AI/Physics/Monetization/3D

Game development and deployment is a huge task, so it is important to realize what exactly we want to cover. This book is very ambitious in this regard: by the end of Volume IX, it aims to cover all the aspects of development and deployment for a multiplayer game, though with two (though all-important) exceptions.

First, in this book, we won't try to answer questions such as "What should your game be about?" or "How should your game look?" or "What should be your game mechanics?" or "How to make money out of your game?"; these are all-important business questions that you need to answer yourself.

When starting development, you should know exactly how you want your game to be played, how you want it to look, how your AI or Physics (if applicable) will work, and how you're going to monetize it.[9] As a result, these questions are completely beyond the scope of this book.[10]

The second all-important topic that did not really make it into this book is 3D graphics. While there is a chapter on Graphics in Vol. V, I shall tell you upfront that at 20,000+ words, it is still *extremely* sketchy and provides only a *very* cursory overview of graphics (especially when it comes to 3D). Unfortunately, modern 3D mechanics is just way too complicated (and way too large) to fit into this book. Fortunately, 3D is a topic that is already covered in nauseating detail in quite a few very good books (see, for example, the list of suggested literature in the *Recommended Reading* section below).

The good news is that as soon as you have answers to all the business questions above, and have learned your graphics, this book, taken as all nine volumes, has got you covered.[11] We'll discuss pretty much everything you will need to release your game and keep it running, from overall architecture to deployment and post-deployment issues.

---

9   Of course, your vision will change as development goes on, but at any point you should have a clear vision of "what you want to achieve."

10   Note that while the business question of monetization is not covered, a technical question of payment methods is covered to the extent possible.

11   At least, I honestly hope so.

In other words, while I'm not about to answer the question *What* do you want to do, I will try to answer *How*-to-do-whatever-you-want-to-do in as much detail as I can fit into nine volumes.[12]

Game Engines: DIY vs. Re-Use vs. 3rd-Party

From our current 30,000-feet point of view, whatever you'll be doing to develop your MOG will more or less fit into one of the following patterns:

The first option (let's name it *Option DIY*) is to do the whole thing yourself, effectively making a DIY game engine. This is what I generally prefer to deal with,[13] but admittedly it is not always feasible. Especially if 3D is involved, you'll need to spend enormous effort on developing such an engine—including not only the engine itself, but also a toolchain for game designers and 3D artists—and the latter is a *huge* amount of work.

The second option (let's name it *Option Re-Use*) is undoubtedly of much interest for AAA development teams. It is about taking an existing millions-lines-of-code 3D/game engine (with all the tools etc.) and building an MOG game engine around it. That is, all the existing graphics, scripts, level editors, etc. should remain the same, but we'll be designing the whole network layer ourselves, with the changes to existing engine being minimal.[14]

The third option (let's name it *Option 3rd-party*) is traditionally attractive for indie developers. It is about taking an existing 3rd-party game-engine-with-network-support (such as Unity or UE) and using it to develop your game. The technical difference from *Option Re-Use* is that not only is the 3D/game-logic engine reused, but all the network layer is also a 3rd-party one.

In this book, we'll discuss all these development scenarios. While most of the discussion will revolve around *Option DIY* and *Option Re-Use* (both implying that we're doing network-related stuff ourselves), in Volume II we will have a separate chapter, dedicated to the question of "How to use Unity

While I'm not about to answer the question What do you want to do, I will try to answer How-to-do-whatever-you-want-to-do.

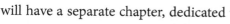

12   As noted above; unfortunately, 3D didn't fit.

13   And sometimes can even find such projects.

14   Note that in any case, there will be *at least some* changes. For example, questions such as "what we should do with a player in a MMORPG when she gets disconnected" clearly belongs to the game designer's zone of responsibility. On the positive side, the number of such exposures-of-network-stuff to game designers can and should be minimized.

5, Unreal Engine 4, or Lumberyard for an MOG" (and yes, you still *do* need to understand how the engine works with networking before committing to using it).

That's all that matters for now; we'll discuss pro and contra arguments for DIY over re-use (and more importantly, *what* to DIY and *what* to re-use) in Vol. II.

IS THIS BOOK FOR YOU?

After describing the question of "What is this book about?" let's proceed with the second all-important question, "Is this book for You?"

CD *not* included

The road to launching your own MOG in a way that scales (and to getting rich as a nice-to-have side effect) is anything but easy, and it is important to realize it *well before* you undertake the effort of developing your own MOG.

First, let's briefly warn some potential readers who may be otherwise frustrated.

I have to admit that this book is not one of those "how to get rich!" books. Moreover, it is not even one of those "how to copy-paste your game engine to get rich!" books. The road to launching your own multiplayer online game in a way that scales (and to getting rich in the process as a nice-to-have side effect) is anything but easy, and it is important to realize it *well before* you undertake the effort of developing your own MOG.

As a logical result of *not* being a book to copy-paste your game engine from, this book does not include any CD, and neither does it include any code for a ready-to-use MOG engine. There are, of course, occasional code snippets here and there, but they're intended to illustrate the points in the text and have *absolutely nothing to do* with a ready-to-use game engine that you can use as a starting point and modify later.

There are several reasons why I am not trying to make such a ready-to-use game engine, but the main one is that trying to do so would restrict discussion to a very limited subset of easy-to-illustrate items, which in turn would tremendously narrow the scope of the book.[15]

---

15   Or would force me to write MOG-engine-which-covers-everything-out-there, and even I am not that audacious.

"Nothing About Everything"

From a certain point of view, all programming books can be divided into "books that tell everything about nothing" and "books that tell nothing about everything." The former are *very* specific, but this universally comes at a cost of narrowing the scope to solving one *very* specific problem, with anything beyond this narrowly defined problem going out the window. These books are often useful, but often their use is limited to beginners for use as a learning project.

The latter type of book, the kind that tells "nothing about everything," is trying to generalize as much as possible, at the cost of not going into implementation details at each and every corner. Usually, such books are of little use for learn-by-example, but can help seasoned developers progress much further by explaining not "how to do low-level things," but rather "how to combine those low-level things into a larger picture, and how to balance them within that larger picture to get the desired result." And when trying to balance things, usually the best (and maybe the only viable) way to do it is to explain it in terms of relevant real-world experiences.

The latter type of book, the kind that tells "nothing about everything," is trying to generalize as much as possible at the cost of not going into implementation details at each and every corner.

Of course, in general, the division between these book types is not that clear, and there are some books in the gray area between these two types, but this book belongs firmly in the "nothing about everything" camp. It correlates well with not having a CD (as mentioned above), and with being oriented toward intermediate developers and up (as mentioned below).

Prerequisite: Intermediate+

This book is targeted toward at-least-somewhat-experienced developers (or, in other words, it is *not* a "how to develop your first program" book with IDE screenshots and copy-paste examples). If your game project is your very first programming project, you're likely to have difficulty understanding this book.[16]

If your game project is your very first programming project, you're likely to have difficulty understanding this book

---

16   Feel free to read the book in this case, but don't complain if it turns out to be too difficult.

I would even go so far as to say that—

> *The target audience for this book is from those intermediate developers who want to progress into senior ones, and goes all the way up to CTOs and architects.*

In particular, there will be no explanation of what event-driven programming is about, what the difference is between optimistic locking and pessimistic locking, why you need a source control system, and so on. Instead, there will be discussions on how *the concept of futures* fits into event-driven programming, when the use of optimistic locking *makes sense for games*, and how to use source control *in the presence of unmergeable files*.

On the other hand, this book doesn't rely on in-depth knowledge in any specific area. To read and understand this book, you don't need to be a network guru who knows every tiny detail of RFC 791 by heart; neither do you need to have hands-on experience with shaders and/or CUDA; even less do I expect you to be a C++ wizard who is capable of writing an arbitrary Turing-complete program in templates, or a DB/2 expert who can predict how execution plan will be affected by adding "1=0" to "WHERE" clauses, or an admin guru able to configure BGP-based DDoS protection without consulting any documentation (BTW, to be honest, these things are beyond my own capabilities too).

Of course, 3D graphics experience may be helpful for 3D MOGs, and knowledge of network basics and sockets won't hurt, but whenever discussing the issues that go beyond "things that every intermediate-level developer out there should know anyway," I will try to provide pointers "where to read about this specific stuff if you happen to have no idea about it."

And last, but certainly not least —

> *Even if you're an experienced developer but have worked on neither single-player 3D games nor on multiplayer games, it would be unwise to start with a multiplayer 3D game.*

Both 3D games and multiplayer games are overwhelming subjects even if taken separately, so trying to learn them within the same development effort is likely to be catastrophic.

That being said, I am sure that going into multiplayer 3D games is possible both from the single-player 3D game side and from the non-3D multiplayer side (the latter includes social games and stock exchanges).

On LAN-Based Games and Peer-to-Peer Games

Historically, lots of multiplayer game development (especially by indie gamedevs) was concentrated on LAN-based and peer-to-peer games.

I have to admit that I am not a fan of peer-to-peer game architectures (not even of the variety that elects one of the peers to act as a temporary authoritative server). One reason is that such architectures are inherently wide open to cheaters, so as soon as your game is large enough to attract hundreds of thousands of people-who-don't-know-each-other, it is going to be hacked (for a discussion on cheating, please see Chapter 2).

As a result, this book mostly discusses things in the context of Authoritative Servers (and BTW, there is more or less a consensus in the industry that these are the way to move ahead); moreover, it assumes that the Server is controlled by your company (and not sitting at home behind NAT on an ADSL connection). Still, quite a few of the concepts described in this book apply to the peer-to-peer games, and even to LAN-based games. However, if your game is LAN-based, be careful and don't rely on *everything* I'm writing; balance of factors affecting decisions is significantly different for LAN-based games and, as a result, quite a few things can be significantly simplified when developing for LAN.

Both 3D games and multiplayer games are overwhelming subjects even if taken separately, so trying to learn them within the same development effort is likely to be catastrophic.

Recommended Reading

Programming in General

► *The Art of Computer Programming* by Donald E. Knuth (especially Volume 1)

  ▪ *Don't* try to solve all the exercises, though—that is, if you want to get to the coding before retirement.

Game Programming (Not Really Network-Related)

► *Game Programming Patterns* by Robert Nystrom

► *Game Engine Architecture* by Jason Gregory

► *Game Coding Complete* by Mike McShaffry and David "Rez" Graham

► *Game Programming Gems* series

  ▪ While the books in this series are extremely popular, a word of caution is necessary. These books consist of various articles written by various authors, and as a result quality tends to vary significantly. IMO, the quality of *Game Programming Gems* (of those parts that I am able to judge) usually varies from "pretty good" to "real gem"; this is *much* better than most of the books out there (though IMO the quality has degraded somewhat over time).

► *Game Engine Gems* series (not to be confused with *Game Programming Gems* series above)

  ▪ In the same manner as with *Game Programming Gems*, the quality of articles IMO varies from "so-so" to "real gem."

3D Programming

► *3D Game Engine Architecture: Engineering Real-Time Applications with Wild Magic* and *3D Game Engine Design: A Practical Approach to Real-Time Computer Graphics* by David H. Eberly

► *Real-Time Rendering* by Tomas Akenine-Möller, Eric Haines, Naty Hoffman

► *GPU Pro* series

Network Programming (Not Game-Related)

▶ *Unix Network Programming, Volume 1: The Sockets Networking API* by W. Richard Stevens

▶ *Honestly, you won't really need anything else in this department (except for this book, of course <wink />). Windows programming is not that different from Unix when it comes to sockets, and MSDN will be enough to figure out the differences if you run into them.*

Game Network Programming

TBH, most of the books written about network games are very poor (and, as noted above, this was the main motivation behind writing this one). However, there are some books worth mentioning:

▶ This book, of course[17]

▶ *Multiplayer Game Programming* by Joshua Glazer and Sanjay Madhav

  - While I think that descriptions of real-world stuff in this book are way too sketchy (all the Server-Side specifics discussed on the five pages within the Scalability section, and three more pages within the Security section. Gimme a break!), and I have quite a few disagreements with this book (especially in the Security section), it is still one of the very few books on the subject worth opening.

▶ *Massively Multiplayer Game Development* and *Massively Multiplayer Game Development 2* (edited by Thor Alexander)

  - Note that these two books (similar to the *Game Gems* series above) are actually a series of articles written by different authors, and quality varies *greatly* from one article to another. For the *Massively Multiplayer Game Development* series, the quality of the articles varies from "outright misleading" to "real gems." In other words: take everything from these books with a really good pinch of salt (i.e. make sure to take even more salt than for this book).

---

17 Yes, I know that being humble isn't one of my virtues.

C++

For those new to C++

- ► *C++ Primer* (5th Edition(![18])), by Stanley Lippman
- ► *Programming: Principles and Practice Using C++* (2nd Edition(!)), by Bjarne Stroustrup

For those experienced with C++,
but potentially needing an upgrade to C++11/C++14

- ► *The C++ Programming Language* (4th Edition(!)), by Bjarne Stroustrup
- ► *Effective Modern C++* by Scott Meyers

Security

- ► *Applied Cryptography* by Bruce Schneier
- ► *Security Engineering* by Ross Anderson

TBH, unless you're dealing with a stock exchange, IMO you'll need only one of these two books.

HOW TO READ THIS BOOK

Conventions

This book uses more or less traditional conventions, but there are still a few things that may require some explanation.

First, there are those pull-quotes in the margins—the ones with my face inside a circle. These are just repetitions of the same sentences that are already present in the text of the book, but that reflect my emotional feeling about them. Whenever I'm telling something, I honestly believe it is true; however, whether or not I like it is a completely different story, and I want to be able to express my feelings about the things I'm saying (and without cluttering the main text with long descriptions of these feelings).

There are those pull-quotes in the margins—the ones with my face inside a circle.

---

18   Earlier editions don't cover C++11

Then there are "wiki quotes." These are intended to introduce certain terms that are more or less well-known in some industries, but which may be completely new for some readers. I am not able to discuss these terms in-depth myself (the book is already over the top, page-wise), but am rather suggesting taking a look at them elsewhere (as always, Wikipedia and Google being the primary candidates).

Wikipedia

Wikipedia is a free online encyclopedia that aims to allow anyone to edit articles.

—Wikipedia

Code Samples

As is expected from a development book, there will be code samples included. Most of the samples in the code are in C++; however, this certainly does *not* mean that the ideas are limited to C++. On the contrary. Most of the examples (except for one C++-specific chapter in Vol. V) are intended to apply to pretty much any programming language and C++ is used as the most common programming language used for game development.[19]

Also, please note that the samples should be treated as just that, samples, to illustrate the idea. Except when speaking about it explicitly, I am not trying to teach you C++ or C++ best practices. Therefore, whenever I am facing the dilemma of "whether to make the big idea behind it more obvious, or to follow best practices," I am likely to sacrifice some of the best practices in the name of the point-at-hand being more understandable.

My Captain-Obvious Hat

With the target audience of this book being pretty broad,[20] I am bound to explain things-that-are-considered-obvious by certain groups of people (but which may still be unclear for another group). Moreover, for each and every bit in this book, there is somebody out there who knows it. So, please don't complain that "most of the stuff in this book is well-known"—it certainly is and, as noted above, the whole point of the book is to "*summarize* a body of knowledge that is known in the industry, but is rarely published."

---

19 And also the one I know the best.
20 I admit being guilty as charged regarding an attempt to reach as many people as I can.

I will try to include notices (like this one) whenever I know for sure that a certain section of the book is not interesting for a certain group of people (for example, my musings on graphics will certainly be way too obvious to 3D professionals).

As a result, please don't hit me too hard when I'm saying things that are obvious specifically to you. I can assure you that there are developers out there who don't know that specific thing (and don't rush to name those idiots, as they're likely to know some other stuff that you don't know yet[21]).

I will try to include notices whenever I know for sure that a certain section of the book is not interesting for a certain group of people (for example, my musings on graphics will certainly be way too obvious to 3D professionals). Still, it is unlikely that I've managed to mark all such places, and I apologize for any inconvenience caused by reading stuff-that-is-obvious-to-you.

Terminology

As for any wide-but-not-so-formalized field, MOG development has its share of confusing terms (and, even worse, terms that have different meanings in different sub-fields, ouch!). I am not going to argue "which terms are 'correct'" (it's all in the eye of the beholder, which makes all the arguments on terminology silly to start with). Instead (and taking into account that using the terms without understanding their meanings is even sillier), I am going to define how-I-am-going-to-use some such terms.

MMO vs MOG

The very first term that causes quite a bit of confusion is the definition of "Massively Multiplayer Online Games" (a.k.a. MMOGs and MMOs).

The point of confusion lies with those games that have tons of players, but don't have all of them within one single game world. As the games with the most players online (think CS or LoL) tend to fall in this category, it is quite an important one. In this regard, one school of logic says, "Hey, it is multi-player, it is online, and it has a massive number of players, so it is an MMO." Another school of thought (the one that happens to take over Wikipedia's

---

21 And if you already know everything under the sun, you probably should have written your own book on MOGs and spared me the effort.

article on MMOGs[22]) says that to qualify as an MMOG, it is necessary to run the whole thing within one single instance of the Game World.

As promised, I won't go into detail on terminology, just noting that to avoid any potential for confusion, I will try to avoid using the term "MMO" (except for the much better defined MMORPG and maybe MMOFPS). Which means that—

> *What we'll be discussing in this book is named Multiplayer Online Games, even when they have massive numbers of players.*

In fact, most of the time I'll assume that we're speaking about the game able to handle hundreds of thousands of simultaneous players; this is the only thing that really matters (and whether to name it MMOG or just MOG is not of that much interest).

Server

In MOG world, the term "Server" is badly overloaded, and can be used to denote several different things.

One such meaning is "server," as in "physical server box"; another is a "place where players can connect" (for example, "West-Europe Server"). However, in spite of the name, the latter is actually almost universally implemented as a bunch of physical Servers (usually residing within one Datacenter). To make things even more confusing, people often use the term "servers" for different instances of your Game World (which in turn can be pretty much anything: from an instance of a battle arena where the play occurs, to the whole instance of a complicated MMORPGs Game World).

To avoid unnecessary confusion, for the purpose of this book, let's name the physical server box a Server, and a bunch of physical servers residing within a single datacenter a Datacenter. As for "game world instances," we'll name each of the logically separated entities running on the physical server

Most of the time I'll assume that we're speaking about the game able to handle hundreds of thousands of simultaneous players; this is the only thing that really matters (and whether to name it MMOG or just MOG is not of that much interest).

---

22   Note that as of the beginning of 2017, the Wikipedia article on MMOGs violates quite a few fundamental Wikipedia policies.

box a Game Server; when speaking about more specific types of Game Server, we'll say Game World Server or Matchmaking Server, or Cashier Server, etc. Once again, it is not because "these definitions are 'right'" in any way—it is just a convention I prefer to use.

Dedicated Server

Another ongoing source of confusion with regard to MOGs is the definition of the "dedicated server." In the hosting industry, there is a very well-established understanding that it is a "server box where you have root/Administrator access"; usually such "dedicated servers" are available for rent, and the term is used to differentiate "dedicated servers" (physical boxes) from "virtual servers" (which is just a *part* of the physical box, and, in some cases, such as within the cloud, can also migrate with time from one physical box to another).

On the other hand, for MOG development, there is a very different common understanding of the term "dedicated server," which roughly means something along the lines of "instance of the game that doesn't have graphics directly attached to it" (this definition is most popular among indie gamedevs and is coming from Client-Centric Development Flow, which we'll discuss in Chapter 1).

For the purpose of this book, I'll try to avoid using the term "dedicated server" at all to avoid confusion; however, if there is an occasional slip of the tongue (or whenever I am speaking about renting Servers from ISPs), I mean the first definition (i.e. a "physical server box, usually rented from hosting ISP").

BYOS (As in, "Bring Your Own Salt")

One last thing I would like to mention before we proceed to more practical matters. There is not one single sentence in this book (or any other book for that matter) that is to be taken as an "absolute truth." In the practical world (especially in game development), for each and every "Do THIS_THING this_way" statement, there exists a counterexample illustrating that sometimes THIS_THING can (or even *should*) be done in a different (and often directly opposing) manner.

In the practical world (especially in game development), for each and every "Do THIS_THING this_way" statement, there exists a counterexample..

All advice out there has its own applicability limits, and so does any advice within this book. When I know of certain game-related scenarios where these limits are likely to be exceeded (and the advice will become inapplicable), I will try to mention it. However, it is extremely difficult to predict all the usage scenarios in a huge industry such as game development, so you should be prepared that some of the advice in this book (or any other book for that matter) is inapplicable to your game without warning.

Therefore, take everything you read (here or elsewhere) with a good pinch of salt. And as salt is not included with the book, you'll need to bring your own. In more practical terms—

> *For each and every decision you make based on advice in this book, ask yourself:*
> **Does This Advice Really Apply to My Specific Case?**

Bibliography

2006. *31 U.S. Code § 5362 - Definitions.*
https://www.law.cornell.edu/uscode/text/31/5362.

Hare, 'No Bugs'. 2015. *How many mistakes can fit into 100 lines of book tutorial code.* http://ithare.com/how-many-mistakes-can-fit-into-100-lines-of-book-tutorial-code-part-1/.

CHAPTER 1.

GAME-DESIGN DOCUMENT FROM AN MOG PERSPECTIVE

So, you have a Great Idea for your Next Big Thing™ multiplayer online game, and know every detail about its upcoming gameplay, physics, and graphics. Now the only tiny thing you need to do is program it.

Unfortunately for you (and fortunately for me as an architect and the author of this book <wink />), development and subsequent deployment for a multiplayer game is not that simple. There are many details you need to take into account to have your game released, to be able to cope with millions of simultaneous players having very different last-mile connections, and to make the game work with 0.01% unplanned downtime while being able to add new game features twice a month.

YOUR GAME AS YOUR BABY

You don't "make" a violin. It is barrels and benches which are "made."

And violins—just like bread, grapes, and children—are born and raised.

—Nicola Amati character from *Visit to Minotaur*

A game being developed is pretty much like your baby. It will go through all the stages that are typical of development, from conception to infancy and then to toddlerhood. While development of your game certainly doesn't stop at that point, in this book we won't discuss how to raise your game beyond toddlerhood; child and teen issues (both with games and real children) are too often of a psychological nature and are beyond the mostly physical issues we're about to discuss.

"You," as used throughout this book, actually means "parent of your game baby." "You" can be anything from a 300-developer team on one side of the spectrum to a single developer on the other. What is important for us now is not the size of the team, but how the team feels about the project.

If you (as a future parent) don't feel that your future game is your baby, think twice before conceiving it. Doing such challenging development with only money in mind might not be the best decision in your life. If you're starting to develop only for money without any feelings for the project, then there are two possible outcomes. In the first case, you will gradually become attached to the project and eventually will get those all-important positive feelings about its development, greatly increasing the chance of success. In the second case, you keep doing it for money; ironically enough, with such a purely money-oriented approach, the chance of making a great game (and making money from it) becomes infinitesimally small.

TL;DR:

> *Don't start development unless your team is passionate about your upcoming game.*

3500-WORD CRASH COURSE FOR FIRST-TIME GAME DEVELOPERS

As I've mentioned, we're working under the assumption that you already have a Great Game Idea™ (with as complete an understanding of planned user experience, physics, and AI as is possible at this time), you're really passionate about it, and you are eager to start development.

This section is not intended for experienced game developers, especially for those coming from AAA gamedev companies. Please skip to the *Three All-Important GDD Rules* section.

What should your first step be? Start coding? Nope. Choose the programming language? By the tiniest of margins closer, still very much a *no*. Your first step should be to understand what exactly you're going to achieve.

For any game, there are quite a few things that are dictated by your future players (and other project stakeholders), and are commonly written down as a Game Design Document (GDD).

On the GDD

In the game-development industry, it is common to have a GDD that describes (from an extremely high level) "how the game should work," and includes characters, gameplay, etc. And not only it is common to have a GDD, but there are also very good reasons to have one. A GDD provides an understanding of what you're going to achieve, and is essentially a prerequisite for successful development. Sure, smaller teams can get away without a formal GDD (effectively keeping it in mind), but even for these, spending half a day to write it down and discuss tends to help a lot.

For those developers coming from other fields, a GDD is pretty much like your typical "Business Requirements" document, as it applies to a game.

Now, let's discuss a few all-important properties of the GDD. For the time being, we'll discuss common properties of a GDD that apply to both single and multiplayer games; we'll discuss the differences of a multiplayer-oriented GDD starting from the *Limited-Lifespan vs. Undefined-Lifespan Games* section below.

Subject to Change, Seven Days a Week

It is to be understood that a GDD tends to change very often, and is certainly not carved in stone. This is to be expected for most software projects, and applies in spades to game development. Therefore:

> ### Expect your GDD to change, and leave **lots** of room for these changes.

Even if you're told that a certain thing will "never ever" change, keep in mind that "never ever" will probably come much sooner than you expect. This is not to say that you should write an "absolutely universal" system able to deal with any change (see about the dangers of being overly generic below); this is to suggest that you not be too upset when you're forced to rewrite 50% of the system when a thing-that-you-were-told-will-never-change does change overnight. Oh, and do keep records of these assurances, so when the GDD changes, you can explain why such a simple thing (from the point of view of the stakeholder) requires rewriting half the system.

Even if you're told that a certain thing will "never ever" change, keep in mind that "never ever" can come much sooner than you expect.

Sure, it is the very same profound truth that the whole agile movement is speaking about since time immemorial,[23] but let's keep in mind that some of the profound truths (this one included) happen to occasionally be applicable in the real world.

---

23   More precisely, since 2001

Being Agile and Writing It Down

One important thing to understand is that a GDD being agile doesn't imply that you don't need to write it down. While each of the GDD requirements may change later, at every point it should be clear (and agreed by both stakeholders and developers) what you're trying to achieve right now. When (not *if!*) the GDD changes—fine, you will update it.

I usually suggest that you treat your GDD as one of the documents under your source-control system. In any case, the GDD tends to have effects similar to those of an extremely high-level header file in C/C++: as with changing a high-level header file, changing a GDD can be very expensive, but in a majority of cases doesn't mean rewriting everything out there, especially if you have prepared for at least *some* of the changes.

The Overly Generic Fallacy

> Sculpting is easy. You just chip away the stone that doesn't look like David.
> —(Mis)Attributed to Michelangelo

When speaking about agility and taking the "be ready for changing requirements" adage to the extreme, there is often a temptation to write a system-that-is-able-to-handle-everything and which therefore will never change (and handling "everything" will be achieved by some kind of configuration or script or...).

As a programmer, I perfectly understand the inclination to "write Good Code™ once so we won't need to change it later." Unfortunately, it doesn't work this way in the real world. The issues with this overly generic approach start with the time it takes to implement, but the real problems come later, when your overly generic framework is ready. When your overly generic code is finally completed, it turns out that either (a) "everything" as it was implemented by this system is too narrow for practical purposes (i.e., it cannot be really used, and often needs to be started from scratch), or that (b) the configuration file/script are at best barely usable (insufficient, overcomplicated, cumbersome, etc.). In an extreme case of overly generic software, its configuration file/script is a fully fledged programming language in itself, so

When speaking about agility and taking the "be ready for changing requirements" adage to the extreme, there is often a temptation to write a system-that-is-able-to-handle-everything and which therefore will never change.

Turing-complete

A programming language is said to be Turing complete or *computationally universal* if it can be used to simulate any single-taped Turing machine.

—Wikipedia

after doing all that work on the overly generic system, we need to learn how to program using this (strange and usually not exactly convenient) programming language, and then to program our game using it—which means that after spending all the time on the overly generic system, we're essentially back to square one.[24]

In fact, systems-that-can-handle-everything already exist and there is nothing bad about them. Actually, any Turing-complete programming language[25] can indeed handle absolutely everything; in a sense, Turing-complete programming language represents absolute freedom. However, as writing a Turing-complete programming language is normally not in the game-development scope, our role as game programmers should be somewhat different from just copying compiler executable from one place to another and saying that our job is done.

What we as programmers are essentially doing is restricting the absolute freedom provided by our original Turing-complete language (just like a sculptor restricts the absolute freedom provided to him by the original slab of stone), and saying that "our system will be able to do this, at the cost of not being able to do that." Just as the art of sculpting is all about knowing when to stop chipping away at the stone, the art of the software design is all about feeling when to stop taking away the freedom inherent to programming languages.

Coming back to Earth from the philosophical clouds—

> *When developing a game (or any other project), it is very important to strike The Right Balance™ between being overly generic and overly specific.*

---

24 BTW, creating a domain-specific programming language optimized for a game may make perfect sense; the point here is not aimed against developing scripting languages where they make sense and provide additional value specific to the game domain, but against being overly generic just for the sake of writing-it-once-and-forgetting-about-it.

25 And I don't know of any practical programming language that is not Turing-complete.

On Project Stakeholders

Each and every software development project out there has project stake-holders. In general, a stakeholder can be an investor, a manager, and/or a customer.[26]

For games, it is often translated into producers[27], marketing and monetizing folks, CSRs (a.k.a. "support people"), and, of course, players. For games, players are an extremely important type of stakeholder.

One thing that is very important for the game to be successful, is to—

> *Have your project stakeholders, including future players, represented in your development process.*

If your project stakeholders don't participate in your development process, chances are that your game will fail in one way or another. And for games, project stakeholders *must* include future players of your game.

How to represent future players within your team is a bit of a different question and is not *that* obvious. Quite often, it is done by a "focus group," but this is not that universal and is even controversial. Actually, the question of "whether to use focus groups" is up to you—

> *What is not up to you, however, is having* **somebody** *represent future players.*

Depending on the development environment, it *may* be a producer who represents the players' point of view, or it *may* be a game designer, but as a rule of thumb, the further this person is from knowing "how the bytes are moved around to make things work," the better; otherwise, there is the risk of her becoming a victim of "not seeing the forest for the trees" syndrome.

CSR

Customer service representatives (CSRs) .. interact with customers to provide answers to inquiries involving a company's product or services.

—Wikipedia

---

26 For game development, the term "project stakeholders" is not really common, but relevant people and dependencies still exist, so I will use the term in the sense that it is common for general software development.

27 I don't want to engage in a discussion of whether a producer qualifies as a "project stakeholder" or a "product owner"; this is not important at this point.

Unfortunately, when we (as programmers) are writing code (and, to a lesser extent, when game designers are designing levels, etc.), it affects our judgment about the game a lot; in other words, we know too much about the game internals (and on efforts we need to spend to develop this or that particular feature) to represent the opinion of "an average player out there." While our suggestions (based on this knowledge) can be very valuable, the decisions about gameplay *should* generally be made by those future players who are not programmers.

On Focus Testing and Playtesting

During game development, there may be two different stages at which players can possibly participate in testing.

At earlier stages, it is known as "focus testing" (disclaimer: Your Terminology Mileage May Vary). The key here is that "focus testing" is usually performed *before* there is something tangible to show the players [Pfister]. In the gamedev world, quite a few prominent developers have said very harsh things about it, such as "screw focus groups" [Brightman] and "focus groups have become an f-word" [Donovan].

At later stages, when there is something that can be played, it is known as "play testing." To confuse things further, there can also easily be "focus groups" during "play testing."

I am not going into a lengthy discussion about this rather controversial subject, but will instead mention a few (hopefully rather obvious) points:

You *should not* use your "focus group" to try and figure out "what the Big Idea is behind your game."

▶ First, it is quite clear that you *should not* use your "focus group" to try and figure out "what the Big Idea is behind your game" (this decision should be yours and yours alone, otherwise you are in a Really Big Trouble™).

▶ On the other hand, ironing out relatively minor details (and these *may* include such things as 3D models and graphics, though you *should* make an effort to put them into context) is often beneficial. This *may* open the door for "focus testing" as defined above, though I won't say that you're necessarily wrong if you're not doing it.

▶ Whether you're doing "focus testing" or not, you would be *really* crazy not to perform "play testing" (this may include "alpha," "closed beta," "open beta," and whatever-other-letter-of-Greek-alphabet-you-prefer).

- This "play testing" *may* or *may not* include "focus groups"; TBH, I am not a big fan of "focus groups" in a traditional sense, where players may interact with one another (as this kind of interaction may easily lead to suppressing opinions from all-but-the-most-vocal-members-of-the-group), but, well, I am pretty sure that it is possible to have a use for the traditional focus group.

- Overall, *how* to do your "playtesting" depends on many factors; the most important thing, however, is to start it very early in the process and adjust it whenever it doesn't work.

On Marketing and Monetization: Critical Mass

On the other hand, having *only* future players as project stakeholders is not sufficient. For your game to survive, you will most likely need some kind of monetization. And those people who're responsible for monetization are also very important project stakeholders and *must* be involved in game development. Otherwise, you can end up with a game that everybody loves, but—as you didn't take monetization into account—you just don't have enough money to run your servers and pay developer salaries.

For your game to survive, most likely you will need some kind of monetization.

Moreover, without help from your marketing and monetization team, you may be missing an all-important item in the whole MOG puzzle. I am speaking about the answer to the "how to achieve 'critical mass'" question. In short, in a classic catch-22 scenario, until your game has X players, it will lose players because there aren't enough other players to play with; this often makes a "critical mass" problem a life-and-death one for indie MOG teams. "Critical mass" depends heavily on the game type (and even more on your matchmaking algorithm), but as an extremely rough rule of thumb, you need to have at least a few hundred players at all times of day to stand a chance.

In any case, within the scope of this book, we won't concentrate on marketing or monetization as such. However, as we'll see below in the *Technical Issues Affecting Marketing* section, there are quite a few mostly technical decisions that will significantly affect your monetization and marketing efforts. See the section below for further discussion.

On Stakeholder Availability

One thing to keep in mind about stakeholders is that it is not a one-way street of: "stakeholders have said; developers are doing it." Ideally, you should have a culture of "if developers are in doubt, they should ask project stakeholders"; from my experience, it is such teams that tend to produce Really Great Games™ (YMMV; batteries not included).

However, for this to work, we *do* need to have a stakeholder available during all stages of the game-development process. In other words, if we (as developers) have any doubt about any issue related to the GDD, we *should* have somebody on hand to ask for their authoritative opinion.

TL;DR on Project Stakeholders

To summarize our discussion of project stakeholders and their role in game development:

Participation of both future players and other stakeholders (such as the marketing and monetization team) in developing the GDD is absolutely necessary.

► Participation of both future players and other stakeholders (such as the marketing and monetization team) in developing the GDD is absolutely necessary.

- The same stands for amending the GDD as the project goes ahead.

► No stakeholders—no GDD—no development. It is that simple. Doing it any other way is extremely risky, at the very least.

On a Typical Non-MOG Team Structure

For a typical non-multiplayer game, the following teams usually participate in game development (listed more or less according to their order in the food chain):

- ▶ Business and Monetization

- ▶ Producer(s)

- ▶ Game Designers

- ▶ Artists (all kinds)

- ▶ Programmers (also known as Engineers)
  - ▪ This certainly includes *runtime programmers*
  - ▪ In addition, for 3D games (and other games with heavy tool-chains), there are also *tools programmers*

I don't want to elaborate further on these teams; Google and other books referenced within the Introduction will provide additional information, if desired. Let's just note that the size of each of these teams can vary from half-a-person (i.e., a person working simultaneously on several teams) to a hundred-people. In other words, another way to see it (especially in small development environments) is to consider these as not *teams*, but *roles*.

What is important, though, is that for an MOG team there will be additional four(!) teams or roles discussed below in the *On MOG-Specific Teams* section.

Time-to-Market, MVP, and Planning

When developing a game (or any other software), it is important to deliver it while it still makes sense, market-wise. If you take too long to develop, the whole subject can disappear or at least become much less popular, or your graphics can become outdated.[28] For example, if you started developing a game about dinosaurs during the dinosaur craze of the 1990s but finished it

---

[28]   Not to mention that you can simply run out of money for the project.

We will be universally pushed to deliver our game ASAP (with a common target date being "yesterday")—there is no way around it.

only in 2015, chances are that your target audience has shrunk significantly (to put it very mildly).

That's why (unfortunately for us developers) we will be universally pushed to deliver our game ASAP (with a common target date being "yesterday")— there is no way around it. If leaving this without proper attention, it will inevitably lead to a horrible rush at the end that results in dropping essential features (while a lot of time was already spent on non-essential ones) and skipping most of the testing. As a result, it will very likely lead to a low-quality game.

Dealing with Time-to-Market

Dealing with this time-to-market problem is not easy, but is possible. To avoid a rush at the end, there are two things that need to be done.

The first is defining a so-called Minimum Viable Product (a.k.a. MVP). You need to define what exactly you need to be in your first release. The common way to do it is to do roughly the same thing you do when packing for a camping trip. Start with things-that-you-*may*-want-to-have and that will make your first list. Then, go through it and throw away everything except the things that are absolutely necessary. Note that you may face resistance from stakeholders in this regard; in this case, be firm: setting priorities (in particular, answering questions such as "do you folks want feature set A on date A, or feature set B on date B?") is vital for the health of the project.

On the other hand, having an MVP does *not* mean having a half-baked product (see, for example, [Joseph Kim]); this is where the art of game design really lies—how to design a game that is delivered "soon enough" but is also fun.

The second endeavor you need to undertake to avoid that rush-which-destroys-everything is as obvious as it is universally hated by programmers. It is planning. You do need to have a schedule (with appropriate time reserves), and milestones, and you more or less need keep to the schedule. As Kim's Law from [Joseph Kim] states:

> *Develop a Minimally Viable Product*
> *with Maximum Viable Planning*

On the Importance of Holding Your Horses

When you're developing your first game, it is often tempting to say "hey, we will be using such-and-such a game engine, so all we need is to implement our game around this engine." Or (especially if you're coming from web development) to say pretty much the same thing, but instead about building the game around the database. Or building your game around some protocol (TCP or UDP).

However, at this stage of the development process, it is extremely important to realize that you still don't really have sufficient information to make architectural decisions. All these engines, databases, and protocols are nothing more than implementation details, and we're not at the implementing stage yet (and by far, too).

While your multiplayer game is likely to have some kind of graphics engine, and very likely to have some DB to provide persistence, and will certainly need to run on top of some IP-based protocol, it is way too early to make any of them a center of your game universe. In particular, even the decision of whether your game should be game-engine-centric, or 3D-engine-centric, or DB-centric, or protocol-centric, requires an understanding of game mechanics.

While your game is likely to have a 3D engine, and very likely to have some DB to provide persistence, and will certainly need to run on top of some IP-based protocol, it is way too early to make any of them the center of your game universe.

Making these decisions (and actually any architectural decisions) before you have your GDD *and* Entities-and-Interactions diagram[29], can severely restrict your choices, and if you have made a mistake with such a decision (and when you're deciding without having sufficient information, mistakes are more than likely), it may easily lead to grossly inefficient and even completely unworkable implementations.

For example, if you decide that "our system should be DB-centric, with 100% of the state being written to DB at all times," and your system happens to be a blackjack site, your implementation will cause about 10x more DB load than an alternative one; plus, you will get a bunch of issues with implementing a rollback in case your site crashes (which causes many games to be interrupted in the middle and, with a multiplayer site, you *do* need some kind of rollback). Usually, the optimal implementation for many of the casino

---

29   Described later in this chapter.

multiplayer games is with state of the table being stored in-memory only (and synchronized with DB only when a single game is completed), but this won't become obvious until you draw your Entities-and-Interactions diagram.

As another example, if you decide that "our system should be game-engine-centric," and your game engine of choice doesn't support so-called "Interest Management" (which will be discussed in Chapter 3), you may end up with a system that works reasonably well for small virtual worlds, but that is completely unscalable to larger ones due to $O(N^2)$ traffic, which pretty much inevitably arises from the everybody-interacts-with-everybody assumption.

TL;DR On a Crash Course for First-Time Developers

A GDD is an absolute *must.*

Phew, it seems that we're done with the crash course for those of us who didn't participate in larger game developer projects. Let's summarize our findings:

► A GDD is an absolute *must.*

► Stakeholders participating in the game-development process is also a *must.*

   ▪ Stakeholders *must* include both somebody-representing-future-players and monetization and marketing teams

      • Developers (even heavily playing developers), while being stakeholders, are not sufficient to represent players. In other words, you *should* have non-developing players as stakeholders.

► Minimum Viable Product and Maximum Viable Planning are Good Things™.

► Before a GDD is written and an Entities-and-Interactions diagram is completed, it is way too early to decide on implementation details, including, but not limited to:

   ▪ Game engines
   ▪ Databases
   ▪ Protocols

THREE ALL-IMPORTANT GDD RULES

There are three extremely important (and unfortunately, way too often over-looked) rules when it comes to a GDD. While they're about different facets of pretty much the same thing, I still prefer to state them separately. The first is:

> ## The GDD **should** be written by Project Stakeholders (and not by Programmers)

As programmers, we *should* by all means be involved in the development of our GDD, and raise hell when something is not doable (preferably in a form more polite than "are you guys crazy or what?"), but we should be ready to accept decisions of stakeholders when they insist (that is, as long as they're staying away from implementation details; see below).

After spending quite a few years programming, I know that this is a tough one, but on the other hand, I am the first to admit that I can get carried away with something that is very nice to implement, but which won't make much difference for the player. BTW, the opposite tendency, avoiding features that are difficult to implement, tends to be equally devastating to the quality of the end product. Either way, however, illustrates the main problem with GDDs being written by programmers: we as programmers are usually too closely involved with implementation details, which makes it too difficult for us to see the Big Picture. In a sense, it is a classical "can't see the forest for the trees" problem and, as with any other psychological problem, it is extremely difficult to find a workaround.

I can get carried away with something that is very nice to implement, but which won't make much difference for the player.

Rule #2 which needs to be kept in mind when writing our GDD is:

> ## The GDD is **not** about "HOW we do it?", but is **only** about "WHAT do we do?"

As a task definition written by stakeholders (and not programmers), the GDD is not supposed to get us into a lengthy discussion on implementation details. Of course, things that are outright impossible to implement should be filtered out and, of course, it is perfectly okay for a programmer to say during a GDD discussion that "hey, implementing this feature will take us an extra three months" (which in turn requires an understanding, but not an explanation, of "how to do it"). However, these two types of feedback[30] are *the only* types of feedback related to implementation details that should be allowed into a GDD discussion (and note that they're also very much along the lines of Rule #3 below).

As a way to make the second rule more specific (which in turn allows us to enforce it), I've found that the following Rule #3[31] tends to work very well:

> *The GDD MUST be written exclusively in players' terms; the rest is implementation details that do not belong in the GDD.*

For example, players do care about the platforms where they will be able to run your game, so "which platforms are to be supported?" is certainly a part of your GDD; but, on the other hand, players don't care about the programming language you will be using (as long as it can run on all those platforms). As another example, players do care about response times and may care about how-your-app-works-over-firewalls, but they don't care if you achieve those response times and working-over-firewalls via TCP or via UDP, as long as the whole thing does work.

On Separating GDD and Implementation Details

Why are Rules #2 and #3 so important? Because writing GDD requirements in terms of implementation rather than in player terms may severely hurt your ability to choose an optimal way to implement your game.

For example, if you write down a *bad* GDD requirement: "We *must* write our app in Java" (instead of the *good* one: "Our app *must* run on Windows, iPhone, and Android"), you won't even start to think about writing your app

If you write down a *bad* GDD requirement: "We *must* write our app in Java" (instead of a *good* one: "Our app *must* run on Windows, iPhone, and Android"), you won't even start to think about writing your app in C++ and porting it to Android using NDK.

---

30 Actually, we can consider it one type of feedback, as "outright impossible to implement" can be re-formulated into "it will take us 100 years to implement."

31 Which, BTW, is a close cousin of "ubiquitous language" from [Elbaum and Scott].

in C++ and porting it to Android using NDK (with a rather minimal Java UI), and you'll miss an opportunity to consider *emscripten* (more on it in Vol.II's chapter on Client-Side Architecture). While there is no guarantee that these options are better, throwing them out of the window without proper consideration is rarely a wise decision.

As another example, if you write a *bad* GDD requirement: "We *must* use UDP" (instead of a *good* one: "In 99.99% of cases, we need an average delay of at most 200ms between the user pressing a button and it showing up for the other users"), you won't even start to learn about the ways to improve TCP interactivity (which will be described in Vol. IV's chapter on Network Programming), and may miss an opportunity to make your app more firewall-friendly and to simplify your development by using TCP. Or, the other way around, you may write a *bad* GDD requirement "We *must* use TCP" (instead of a *good* one: "We *must* have TLS-class security"), and may miss an opportunity to make your app more responsive via implementing it over UDP (using DTLS and/or TLS-over-reliable-UDP for security purposes, as it will be described in Vol. IV).[32]

In short, we can say that writing a GDD in player terms allows you to keep your options open—and keeping your options open is in general a Good Thing™.

Dealing with "Difficult" Stakeholders and (Jobs Forbid) Managers

The separation between the GDD and implementation details means that if your project stakeholder (future player, marketing guy, manager, investor, etc.) says "we need to write into our GDD that our game *must* be written in Java" (or "*must* use TCP," etc.), you need to explain that this is an implementation detail, and ask for a definition in terms that are obvious to the player.

---

[32] Note that while "we need to use UDP" (or TCP for that matter) may be a valid GDD requirement in some cases (for example, when you're writing a communication library, and your user is a programmer, so she knows about UDP), it doesn't apply to games. You *may* need to use UDP for your game—it is not just a GDD requirement, but a technical decision of "how to implement these GDD requirements."

Moreover, if such a "difficult" stakeholder is a manager and after all the explanations[33] is still insisting that using {Java|TCP|UDP|whatever-other-implementation-detail} should be a part of the GDD, you really need to think about whether you want to work on this project, as such a deep misunderstanding of a basic concept is often a symptom of super-micromanagement and upcoming deep conflicts with this specific manager.

LIMITED-LIFESPAN VS. UNDEFINED-LIFESPAN GAMES

One of the GDD requirements for your upcoming MOG is very important from a development perspective, but is not too well known (and is more or less multiplayer-specific too), so I'll try to explain it. This GDD requirement intends to describe the projected lifespan of your game. As we will see further down the road, game lifespan has significant implications on the game architecture and design.

It had a naturally limited lifespan, such a game, for one simple reason: to make more money, the producer needed to release another game and charge for it.

Starting from the times of the Ancient Gamedevs (circa 1980), most games released were sold (more or less like a book is sold). It had a naturally limited lifespan, such a game, for one simple reason: to make more money, the producer needed to release another game and charge for it. This is a classical (not to say necessarily outdated) game business model, and multiplayer online games that are intended to have a limited lifespan share quite a bit with traditional game development. In particular, limited-lifespan games are normally built around one graphics engine. Moreover, more often than not, such an engine is tightly coupled with the rest of the game. And for a game that is not going to be sold two years from now, it makes sense: then, there will be another game, and another (bigger and better) game engine.

However, as game development was evolving from Ancient Gamedev Times toward the XXI century, game producers came up with a brilliant idea of writing a game once and exploiting it pretty much forever (monetizing it via either subscriptions or ongoing in-game purchases); this plays especially

---

33   BTW, in some cases, a reference to [Elbaum and Scott] may help. No warranties of any kind; batteries not included

well for the likes of an MOG: if your game is good enough, once you get loyal players, you can make sure that they're playing for years and years. As a result, these days quite a few multiplayer games are intended to have a potentially unlimited lifespan. The idea behind it runs along the following lines:

> *"Let's try to make a game and get as much as we can out of it, keeping it while it is profitable and developing it along the road."*

Indeed, games such as stock markets, *World of Warcraft*, poker sites, or *Top Eleven Football Manager*, are not designed to disappear after a predefined time frame. Most of them are intended to exist for a long while (providing jobs to developers and generating profits for owners), and this observation (actually, a GDD-level requirement) makes a substantial impact on some of the architectural choices.

Indeed, games such as stock markets, poker sites, *World of Warcraft*, or *Top Eleven Football Manager* are not designed to disappear after a predefined time frame.

Most importantly for us now, for undefined-lifespan games, there is too much risk in relying on a third-party game engine. If your engine is not 100% your own, a question arises: "Are you 100% sure that the engine will be around and satisfy the demands of your players in 5-10 years?" This, in turn, has several extremely important implications, shifting the balance toward DIY (more on DIY in Vol. II) and/or going for an ability to switch the engines (which, in turn, requires severely reduced coupling with the graphics engine, using isolation layers such as Logic-to-Graphics Layer discussed in Vol. II's chapter on Client-Side Architecture).

There are also several other cases where being an undefined-lifespan game affects architectural decisions; I'll try to mention them in appropriate places in the book.

CLIENT-DRIVEN VS. SERVER-DRIVEN DEVELOPMENT WORKFLOW

With preliminaries more or less out of the way, let's discuss one more issue that is specific to multiplayer games; it is the difference in development workflows depending on the specifics of your MOG.

From my experience, for MOG development there are two quite different development patterns; let's name them "Server-Driven Development Workflow" and "Client-Driven Development Workflow." It is not that one is *better* than the other for *all* of the games; rather, each is optimal for a range of game genres.

Server-Driven Workflow

Server-Driven Development Workflow usually arises when the game is (almost) completely defined by its rules[34], and no (or little) visual stuff is needed for game designers to work. In other words, game designers live in the world of game rules, and pretty much nothing more; in particular, level design is either non-existent or is very rudimentary. This happens for quite a few games out there, usually whenever 3D is not necessary (or at least not mandatory): stock exchanges, casino-like games, social games—all of these (and quite a few mobile-oriented games too) are often made using Server-Driven Development Workflow.

With Server-Driven Development Workflow, toolchains are rudimentary and Server Team is the one implementing the rules of the game, and the Client is merely executing instructions coming from the Server-Side. In short, Server is king.

Client-Driven Workflow

In contrast, Client-Driven Development Workflow is more typical for 3D-based simulation-related games (think MMORPG or MMOFPS), and is much closer to the workflow that is used for classical single-player games. In

---

34   N.B.: rules may include using randomicity.

this case, game designers cannot just lock themselves up inside rule world, and during design they need to see the things as they will look on the Client. Heavy dependency of the gameplay on game levels, combined with the need to render it in a 3D engine, is a very strong indicator of the Client-Driven Development Workflow coming in.

With Client-Driven Development Workflow, game designers work with visual stuff (such as level design) a lot, and toolchains are universally heavy.[35] Usually it leads to a situation where game designers design a Game World without caring too much about the distributed nature of the game, but in terms of "whenever PC comes within 30m of *this point* while not having level 29, he gets beaten badly" (with *this point* defined via clicking at the visual map). Moreover, working in these terms is probably the only feasible option for these game genres (otherwise game designers wouldn't be able to do their job at all, as there are too many things for them to care about).

For MMORPG or MMOFPS, game designers cannot just lock themselves up inside a rule-based world, and during design they need to see the things as they will look on the Client.

Overall, for Client-Driven games, development workflow revolves around the Client-Side, with minimal involvement of the distributed machinery (at least as it is seen by game designers). In short, Content (and Client) are pretty much Kings.

BTW, Client-Driven Workflow doesn't mean that your game will have Authoritative Clients or anything of the kind; all those Server-Side authoritative objects and Client-Side proxies of those objects can[36] appear within your Client-Driven game too. However, your workflow, when adding new NPCs (or any other in-game entities), will be about creating them within some kind of level editor, which is essentially a Client-Side tool.

Dealing with Client-Driven Workflow

When facing Client-Driven Workflow, there are two distinct options, with game designer experience looking quite similar on the surface, but all the other things being quite different under the hood.

---

35 Okay, sometimes they're *very* heavy.
36 And as we'll see in Chapter 2, *should*.

Option 1. "Continuous Conversion"

The first option (and this is what is often done by indie guys using 3rd-party game engines) is to make all the development "as if" it is a single-player game and then to "convert" it to a multiplayer one as a separate effort (though it *must* be a *continuous* one; more below). In other words, all the toolchains of existing non-MOG game engines work without even knowing about the multiplayer stuff, and it is considered a job of the Server Team to "convert" the game into a real MOG. This approach *might* work, though you *must* make sure to start this "conversion" long before the game development is completed (in fact, it should be done right after the game rules are more-or-less established, and in parallel with level design). Such *continuous* "conversion" (and associated testing with simulated latencies, packet loss, etc.) is absolutely necessary to make sure that all the distributed problems that weren't accounted for by your game designers[37] are ironed out as soon as possible. Postponing such "conversion" to later stages of game development means postponing multiplayer testing, and is known to be completely suicidal.

Postponing such "conversion" to later stages of game development means postponing multi-player testing, and is known to be completely suicidal.

If going this way (and for indie development, you'll probably want to do it), you basically have two further choices:

▶ Option 1a, to use game-engine-integrated support for the Server-Side

▶ Option 1b, to write:

  ▪ An export tool to export level information from Client-Side 3D engine into your-own-format

  ▪ Your own Standalone Server (using your-own-format to obtain level information).

As for specific 3rd-party game engines (and associated network libraries) that can be used for Client-Driven Workflow, we'll discuss them in Vol. II's chapter on 3rd-party Game Engines.

---

37 And you can be 99% sure that there will be *plenty* of such unaccounted-for-by-game-designers {multiplayer|latency|packet loss} issues.

Option 2. "Integrate Server into Toolchain"

The second option (the one I would suggest—that is, if you can afford it), is to incorporate your Server-Side into your toolchain. This means that each time a game designer launches the game to see what has changed due to her last level change, it is in fact not only her Client that is launched, but rather a bunch of processes:

- ▶ her Client, *plus*
- ▶ a full-scale Server, *plus*
- ▶ some simulated players, *plus (ideally)*
- ▶ simulated network with simulated network problems.

Of course, such an integration is much more difficult to implement than just using "Continuous Conversion," but on the other hand, it provides much better feedback for the game designers. While this approach is still not sufficient to get rid of *all* the network-related issues and bugs,[38] it does allow you to catch some of the bugs and issues earlier (which in turn speeds up development and improves overall quality).

ON MATCHMAKING AND THE SOCIAL ASPECT OF YOUR MOG

N.B.: In this section—as well as across the whole book—we'll be using the definitions of Servers and Datacenters that were given in Introduction. Very briefly: "Server" is a physical server box, and "Datacenter" is a bunch of Servers sitting within the same ISP.

For a successful MOG, it is very common to have megatons of players playing on tons of different Game Worlds. In this context, the question of "how

---

38   They will still need to be found out during beta testing, ideally by relying on deterministic behavior to reproduce situations that lead to player complaints in your lab, as discussed in Vol. II's Chapter on (Re)Actors and in [Aldridge].

we assign players to different Game Worlds?" arises.[39] This process is usually referred to as "matchmaking."

Matchmaking That *Doesn't* Work (As a Rule of Thumb)

As we'll see in Vol. III (chapter on Server-Side Architecture), implementation-wise it is often tempting to consider all your players a commodity, and to *permanently* assign players to your Game Worlds prohibiting any communication between players in those Game Worlds. Implementation-wise, it corresponds to an architecture[40] with each of the Game Worlds having its own database, absolutely separated from anything else.

However, you should be *really* careful with this kind of "random permanent matchmaking," as it has a lot of negative implications in the context of socializing.

However, you should be *really* careful with this kind of "random permanent matchmaking," as it has a lot of negative implications in the context of socializing.

Let's note that pretty much any kind of out-of-game integration (Facebook and any kind of game-specific forum included) requires some kind of interaction between players just because they *want* to interact (and not because your rule engine decided that these two players permanently belong to the same Server). This leads us to the following all-important observation—

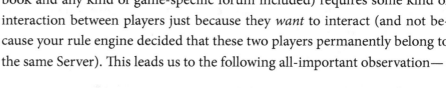

If you don't think that interaction of players just-because-they-happen-to-want-it is a GDD Requirement, think again.

As an example, even a simple "Play with your Facebook friends" feature requires players to "know" about one another, and to interact with one another. This is not to mention that some players may want to play with some specific player (either because they like the guy, or because they like *beating* the guy; regardless of their motives, the end result is still pretty much the same). And

---

39 I consciously avoid speaking about "shards" in this chapter, as I consider a "shard" an implementation detail, and we're not there yet. At this point, we're speaking only about separate "Game Worlds" as it is visible to players.

40 And exactly because of the reasons we discuss here, this architecture tends to fail badly when facing real-world games.

there are also forums ("it would be cool to play with you, what's your handle?"), and off-line tournaments, and who-knows-what.

One of the very popular social(!) games I've seen relied on limited kinda-socializing within a single Server, with players randomly (and permanently!) assigned to each of the Servers (basically, just load-balancing them); as a result, the socializing aspect of the game (which the game was trying to push) was experiencing problems because of such random and permanent assignments; all kinds of makeshift quick-and-dirty sorta-fixes were applied—and it still didn't work as expected for a long while, causing all kinds of complaints from the players.

Sure, for non-social games, socializing capabilities are traditionally considered unimportant, but from the data I've seen, IMO it follows that to make the game successful, every bit that can help to improve popularity counts, and this socializing bit is usually of significant importance. OTOH, as always (and especially in this case), don't take my words for granted and make sure to ask your monetizing and marketing team whether they feel such an interaction *might* be necessary from the point of view of their monetizing and marketing strategy.

Sure, for non-social games, socializing capabilities are traditionally considered unimportant, but from the data I've seen, IMO it follows that to make the game successful, every bit that can help to improve popularity counts.

Matchmaking That Works

Now, let's see how this requirement of allowing-people-to-play-with-those-they-know is usually satisfied in practice.

From what I've seen, the following approaches seem to work reasonably well from a socializing point of view:

► Separate Datacenters, with players able to select a Datacenter. This is the approach MOGs are using since time immemorial (though Datacenters are usually named "Servers," adding to the confusion), especially for those games that are very latency-sensitive (see the discussion on it in Vol. III's chapter on Server-Side Architecture). On the other hand, while this approach works, it tends to cause split communities, which can be a blessing or a curse depending on the specifics of your game.

- Note that, as discussed above, it is rarely a good idea to permanently assign your players to individual Servers within a Datacenter; in other words, each Datacenter (such as a North-America Datacenter, which is usually presented as an "NA Server" to players) is better kept as a single entity from the players' point of view, with no further (and rather artificial) subdivisions such as "NA1," "NA2", etc.

- Even in this case, it is usually quite beneficial to have player accounts the same across the different Datacenters. Even if you don't want to allow players to transfer their respective in-game assets (such as current level, artifacts, whatever else) between Datacenters, having players have one unified account across all your Datacenters (or at the very least ID/login, which is unique across the board) is a Big Help™ when it comes to such things as fighting cheaters, credit-card fraud, and monetization (and don't forget about your poor CSRs, a.k.a. support, who need to deal with this mess).

Whether your players have selected their Datacenter, or you have one big DB handling all of your players, there is the question of "how Game World Instances are created."

► Whether your players have selected their Datacenter, or you have one big DB handling all of your players, there is the question of "how Game World Instances are created." For this, I've seen or heard of the following approaches:

- Game World Instances created on-demand by Matchmaking process/Server (for example, when there are enough players to start a tournament, match, or something). Usually such systems are lobby-based, and allow you to express your interest in playing some kind of game.

  - In this case, consider allowing players to select who-they-want-to-play-with (for example, via joining a "party," but implementation details may vary). It does help to invite friends from Facebook to play.

    ▷ You may even want to allow players to have their own "events" (with them controlling who's invited). However, this tends to work reasonably well only for really-popular-games with really-popular-forums.

- Alternatively, you *may* want to have a ranking-based matchmaking, but this usually lacks a socializing aspect (and once again, it may be a blessing or a curse depending on the specifics of your game).

- For MMORPGs, splitting players between different Game World Instances is a well-known technique. One thing to keep in mind is to know that Game World Instances can be spread over different Servers (and even over different Datacenters), so there is *no* 1-to-1 match between Game World Instances (which are user-visible, and therefore are subject of GDD) and Servers (which are an implementation detail). With regard to socializing, I've seen two quite different approaches when assigning players to different MMORPG Game World Instances:

  - Completely random, without any affinity between players and Game World Instances.

  - With "probabilistic" distribution of players to different Game World Instances, with "probabilities" taking into account affiliations between players. One example of such a system is *Guild Wars II* megaservers; while introducing megaservers into *Guild Wars II* did cause significant controversy (as absolutely-any-change-of-this-scale for an existing game would), they seem to work pretty well from a socializing point of view.

Let's also note that anything else (beyond user-selected Datacenters and user-visible Game World Instances) is of no direct interest to players, and therefore qualifies as an implementation detail. All the intra-Datacenter partitioning, sharding, etc. fall under this category. And as with any other implementation detail, they *should not* affect your GDD (well, at least in theory).

TL;DR of this section on Matchmaking and Socializing—

> *When thinking of your matchmaking algorithms, make sure to take socializing capabilities into account.*

Sure, it might happen that your specific game will be better without socializing; however, it should be a very conscious decision to reject socializing rather than to realize that "it just so happened" when it is too late to change things.

ON SUPPORT FOR SMALLER GROUPS OF PLAYERS

One very important (and IMO way-too-often-ignored) GDD-related question is related to providing support for relatively minor groups of players. This includes questions such as "Our game is Windows-based, should we spend time to support players with Windows 7?" and "Should we support players with a merely DirectX 10 GPU?" or "Should we support those players who don't have UDP access to the Internet?"

Usually, game developers prefer not to bother with such support (concentrating on supporting just the "latest greatest" hardware and software); however, the answer to this question is not *that* obvious, and its discussion SHOULD involve *both* the development team *and* the marketing team.

One all-important issue to be kept in mind when making this kind of decision is a second question of "how competitive the market for our game is?" In other words:

► If your game is the only kid on the block and has no competition, it is often better not to bother with support for Windows 7 or for TCP and to invest your efforts elsewhere.

► On the other hand, if your game enters a highly competitive field (think "social farming games," "casino games," or MOBA), then the whole picture can be *very* different. For example, if we have 5-10% of players who don't have UDP access, at first glance it *looks* like quite a small percentage. However, if most of the well-established competitors do *not* support UDP, then this 5-10% can become our ticket to start growing—just because this 5-10% of players have nowhere to play except for our game(!). For example, if speaking about the non-competitive market, 5% of the market is just 5% of *our* players; on the other hand, if we're entering a market that has 10 competitors with equal-with-us-strength-but-without-support-for-non-UDP-players, the market share analysis changes drastically. In the latter case, and with players distributed as 95% with UDP support and 5% without, we'll get $1/11^{th}$ of UDP-supporting 95% (~=8.5%); *plus*, we'll get the *entire 5%* of non-UDP-supporting players. This, in turn, means that adding TCP support to our game would increase our overall player base not by 5%, but by (13.5/8.5-1)=59% (!).

If most of the well-established competitors do *not* support UDP, then this 5-10% can become our ticket to start growing—just because all this 5-10% of players have nowhere to play except for our game.

Of course, spending time on supporting really ancient technologies (which are *both* too different from the modern ones *and* aren't being used, like WinXP in 2017) is rarely worth the trouble; however, aspects of support for less-competitive (but still at least somewhat-popular) portions of the player population *do* need to be taken into account when making decisions about supported platforms and technologies.

TECHNICAL ISSUES AFFECTING MARKETING AND MONETIZATION

Regardless of the specific genre of your MOG, chances are that you're making it for profit. Or at the very least, you need to pay for your servers. In any case, as noted above, you're likely to need marketing and monetization teams.

Within the scope of this book, we won't discuss marketing questions such as "How to make gameplay more enjoyable" or "How to get that critical mass," etc. Instead, we will concentrate on the *technical* issues that *may* affect your marketing and/or monetization, so that you can take them into account (and tell your marketing folks in advance too, so it won't be an unpleasant surprise for them later, huh). Off the top of my head, I can think of several *technical* fields that *may* affect marketing efforts for your MOG:

Within the scope of this book, we will concentrate on the *technical* issues that *may* affect your marketing and/ or monetization, so that you can take them into account.

▶ Support for not-so-latest-and-greatest hardware/software, as discussed above.

▶ Matchmaking issues, as discussed above.

▶ "Soft" launch. "Soft" launch usually means releasing your game at different times for different regions (and/or for different platforms). And while it does reduce the pressure on technical teams (especially if "soft-launching" on one platform), we need to keep in mind that for MOGs "soft launch" often affects "critical mass" in a negative way (especially if the competition is significant).

■ In turn, it does affect the question of "whether we want to get all the platforms at once, or one at a time."

▶ Minimizing steps for a potential player on the way to start playing. In general, the smaller the steps your potential player needs to take to start playing your game, the better (that is, if after each step your player gets *something* of value; for example, can see a bit more). This, in turn, can be aided and abetted by the following technical means:

■ Making your *first* download smaller. The shorter the time your player needs to wait before seeing *something*, the better; you can download other optional stuff such as themes, additional characters, additional levels, etc. later on from the game itself. As an additional (though admittedly rather minor) benefit, you won't be paying for the traffic of full downloads of those players who throw away your game after the first thirty seconds.

• Note that having a separate downloader (which does nothing but starts a large 10G download) does *not* qualify as "making your first download smaller" for this purpose. To keep your player happy, it is paramount to show her *something of value* (and seeing "Please wait… ETA—10 hours" clearly does not qualify as such).

To keep your player happy, it is paramount to show her *something of value* (and seeing "Please wait.. ETA—10 hours" clearly does not qualify as such).

- Allowing loginless spectators. If your potential player can download something quickly *and* can watch some of your games in real-time (as well as observe that "see, there are lots of people playing; it should be interesting") without having to go through your registration form, it tends to help increase your player numbers (from what I've seen, it helps *quite a bit*, though your mileage may certainly vary). And even if your game is a competitive one, so cheating is an issue, you can still usually show some of the low-level games (where cheating will have much less impact), and/or show games with a delay, and/or show just *recordings* of the Big Games of Pros. Of course, it is up to your team to decide whether you want it, but *both* the technical team *and* the marketing team should be involved in this discussion (and the result of this discussion should certainly belong to the GDD). Also note that loginless spectators tend to go very well with web-based Clients (discussed a bit below).

- Allowing 3rd-party social logins (Facebook or Twitter or Google+ or Steam or…). Filling out a registration form is usually a rather big step for the player, and 3rd-party social login tends to simplify the process significantly (though TBH, I don't have stats on player acceptance for social logins in games).

  - If you're bold enough, you may even restrict your logins to *only* some kind of social login. This "social-only" login policy has two benefits:

    - ▷ First, you'll be getting all-important information about whether the account is associated with a real person, which provides *big* advantages from an anti-cheating point of view (more in Vol. IV's chapter on Basic Security and Vol. VIII's chapters on Bot Fighting and Other Player Abuses).

> ▷ Second, implementing your own login properly requires a lot of effort (usually much more than integrating three of the popular social logins, though see below on browser-less apps). More on it in Vol. IV's chapter on Basic Security.

> ▷ If you're using a downloadable Client, make sure to double-check how you're going to integrate it with your social-login platforms. While there exists a generic way that works pretty-much everywhere-where-you-can-open-a-default-browser-window (see Vol. II's chapter on Client-Side Architecture for details), it is still better to double-check that it *is* working for your platforms/3rd-party logins.

- No-download web-based Client (even if it is a spectating-only one). If you can show your players what your game is about, without requiring them to install your app, you can often improve your conversion rates for people coming to your site quite a bit. Such spectator-only web clients go hand in hand with loginless spectators, mentioned above.

If you can show your players what your game is about without requiring them to install your app, you can often improve your conversion rates for people coming to your site quite a bit.

  - Keep in mind that you indeed *may* want to restrict such a web-based Client to be spectating-only (or play unranked games only, or something else along the same lines), at least to deal with cheaters (more on cheating in Chapter 2 and Vol. VIII). And, while we're at it, when implementing such a web-based Client, keep in mind that leaks of code from a web-based Client into a "real" one can defeat many of your defenses, so you might want to separate code bases for a hackable web-based Client and a "real" one.

► A *very* different thing from having a full-scale web-based Client is forcing your players to use *both* your downloadable Client (for the game itself) *and* a web-based interface (for "side" stuff such as stats, purchases, etc.) on the same platform, and this is IMO generally a Bad Thing™ for the game.

■ Of course, if your game has a downloadable Client, having two separate interfaces (one primary, for game-only via game Client, and another secondary, for "side" stuff) might look technically appealing on the first glance (it often requires significantly less effort to implement than doing everything via your game Client). However, this split-interface approach does have its drawbacks (and quite significant ones at that). These drawbacks are both technical (mostly security-related) and marketing and monetization ones. Among the latter are such things as inconvenience of the switch-from-client-to-web for the player (hey, you don't want to make the payment more difficult than is necessary, do you?), complicated integration between two interfaces (limiting options available to marketing and monetization teams), and creating an unwelcome feeling of an "unfinished product." Overall, as a player, I *hate* using *both* Client *and* web browser for the same game (though web-based social login is usually okay).

• Note that using an in-app web-browser (the one that *looks* like part of your Client) is a completely different thing from a GDD perspective (and usually qualifies as an "implementation detail" of overall Client, but is not without its own drawbacks); what matters for GDD is whether in-game purchases, stats, etc. will *look* like a part of the Client from the player's perspective. For the discussion on *implementing* it, see Vol. II's chapter on Client-Side Architecture.

■ On the other hand, if you *really* feel that such an abomination will speed development up significantly, you may want to raise a question whether it is okay to do it this way during your GDD meeting (and make sure to write this "okay" down in GDD). What you *must not* do, though, is start to implement it without having an okay from your marketing and monetization teams (I know of a few cases where they were jumping pretty high at the very mention of this thing).

YOUR GDD REQUIREMENTS LIST

By this point (and with or without reading all the stuff above), you've got your list of GDD requirements for your game. While your list is unique for your game, there are some things that need to be present:

▶ **A very detailed description of the user experience** (including game logic, UI, graphics, sounds, etc.). This is what is traditionally present in traditional (non-MOG) GDDs. While it is going to take most of your GDD, it is game-specific so we cannot really elaborate on it here. However, there are lots of much-less-obvious (and MOG-specific) things that need to be written down; see below.[41]

Note that at least in theory, dual 2D/3D interface can be implemented, especially for those games with an "undefined" lifespan.

  ▪ One thing of specific interest for our purposes: Is your game supposed to be 3D or 2D? Note that at least in theory, dual 2D/3D interface can be implemented, especially for those games with an "undefined" lifespan.

  ▪ Another question that is extremely important for us is related to development flow. Is your development flow going to be Client-Driven or Server-Driven (in the sense defined above)?

▶ **Projected lifespan of the Game** (is it "release, then three DLCs over two years, and that's it," or "running forever and ever, until death do us part"?). For further discussion, see the *Limited-Lifespan vs Undefined-Lifespan Games* section above.

---

41 Obviously, it doesn't really matter whether you write all the MOG-related stuff into a GDD itself, or into a separate document that accompanies the GDD; however, it is *as important as the GDD itself, and should be treated as such.*

▶ **List of platforms you would like to support for the Client-Side app.**

  ▪ One interesting twist is that you *may* want to implement a web-based Client, even if you can provide only spectator-only functionality over the web (see brief discussion in the *Technical Issues Affecting Marketing and Monetization* section above).

▶ **List of supported video cards** (DirectX/OpenGL versions, etc.).

▶ **List of platforms/video cards you want to support in the very first release** (for the Client, that is)

  ▪ You need to keep in mind that the role of different platforms is quite different for MOGs than for traditional games. As mentioned above, a "soft launch" may be detrimental for "critical mass," and if your marketing folks think this is the case, it *may* be an argument for going for "release all the platforms at once" (or at least "release those platforms that are rather technically similar at once").

Note that the list of platforms for the Server-Side is normally an implementation detail, and as such doesn't belong to the GDD (for further discussion, see the *Three All-Important GDD Rules* section above). Neither do programming languages, frameworks, etc.

▶ **In-game timing requirements** (i.e. "how long it *may* take for the player to see what is going on"); note that they should include *both* "how long it *may* take for the player to see the result of her own actions" (this is known as "Input Lag," which will be discussed in detail in Chapter 3), and "how long it *may* take for the player to see the result of the actions of others." With regard to such timing requirements, writing "As fast as possible" is not really useful, but statements such as "our game should be at least as fast as such and such a game," or "it should be fast enough so nobody on our team can say it is sluggish" is much better (if you can get "at most X milliseconds delay between one user pressing a button and another seeing the result," it's even better, but don't count on being able to write it down correctly from the very beginning).

"As fast as possible" is not really useful, but "at least as fast as such and such game" or "fast enough so nobody on our team can say it is sluggish" is much better

- Closely related to timing requirements is the question of your game being "synchronous" or "asynchronous." In other words, do your players need to be simultaneously online when they're playing?[42] Most of the time, fast-paced games will be "synchronous" (it doesn't make much sense to play MMOFPS via e-mailing "I'm shooting at you; what are you going to do about it?"), while really slow-paced ones (think chess by snail mail) will be "asynchronous."

▶ **What types of client connection do you need to support?** Do you need to support dial-up (hopefully not)? What about playing over 3G? What about supporting play over GPRS?

- What about firewalled connections? According to [Roskind], 6-9% of Internet users cannot use UDP—and, most likely, it happens because of firewalls.

▶ **What is your target geographical area?** While "worldwide" always sounds like a good idea, for some very fast-paced games, it might be not an option (this will be discussed in Chapter 3 and Vol. III's chapter on Server-Side Architecture), and you *might* need to support regional Datacenters. In addition, considerations such as "when most of the players are available" can affect some types of gameplay (for example, if in your game one player can challenge another, with a loser losing by default, you will most likely need to have "time windows" where such challenges are allowed, with the timing of these "time windows" tied to real-world clock in the relevant time zones).

- If it is "worldwide," a closely related question is "are you allowed to split your players into separate groups geo-wise (with only players within the same geo group being able to play with one another)?" While, say, continent-specific servers *may* be necessary from a technical standpoint (usually due to latencies, see Chapter 3 for discussion), it may also

---

42 I don't want to get into a lengthy hair-splitting discussion of whether this property should be named "temporal" or "synchronous"; let's simply use the name "synchronous" for the purposes of this book.

Make sure to pressure your monetization team about this one to make sure that you know as much as possible in advance.

easily affect marketing efforts, so you *do* need to agree with your marketing team whether it is allowed or not.

▶ **Which socializing features do you want to have**? Do you want an "Invite your Facebook friends to our game" feature? Do you need a feature such as "hey, there are five of your Facebook friends on server XX right now; would you like to join them?" And so on and so forth.

- Make sure to pressure your monetization team about this one to make sure that you know as much as possible in advance. In particular, if they tell you "inviting Facebook friends will be *the only* thing we'll *ever* need," don't trust them; I have never seen a game for which this is really the only thing necessary, social-wise.

▶ **A detailed description of your Matchmaking Algorithm:** how Game World instances are created? How they're populated? And don't forget about social implications of these decisions (see the *On Matchmaking and the Social Aspect of Your MOG* section above for more discussion).

▶ **Do you want/need to support "instant gameplay"** (i.e. the player being able to start enjoying your game without waiting for a huge download)? While potentially possible – it is not that easy, and needs to be planned well in advance (see Vol. II's chapter on Client-Side Architecture for a brief discussion of progressive downloads).

▶ **Are you going to support spectators**? In other words, will it be possible just to observe the others playing without playing yourself? If spectators are possible (and game download is small enough), it tends to work as quite a big incentive to start playing ("I've seen it, and I like what's going on, so why not try playing it myself?").

- As noted above in the *Technical Issues Affecting Marketing* section, even if your game is highly competitive (and observing can reveal information causing cheating), there are usually things that you can show without compromising the integrity of your game (examples include showing low-level games, showing games with delay, and recordings of high-profile games).

- If spectators are possible, will you require a login for spectators? For free-downloaded games of a smaller size, I've seen the ability to observe the game without the need to enter *any* information, providing a significant advantage (which comes at almost-zero cost if your infrastructure is good enough). See also the *Technical Issues Affecting Marketing* section above.

▶ **Are you planning to have your big finals shown in real time to thousands and hundreds-of-thousands of spectators?** *NB: We'll see why it is important from technical perspective, in Vol. III's chapter on Server-Side Architecture.*

- What about recording big finals and allowing spectators to watch them later?

▶ **What do you need to write into your database** (so that your Customer-Support and Marketing-and-Monetization Teams are capable of doing their job)? While writing each and every move is not realistic (neither is it necessary), you will be surprised by how many things Marketing will want to know, and it is better to account for it from the very beginning.

▶ **Do you need to implement i18n in the very first release or it can be postponed?**[43]

- For your i18n, do you need to support Asian languages?
  - If yes, do you need to support Japanese kanji or Chinese?
  - What about Korean Hangul?
- For your i18n, do you need to support right-to-left languages (Hebrew or Arabic)?

i18n

Internationalization (frequently abbreviated as i18n) is the process of designing a software application so that it can potentially be adapted to various languages and regions without engineering changes

—*Wikipedia*

---

43   Okay, okay, in some cases you might want to ignore it completely.

▶ **Is it acceptable to have a separate Client and web-based second-ary interface in a separate browser window** (such as "we'll use web browser with a separate login for in-game purchases")? While I am usually quite a strong opponent of the separate-browser-window sec-ondary interfaces (both on technical and marketing grounds; see the *Technical Issues Affecting Marketing and Monetization* section above), it can still save you a bit of development time, so having it as an open *option* (in case you run out of time—and this, as we all know, is ex-actly what usually happens) might be useful.

▶ **What about 3rd-party (social) logins?** Do you need them? Is it okay to use *only* 3rd-party logins? (see discussion in the *Technical Issues Affecting Marketing and Monetization* section above).

▶ **Client-update requirements.** There is a requirement that is (almost) universal for all multiplayer games: "We do need a way to update the Client automatically, simply when the player starts the app"; still, make sure to write it down. However, there are two more subtle ques-tions for a Client update:

Is it acceptable to stop the Game World while the Clients are being updated?

- Is it acceptable to stop the Game World while the Clients are being updated? How long is this stop-the-Game-World al-lowed to take?

- Is it acceptable to force-update Client apps (or at least not allow playing with an out-of-date Client)?

  • If not, for how long (in terms of "months back" or "versions back") do you need to support backward compatibility?

▶ **Server-update requirements.** Most of the Server-Side stuff qual-ifies as "implementation details"; however, whenever the Server is stopped, it's certainly visible to the players, so "how often we need to stop the Server for software upgrades" is a perfectly valid GDD-level question. Is it acceptable to stop the game while the Server is being updated? How often are Server updates planned? With the game be-ing multiplayer, stopping and then resuming the Game World may become quite a Pain in the Neck™ for players. However, allowing for Server updates without stopping the game world can easily become a much bigger Pain in the Neck™ when developing your system (see Vol. IX for some hints in this direction), so you need to think in advance about whether the effort is worth the trouble. Unless a non-stopping Server requirement is really significant for your game (or your monetization), you may want to try dropping it from the GDD and explicitly state that you can stop the server once-per-N-weeks (and also whenever an emergency Server update is required) to update Server-Side software (where N depends on the specifics of your game).

▶ **Fault-tolerance requirements.** This one requires a bit of explanation. Most likely, your game will be running on several commodity Servers. And commodity Servers do fail from time to time (in the very best case, once per Server per 3-5 years or so; however, if you're running 100 of such Servers, the probability of *one* of them failing is more like several-times-a-month). The Big Question™ we're asking here is the following: what is an acceptable behavior when such a hardware (or OS) failure occurs? Is it okay for the whole game site to go down? Or is it acceptable for those games that were running on the failed Server to be restarted from scratch—while all other games continue without a blink? Or you want a full-scale fault tolerance (i.e., whatever happens, the Server goes ahead without a hitch) for some of the critical Servers (like "The Server Running Tournament of the Year")? Or maybe you want such a full-scale fault tolerance for *all* your Servers? All of these are possible, but making it happen requires a *lot* of planning in advance. And if you have any doubt as to what-exactly-you-want in this department, make sure to read the rather detailed discussion of Fault Tolerance in Vol. III.

▶ **In-game payment systems,** which may need to be supported in the long run (these have implications on security, not to mention that you need to have a place for them within your architected system). Even if it is "the game will be free forever and ever," or "all the payments will

Even if it is "the game will be free forever and ever" or "all the payments will be done via Apple AppStore," it needs to be written down.

be done via Apple AppStore," it needs to be written down. Oh, and if it is "all the payments will be done via Apple App Store" and there is a "Windows" in the list of the platforms to be supported, there is a likely inconsistency in your GDD, so either drop "Windows" or think about specific App Stores for the Windows platform, or be ready to support payments yourself (which is doable, but is a really big Pain in the Neck™, so it's better to know about it well in advance).

Yes, it is a long list, but as we will see over the course of the book, we will indeed need all these things to architect your MOG. It means that if your list is missing any of these, at some point you will need to go back to the drawing board and get them out of the project stakeholders.

ON MOG-SPECIFIC TEAMS

One question that is closely related to the GDD (at least because all the teams *should* be represented during GDD discussions—at least by their respective team leads—is the issue of MOG-specific teams. That is, in addition to those traditional teams participating in the game development (see the *On a Typical Non-MOG Team Structure* section for a more-or-less-typical list), for an MOG there are usually four additional teams: *Network Team, Server Team, Database Team*, and *Back-End Team*.

Network Team

Your Network Team is responsible for development of a network communication layer. At the very least, it includes marshalling and dealing with stuff such as UDP and TCP. I usually argue that the Network Team is also responsible for developing an infrastructure (or "middleware") for event-driven programming and/or (Re)Actors (see Vol II for a detailed discussion on the benefits of event-driven programming and/ (Re)Actors); however, this is not strictly required. In any case, the idea here is very simple—

> *You certainly don't want your game programmers to deal with **both** your game logic **and** network peculiarities at the same time.*

Even if you're a small development shop and your programmers need to work part time on game logic and part time on network stuff—it is still beneficial to keep infrastructure-level code and game-logic code as separate as possible. Moreover, in my experience, doing it in a different manner (i.e., intertwining socket-handling code with game logic) is an almost-guaranteed way to ensure a disaster.

Server Team

Your Server team (at least in terms-that-are-used-within-this-book) is responsible for Server logic (this includes both Server simulation logic and any other logic, such as payment logic, tournament logic, etc.). Of course, diversity of the tasks involved can mean a further splitting of the Server Team into smaller task-specific teams.

We won't go into further detail on the responsibilities of different Server Teams here, but they will become obvious throughout the book. Just one thing to note is that in most cases, even if your development flow is Client-Driven as defined above, you will still need your Server Team[44] to deal with that "ongoing conversion" from Client to Server mentioned above (or with integrating the Server into your toolchain), with optimizing Server-Side, with non-Game-World game entities (Cashier, payment gateways, etc.), and so on and so forth.

Even if you're a small development shop and your programmers need to work part time on game logic and part time on network stuff, it is still beneficial to keep infrastructure-level code and game logic code as separate as possible.

---

44 As with anything else, for small development teams it might be a part-time role instead of a dedicated team.

Database Team

Pretty much any MOG has its own database,[45] and as a Big Fat Rule of Thumb™, you'll need a Database Team to deal with it. Not surprisingly, the Database Team is responsible for your database(s), and I usually argue for it handling *all* the aspects of the database, from development to DBA tasks, and from OLTP to analytics (more on it in Vol. VI's chapter on Databases).

This team is routinely responsible for maintaining database structure (both logical and physical), for ensuring data consistency (which goes above and beyond simple SQL-level constraints), for providing DB manipulation APIs to other teams (with these APIs ensuring data consistency), for replicas, for database performance, for optimizing DB requests, and last but certainly not least, for scalability.

BTW, about DB and scalability: for a properly architected Server-Side, the database almost universally becomes *the* bottleneck of the whole system; it means that the ability of your game to scale will depend on the Database Team in a big way. We'll discuss DB scalability in Vol. VI's chapter on Databases and in Vol. IX.

The ability of your game to scale will depend on the Database Team in a big way.

Back-End Team

Back-End Team is the team that is probably the most persistently ignored/downplayed, and ignoring it is a mortgage-crisis-size mistake.

In general, the Back-End Team is responsible for providing all the tools necessary for your support people/CSRs to do their job. And, believe me—

> *For an MOG, support can provide a **big fat advantage** over the competition.*

Sure, if your game is one-of-a-kind with no rivals in sight, support isn't too likely to be *that* important; however, as soon as there is competition, support can easily become the reason players prefer you over the competition.

---

45   Or a reasonable facsimile; even if you're storing your persistent objects in files, we'll still name it "DB" for the purposes of our current discussion.

BTW, whenever I speak about "support" or "CSRs," I mean the whole spectrum of support tasks, from the handling of trivial "I forgot my password" requests[46] all the way to sophisticated cheating investigations that can easily take several days to accomplish (and can have a profound effect on players, including such unpleasant-but-sometimes-necessary decisions as disqualifying a tournament winner due to cheating).

Back to the Back-End Team and its role. As noted above, the Back-End Team is responsible for making the work of the support team as efficient as possible, and it can make a *really big difference.*

In particular, it is a big mistake to think that 3rd-party tools taken "as is" (i.e., without any adjustments for your specific game) will work—they won't. In other words, even if you'll be using a 3rd-party Customer Relations Management (CRM) tool,[47] you'll need to integrate it with your databases for your support processes to make any sense.

And there will be reports over your own databases (in one game I know, there are over 500 such reports), and tools to manipulate the DB, and access to the monitoring tools (integrating them with other tools, like "tell me, wasn't our system overloaded at the moment when this e-mail came in?"), and alerts so that CSRs on duty know when something goes wrong with the servers (and can call admins or developers or…), and so on.

Timeline for the Back-End Team

As we can see, there are *lots* of things for the Back-End Team to do. However, unlike with all the other gamedev teams (whether MOG-specific or not), for the Back-End Team most of these tasks will become clear only when you have your game more-or-less ready. Sure, there are some things that are obvious from the beginning (like "I forgot my password" one), but, most of the time, load on the Back-End Team will increase dramatically after the launch of the "public beta."

For the Back-End Team, most of these tasks will become clear only when you have your game more-or-less ready.

---

46   However good your UI/help/FAQ is, there will be lots of people writing about it.

47   And the "3rd-party vs in-house" decision is not really as obvious as it might look at first glance.

As a result, my suggestion with regard to the Back-End Team is usually along the following lines:

► From the very beginning, *do* have the Back-End Team, but with minimal resources (as in "just a Back-End Team Lead" if you can afford it, or a partial-time role if you cannot).

  ▪ For the time being, the Back-End Team should deal with tasks-that-are-necessary-for-a-pretty-much-any-game, including things such as:

    • Identify the 3rd-party CRM you'll be using (or develop your own)

    • Play with your CRM and integrate it with your DB

      ▷ Make sure that all incoming e-mail requests have respective player accounts identified (if there is *any* reference of this e-mail in *any* of your DBs, it should be automagically identified)

      ▷ Spend time on a few very obvious requests (such as "I forgot my password"). Make sure that these requests can be handled *absolutely efficiently* (i.e., there are only 2-3 clicks to handle it; more details will be discussed in Vol. VII's chapters on Back-End Tools and CRM).

    • Develop a few very simple reports against your DB (like "show me all the details and all the playing history of the player by his ID").

    • Develop a few very simple tools to manipulate your DB (normally via APIs provided by your Database Team). Such tools should include at least such things as "add new CSR," "assign roles to a CSR," and so on.

- In other words, the idea is to prepare the framework to deal with the future tasks that will be coming. At the very least such a framework should include:

    - CRM system—including integration with your DBs(!)

    - Reporting system (read-only reports over DB), usually directly using SQL (or NoSQL; more in Vol. VI's chapter on Databases)

    - DB manipulation system (usually via calling APIs provided by Database Team)

▶ As the game is about to be open to the public (as a launch or a "public beta"), make sure to allocate additional resources to your Back-End Team (it will certainly become a full-size team if your game is successful) and start working closely with the CSR team lead to see what they need to improve their performance (most of the time it will be identifying the most time-consuming and mundane tasks and automating them).

All MOG-Specific Teams Must Be First-Class Citizens

Unfortunately, in quite a few development companies, MOG-specific teams (Network Team, Server Team, Database Team, and Back-End Team), while present, are treated as second-class citizens when compared with the huge and all-important 3D Team.[48] Most importantly, Network, Server, and Database Teams are often disregarded by the company management and (as a result) by fellow programmers. If 90% of the arguments between your Server team lead and your 3D team lead end up in favor of the latter (either because he is also an overall architect, or just because it "so happens"), you're very likely to have this problem.

In quite a few development companies, MOG-specific teams (Network Team, Server Team, and Database Team), while present, are treated as second-class citizens when compared with the huge and all-important 3D Team.

---

48   Closely related is an erroneous belief that back-end performance is not important; it is—see below for a discussion about Server costs.

With the Back-End Team, the situation is even worse. While in most environments, the necessity of Network, Server, and Database Teams is at least acknowledged, the Back-End Team is all too often created as an afterthought.

I tend to attribute this phenomenon to historical reasons. Quite a few companies out there moved from single-player game development to MOG development. And for single-player games, there is the adage "content is king" (with programmers routinely interpreting it as "3D is king"). And as a natural result of this perception (exacerbated by the fact that those pesky network and Server folks came into a well-established company, with a well-established culture of "3D is all that matters"), it is almost inevitable that without any additional effort to alleviate this problem, network, server, and database gals and guys are treated as second-class citizens.

However, I would argue that for MOGs the answer to the question "who is king?" is substantially different.

However, I would argue that for MOGs, the answer to the question "who is king?" is substantially different. IMNSHO, for MOGs it is gameplay that is king (yes, even more king than the content). If you have any doubts, you can take a look at many highly successful MOGs (including, but not limited to, *Lords & Knights* and *Top Eleven*), all having little to virtually zero content (at least under a traditional definition of the term).

As a result, MOGs are not only no longer about content and 3D and there are other teams that have the-same-order-of-magnitude impact on the end result. Please do your game a favor and openly acknowledge it[49]; it will significantly improve overall results. These improvements can be two-fold: (a) better decisions can be made (because the needs of the Server-Side won't be neglected anymore), and (b) because of better morale of the MOG-specific teams.

BTW, I am not saying that Network, Server, and Database Teams are *the only* teams that deserve respect. What I am arguing for is—

> **All** *programming teams, from the 3D Team on one side to the Back-End Team on the other side, are equally important for the MOG to succeed.*

---

49   Of course, as I am usually in the Network Team, it will also be a favor for me, but I prefer to keep this consideration under wraps.

At the very least, it stands because you cannot possibly release your game without any of these teams. And any attempt to shift the balance in favor of one of the teams is usually devastating to the overall game quality.

Note that this observation doesn't really depend on you using Client-Driven Development Workflow, or a Server-Driven one. Even for a game with a Client-Driven Development Workflow, network, server, database, and back-end folks are *really* important (or, to quantify this statement, if they're doing their job poorly, your game won't fly regardless of the brilliant efforts of the other teams).

RUNNING COSTS BREAKDOWN

One additional thing that you should do alongside writing your GDD is calculating the breakdown of running costs for your game when it becomes operational. The reason for doing it now (and not "some time later") is apparent: if the per-player cost of running your game is higher than your expected per-player monetization—in this case, you obviously have a Big Fat Problem™ on your hands (which in turn will affect your GDD). In addition to the usual and obvious things such as initial development costs, an MOG introduces quite a few new items to the list:

If the cost of running your game is higher than your expected monetization, you have a Big Fat Problem™ on your hands.

▶ **Software maintenance costs.**[50] If you think that your programmers will have nothing to do when the game goes live, forget it. For most successful online games, teams tend to increase (rather than decrease) after the game is launched, but in any case there are *lots* of things to do. It is especially true for your Server Team and Back-End Team (which tend to grow like crazy for pretty much any successful MOG).

▶ **Game Server costs.** Regardless of whether you are using a cloud or renting a "dedicated server" from your ISP, there will be costs. It is impossible for me to tell you how many Servers you will need; you will need to estimate this yourself (and it is *not* going to be easy).

---

50   While not really "new," it is different enough to be mentioned.

Rack Unit (U)

A rack unit (abbreviated U or RU) is a unit of measure defined as 1.75 inches (44.45 mm). It is most frequently used as a measurement of the overall height of 19-inch and 23-inch rack frames, as well as the height of equipment that mounts in these frames.

—*Wikipedia*

Contrary to popular belief, cloud Servers, while providing additional elasticity and per-hour billing, tend to be more expensive than dedicated ones even when rented on a per-month basis (the cost benefit of the cloud comes when you need your Servers only for not-so-many hours a month).

- However, as soon as you have your number-of-players-per-Server (which can easily vary from 1,000 players/workhorse-Server[51] to 50,000 players/workhorse-server depending on your game), you can estimate server costs per player with certain confidence.

- As of the beginning of 2017, one "workhorse" 1U/2-socket Server (with 2x8 cores and 64G RAM,[52] and not including OS) in a decent datacenter[53] could be rented for about $150-$200/month.[54] Contrary to popular belief, cloud Servers (more specifically IaaS virtual servers), while providing elasticity and per-hour[55] billing, tend to be more expensive than dedicated ones even when rented on a per-month basis (the cost benefit of the cloud comes when you need your Servers only for not-so-many hours a month). More on renting "traditional virtualized cloud vs. bare-metal cloud vs. dedicated Servers" when it comes to games will be discussed in Vol. VII, but for an original very rough estimate, the data above should be more-or-less sufficient for you to get the order of magnitude of your Game Server expenses.

- If your game needs Server-Side GPU, then things will become more complicated. There will be some discussion on it in Vol. III's chapter on Server-Side Architecture, but overall perception at the moment is as follows—don't hold your

---

51   For simulation-based MOGs, 1,000 players/Server, or 100 players/core seems to be a kind of "de-facto industry standard" in a sense that this number was observed in quite a few very different simulation-based games.

52   This is more or less a "sweet spot" for quite a few games, though your own "sweet spot" can be quite different.

53   But with you being responsible for all the server management, except for hardware replacements. Also note that exotic locations tend to be *much* more expensive than "mainstream" ones, so if your game (usually a stock exchange, casino, or bookmaker) has some strange legal requirements of "where the servers should be located," check specific prices for a specific location (and, while you're at it, also change the quality of connection at their location, the more exotic the location, the more quality varies).

54   Prices mentioned in this book are toward the lower end of the spectrum. In other words, you won't usually be able to find reasonable-quality things at 2x a lower price (but you will easily be able to find the same things as 5x or 10x more expensive).

55   Or even "per-second."

breath over it, as Server-Side GPUs tend to be significantly more expensive than desktop ones.

▶ **Database Server/Backup costs.** Even if your game is a simulation, you can count on all kinds of things going into the database (and on your Marketing and Monetization Teams asking for all kinds of reports over this database). What kind of information you're going to save in your database follows from your GDD requirements, so you should be able to get a very rough estimate for the amount of storage you'll need. 4-socket DB server (say, 4x8 cores with 128G RAM and 6x500G SSD) is going to set you back around $1,500/month, and additional HDD storage can be obtained (*very* roughly, as pricing depends on implementation details greatly) at approximately $10/month per 1TB of non-RAID-ed HDD storage (RAID-ed SSD can go as high as $100/month per 1TB; more on it in Vol. VII's chapter on Preparing for Launch).

▶ **Admin costs.** All those Servers need to be administered, and the more Servers (and, even more importantly, types of Servers) you have, the more admins you will need. For quite a few games, at some point you're likely to also need a DBA.

▶ **Costs of outgoing traffic.** Exactly as it was for CPU costs, only you can tell how much traffic your game will need. However, as soon as you've estimated your traffic, you can estimate your traffic costs. Estimating traffic is generally an even worse exercise in guesswork than estimating CPU, but it still needs to be done.

    ■ In the real world, I've seen games with traffic being anywhere between 1kbit/s/active-player to 200kbit/s/active-player, depending on the nature of the game;[56] note that for social and other asynchronous games, the concept of active-player doesn't apply, so calculations will be quite different but still necessary and doable.

---

[56] Note that achieving this kind of numbers is not trivial, and your Network Team will spend a lot of time and effort to get there. See more discussion on traffic and optimization in Chapter 3.

If your game is successful, you will likely need to protect it from DDoS.

- As of the beginning of 2017, reasonably good pricing (at a reasonably good datacenter) for traffic went at about $300/month for an "unmetered" 1Gbit/s connection, and at around $2,000/month for an "unmetered" 10Gbit/s.[57]

▶ **DDoS protection costs.** If your game is successful, you will likely need to protect it from DDoS (details of DDoS protection will be discussed in Vol. VIII, but for now let's note that for synchronous games you will likely want DDoS protection based on BGP-level traffic redirection in case of attack). As for the costs of such BGP-level DDoS protection, they depend greatly on a vendor, your incoming bandwidth, and the capacity of DDoS attacks you want to deal with. However, to get an extremely rough (i.e., within an order of magnitude) idea about the cost of such DDoS protection, you may take something like $5K/month per 1Gbit/s of your normal incoming(!) traffic (YMMV; batteries not included).

▶ **Last, but certainly not least, there are support costs.** These are quite difficult to estimate in advance, but I can share one real-world observation in this regard. A game that had some hundreds of thousands of simultaneous players had received dozens of thousands of e-mails per day(!). To deal with it, they needed to keep a support team of hundreds of people (distributed over twenty-four hours) just to answer e-mails. That being said, their support was almost universally "the best e-mail support you could wish for" (and they probably could get away with much smaller support teams if they'd left their players less satisfied[58]), so it is more of an upper-bound for the number of e-mails; on the other hand, their support was extremely well-organized (100+ e-mails per person per day requires quite a bit of organization, especially as trivial e-mails such as "I forgot my

---

57 Therefore, even for a rather "traffic-hungry" game of 200kbit/s/player, you should be able to run up to 50,000 simultaneous players (at peak time) over that $2k/month unmetered link. That is, *if* your Network Team can squeeze your game into 200kbit/s/player. Also note that for cloud servers, traffic can be up to 10x more expensive (!).

58 In particular, because the better support experience your players have, the more they are inclined to use it again.

password" represent only 80% of all incoming traffic, and the rest can require *much* more time to analyze and respond to).

- BTW, if you dream of providing phone support, your costs will go off the charts *really quickly*. One potential exception is if you have a small team that initiates voice conversations from its side based on e-mails; however, opening your support to a well-known phone number is going to cost you *way* too much.

- Live chat support is not necessarily prohibitively expensive, though it easily *might* become so. I'd suggest to stay clear of it for as long as possible (at least until you have all the machinery and people for e-mail support).

Of course, the numbers above provide only a very rough idea about the costs, but let's hope that your estimates will show that you have ample reserve so that your game remains viable even if the original costs are somewhat underestimated. In practice, most of the prices for services tend to drop rather than rise as the time goes by, but as they love to say in the financial industry, past performance doesn't really guarantee anything (and also there are always things that were originally unaccounted for or estimates being too optimistic).

COMMON GDD PITFALL: JUST THROW IN A MULTIPLAYER FOR FREE

One scenario that never works but is still reported to be tried as late as 2016 is when your game is planned as a single-player one and then somebody says "hey, let's add multiplayer capability to our game!—shouldn't be difficult compared to what-we've-already-done." Of course, this sounds very attractive to managers and marketing, as they get "something they can sell" and "for free." There is only one problem with this approach—

Hey, let's add multiplayer capability to our game!— shouldn't be difficult compared to what-we've-already-done.

I don't know of one single instance where it worked

As noted above, MOGs are *very* different from single-player games; there are several new teams involved, and even for a Client-Driven Workflow, integration with the Server-Side (and testing the game in a multiplayer environment) should be done all the time, otherwise multiplayer aspect(s) of your game won't work.

If your manager won't believe me on this account, ask him to take a look at well-known efforts by major gamedev companies. Just one example: when it took the makers of *Elder Scrolls* about seven years to get to their very first MOG (and not as-top-notch as their single-player stuff), this should provide a hint that adding multiplayer functionality is usually not as easy as it sounds. There are *tons* of other similar examples out there, but I will leave Googling as a reader exercise.

In other words, if you want multi-layer capability for your game, it can be done. However, it won't be easy, and making your game an MOG will likely significantly change lots of processes within your software development life cycle.

GAME ENTITIES AND INTERACTIONS

After you have your GDD with all the requirements listed, I argue that the next step for an MOG should be to draw an Entities-and-Interactions diagram specific to your game.

While you may think that such a diagram is "obvious," it is still *much* better to have it drawn and discussed, at the very least to make sure that everybody has the same understanding of what exactly constitutes "obvious." In particular, it is important to remember all the non-Game-World entities such as Cashier, payment processors, and social networks (while the two last ones are not really something you're going to implement yourself—most likely, you *will* need to implement integrations with them, so they *do* belong to your Entities-and-Interactions diagram).

Game Entities: What Are You Dealing With?

In each and every game, you have some Game Entities that you'll be dealing with. For example, in an MMORPG, you're likely to have PCs, NPCs, zones, and cells; in a casino game, you have lobbies, tables, and players; in a social farming game, you have players and player farms. Of course, every game will contain many more entities than I've mentioned above, but they depend on the specifics of your game, so you're certainly in a much better position than I am to write them down. And if you feel that you're about to be hit by "not seeing the forest for the trees" syndrome, you can always replace your diagram with several (organized in a hierarchical manner), so that each contains only a manageable number of entities.

Interactions between Game Entities

Pretty much inevitably those Game Entities of yours will need to interact with one another. Players reside within cells that in turn reside within zones, PCs interact with NPCs, players sit and play on casino tables, and players interact with other player's farms. All these interactions are very important for the game architecture, and need to be written down as a part of your Entities-and-Interactions diagram. Even more importantly, you need to be reasonably sure that you have listed *all* the interactions you can think of at the moment.

Even more importantly, you need to be reasonably sure that you have listed *all* the interactions you can think of at the moment.

What Should You Get? Entities-and-Interactions Diagram

As a result of the process of identifying your Game Entities, you should get a diagram (let's name it "Entities-and-Interactions diagram") showing all the major Game Entities and, even more importantly, all possible interactions between these entities.

One thing that *must* be included in the Entities-and-Interactions diagram (alongside gameplay-related entities) is entities related to monetization (payments, promotions) and entities related to social interactions. In other words, if you're going to rely on viral marketing via social networks, you'd better know about it in advance; as discussed below, the impact of social interactions on architecture can be much more significant and devastating than a simple "we'll add that Facebook gateway later."

Examples of Entities and Interactions

To give you a bit of an idea on entities and interactions, I'll try to describe typical entities for some popular game genres. Note that as with any other advice, in this book or elsewhere, your mileage may vary, and you need to think about specifics of your game rather than blindly copying typical entities mentioned below!

Also, please note—

> *Example diagrams provided here are extremely sketchy and illustrate only a few aspects of each game*

(to give a very general idea of what the Entities-and-Interactions diagrams might contain in general). In practice, your own diagrams will usually be *much more elaborate.*

As we'll see from the diagrams, quite a few include Game Entities that can be named Game World entities (places where actual gameplay and most inter-player interaction is happening) and/or Matchmaking entities. While these terms are sometimes not that well defined and are not universal, we will still use them as a way to generalize certain observations throughout the book (in particular, in Vol. III's chapter on Server-Side Architecture).

And, last but not least, while you may (and actually *should*) think that you already know everything about your game by this point, it is still very important to have this diagram drawn; otherwise you may easily end up with differing vision among team members, which can cost you *much* more than time spent on this diagram (in particular, forgetting about the Cashier and associated interactions is rather common at the early stages of development and, if it happens, can cause quite a bit of trouble later on).

Okay, with all the preliminaries aside, we can finally get to the example diagrams.

Social Farming and Farming-Like Games

While the social games genre is wide and difficult to generalize, one sub-genre, social farming games, is straightforward enough to describe. In farming and farming-like games, the number of different entities and especially interactions between them are quite limited. Entities are usually limited to players and their farms (the latter including everything-that-can-be-found-on-the-farm). Interactions (beyond the player interacting with their own farm) are also traditionally very limited (though they are all-important from the social point of view).

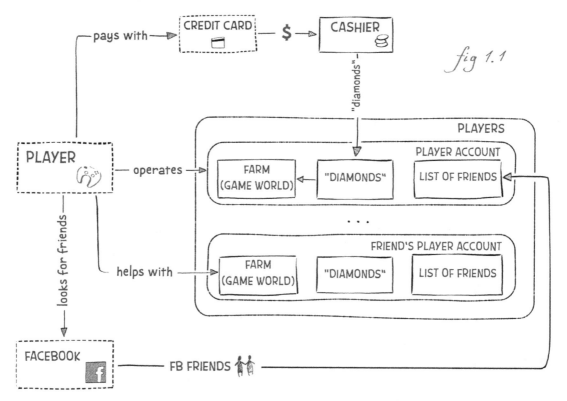

fig 1.1

> NB: On all our example Entities-and-Interactions diagrams, we will draw external (to our game) entities as dotted.[59]

You should keep in mind that in most cases there is one significant caveat to remember: it is a mistake to think that you can randomly separate players on different servers and allow only interactions within one such server; see more discussion on it in the *On Matchmaking and the Social Aspect of Your MOG* section above.

Casino Multiplayer Games

With casino multiplayer games, everything looks quite simple: there are tables and players at these tables. However, in some of the casino games (notably in poker), choosing an opponent is considered a skill, and therefore players should be able to choose who they want to play against. It implies another game entity—a lobby, where the opponents can be selected. An example Entities and Interactions diagram for multiplayer blackjack is shown in Fig 1.2:

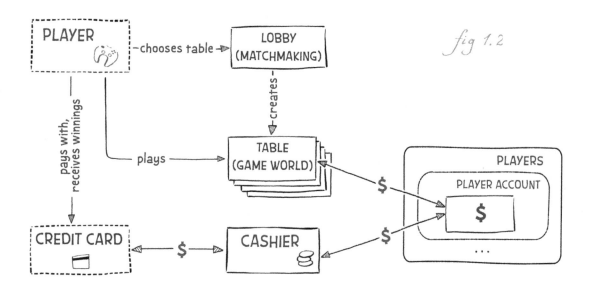

fig 1.2

---

59   At the architecture stage, we'll need to make appropriate gateways to communicate with external entities such as "Facebook" or "Credit Card," but we're not there yet; see Vol. III's chapter on Server-Side Architecture for an appropriate discussion.

Note that for this example diagram, among quite a few other things, we've omitted social interaction; you will need to add it yourself, as it is appropriate for your specific game.

Stock Exchanges, Sports Betting, and Auction Sites

As was already noted in the Introduction, stock exchanges and auction sites are so close to betting that you'll be facing significant difficulties when trying to describe the difference between the three (except, obviously, for the social stigma traditionally attached to betting). With stock exchanges, auction sites (think "eBay"), and betting sites, the entities involved are the same. It is players (though, of course, for a stock exchange you need to describe them as "traders" or "dealers"), and listed shares (or sporting events or products). Players don't interact directly, however, indirect interaction does exist via creating some actions ("orders" or "bets") related to stocks or events or products.

Fig 1.3 shows an example Entities and Interactions diagram for a stock exchange:

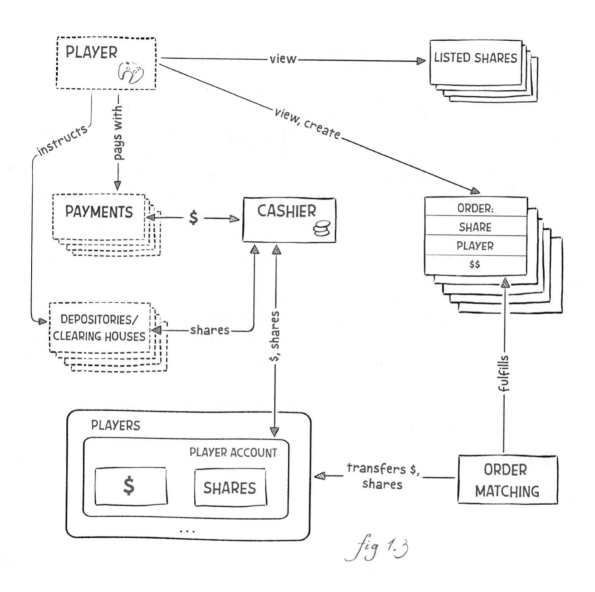

fig 1.3

Large Virtual-World Games (MMOTBS/MMORTS/MMORPG/MMOFPS)

Despite all the differences (including very different latency tolerance, which can significantly affect architecture and protocols; see the discussion on handling latencies in Chapter 3), from the point of view of the Game Entities involved, all the virtual-world games tend to be more or less similar. In particular, in these games there are players (PCs), there are NPCs; also there are usually cells and zones containing those cells,[60] which represent a virtual world (VW) where interactions between PCs and NPCs are occurring. The player option of choosing who she wants to play with may or may not be provided; however, even if it is not provided, and you think that you can toss your players around your virtual worlds as you wish, arbitrary player separation (assigning player to servers without any inter-server interaction) becomes infeasible as soon as you introduce a social feature such as "Recruit a Friend (and play with her later)." See further discussion on arbitrary player separation in the *Matchmaking That Doesn't Work (As a Rule of Thumb)* section above.

Fig. 1.4 shows an example Entities and Interactions diagram for an MMORPG:

---

60   While names may vary, the concepts behind are usually more or less the same.

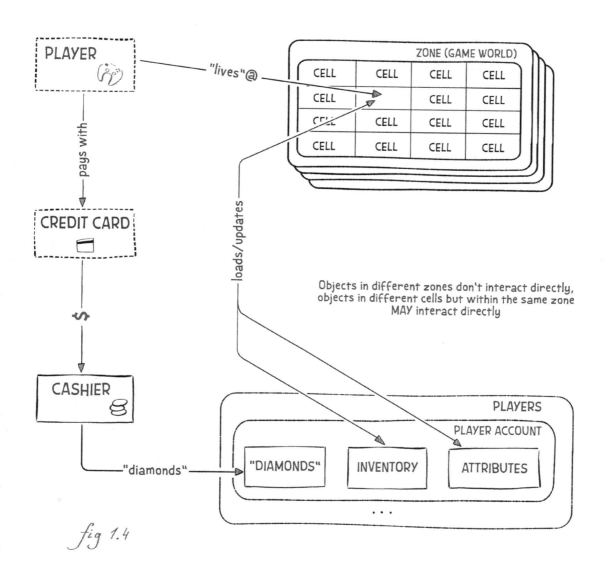

fig 1.4

Team Competitions/eSports

Last but not least, let's describe two game genres that are currently the most popular multiplayer games out there; I'm speaking about Multiplayer Online Battle Arenas (MOBAs) and team-based First-Player Shooters (FPS).

While the mechanics of MOBA and FPS-based games are very different, once again, from an Entities and Interactions point of view, most of these games will follow pretty much the same pattern shown on Fig 1.5:

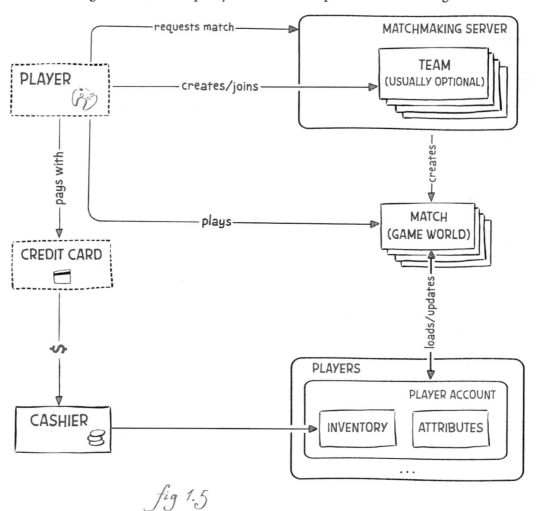

fig 1.5

BTW, if you feel that this diagram looks very similar to Fig 1.2 (the one about casinos), well, that's because these diagrams *are* similar. In any case, players come to a Lobby or Matchmaking server and then play in a Game World based on their selection or matchmaking—that's pretty much it. The only significant differences from an Entities-and-Interactions point of view between team competitions and casino-like games are that (a) with team competitions, well, there are teams (which are optionally used as a part of matchmaking process), and (b) unlike with casinos, for team competitions, Game Worlds where all the play happen, are usually assigned instead of being selected by players.[61] How the money obtained via the Cashier is spent depends on the game and its monetization, but usually there are quite a few things to buy (as well as *tons* of discussion on the Internet regarding which of these items are "pay to win" and which aren't; fortunately, within the scope of this book, we don't need to get onto this discussion minefield).

Entities and Interactions Diagram As a Starting Point to Architect Your Game

This Entities-and-Interactions diagram you've got is one of those things that will affect your architecture greatly. In particular, it is a starting point to realize what kinds of "implementation entities" (such as Servers, OS processes, DB tables, rows, and columns, etc.) you need to implement your Game Entities and how to map your Game Entities into your implementation entities.

In Vol. III (more specifically—in the chapter on Server-Side Architecture), we'll discuss Game Servers as a way to implement some of the Game Entities mentioned above; as a rule of thumb, the types of Game Servers you have will map one-to-one to such Game Entities as Game Worlds, Tournaments, Cashier, and gateway-with-Facebook.

---

61 i.e., while players can select a *type* of the Game World, they normally cannot select specific opponents to play with.

CHAPTER 1 SUMMARY

To briefly summarize the main takeaways from Chapter 1:

► GDD is an absolute *must*.

- The GDD *must* be written with both Project Stakeholders and developers participating, but with Project Stakeholders having the final say.

- The GDD *must* be written *only* using those terms that are understandable to Players.

► There are significant peculiarities related to MOG GDDs (and MOG development in general), in particular:

- MOGs often have undefined or unlimited lifespans, which brings lots of further implications.

- There are two distinct workflows for MOG development: Client-Driven and Server-Driven.

- Matchmaking mechanisms happen to be extremely important both gameplay-wise and architecture-wise.

- Marketing and monetization approaches *must* be taken into account from the very beginning.

  • And there are quite a few technical decisions that can also help them(!).

- Compared to single-player game development, for an MOG four more teams are necessary. These are Network Team, Server Team, Database Team, and Back-End Team.

  • Contrary to current practices in quite a few gamedev companies, these teams *must* be treated as first-class citizens.

- Running costs can kill your MOG and *must* be estimated from the very beginning.

► Make sure to draw your Entities and Relations diagram before going any further.

- This diagram *should* contain not only your Game World entities, but also all of your {monetization|socialization|payment|...} entities, and all the known interactions between the Game Entities too.

Bibliography

Aldridge, David. 2011. *I Shot You First: Networking the Gameplay of HALO: REACH.* http://www.gdcvault.com/play/1014345/I-Shot-You-First-Networking.

Brightman, James. 2012. *GDC: Cliff Bleszinski: "Screw focus groups, they suck".* http://www.gamesindustry.biz/articles/2012-03-09-gdc-cliff-bleszinski-screw-focus-groups-they-suck.

Donovan, Tristan. 2011. *Focus Groups, Testing, And Metrics: Developers Speak.* http://www.gamasutra.com/view/feature/134870/focus_groups_testing_and_.php.

Elbaum, Dan, and Carlin Scott. 2013. "The Perfect Couple: Domain Models & Behavior-Driven Development." *PNSQC 2013 Proceedings.*

Kim, Joseph. 2015. *Mobile Game Design: Iteration vs. Planning, MVP = Dangerous!* http://www.gamasutra.com/blogs/JosephKim/20150224/237157/Mobile_Game_Design_Iteration_vs_Planning_MVP__Dangerous.php.

Pfister, Andrew. 2015. *Coming into Focus: Understanding Video Game Market Research.* http://www.gamasutra.com/blogs/AndrewPfister/20150529/244601/Coming_into_Focus_Understanding_Video_Game_Market_Research.php.

Roskind, Jim. 2013. *Quick UDP Internet Connections.* https://www.ietf.org/proceedings/88/slides/slides-88-tsvarea-10.pdf.

CHAPTER 2.
ON CHEATING, P2P, AND [NON-]AUTHORITATIVE SERVERS

When developing an MOG, there is one extremely important thing to remember. This phenomenon is virtually nonexistent for non-multiplayer games,[62] and is usually of little importance for LAN-based multiplayer games—but is absolutely critical for over-the-Internet games. I'm speaking about player cheating.

---

62   Well, except for "unlock level" and "infinite health" kinds of cheats, but these rarely cause too much trouble for the game ecosystem.

Player cheating is One Big Problem™ for all successful MOGs. The problem is *that* ubiquitous for multiplayer games that we can say—

> If your MOG doesn't have players cheating,
> it is either that you're not looking for cheaters
> thoroughly enough, or you are not successful yet.

Note that in this chapter we will only briefly mention most of the cheats, and will concentrate only on those cheats that are essential for our architectural decisions. In-depth discussion on the subject of "how to deal with cheating" belongs in Volume VIII (chapters on Bot Fighting and Other Player Abuses).

IF YOU'RE POPULAR ENOUGH, THEY WILL FIND REASONS TO CHEAT

Khajiit… are intelligent, quick, and agile.
They make excellent thieves due to their natural
agility and unmatched acrobatics skill.
　　—*Elder Scrolls*

You may think that players have no reason to cheat for your specific game. For example, if your game has nothing that can be redeemed for money, you may think that you're safe regardless of the number of your players. In practice, it is *exactly* the other way around: if your game is popular enough, they will find a reason to cheat regardless of (a lack of) direct monetization options for the cheating.

Just one example from real life. Once upon a time, there was a free poker site out there where players got "play chips" for free, and were able to play with them. There was nothing that could be done with those "play chips," except for playing (so they could not be redeemed for anything-which-has-real-value). At that time, it seemed to the team that there was no reason to cheat on the site; none whatsoever, right? Real life has proven this assumption was badly wrong.

The thing was that the players were able to put all their "play chips" on the table; while doing so made very little sense from a poker point of view, they were using the amount of their chips to brag about "how good a player I am." And as soon as they started to brag about their play chips, one guy had the thought, *Hey, I can sell these play chips on eBay, and players will pay—just to look better than they are!* And as soon as eBay sales started, the cheating became rampant (with lots of multiple accounts to get those free chips, and with lots of "chip dumping" to pass them along).

The thing was that the players were able to put all their "play chips" on the table; while doing so made very little sense..they were using the amount of their chips to imply "how good a player I am."

While I (and probably you) cannot imagine spending twenty real dollars to get two million "play chips" with no other value than helping you boast that you're a "really good player" (when you're not), we know for sure that there is a certain percentage of people out there who will do it. It is just a matter of probabilities, so if your game has enough players, you can count on such things happening.

BTW, the same aspect of human nature is currently being successfully exploited for monetization purposes by numerous modern games (especially social games); however, at this point, we're not concerned with exploiting human vices ourselves (it is a job for monetization guys, and beyond the scope of this book), but with the technical aspects of preventing cheating.

For us gamedevs, the moral of the story is—

> *Even if you think that players have zero reason to cheat, given that your site is popular enough, they will find a reason.*

As soon as your game reaches 1,000 simultaneous players, you're likely to have singular cheaters. And when the number goes up to 100,000, you can be 100% sure that cheaters are there (and if you don't see them, it just means that you're not looking for them hard enough). While the number of cheaters does depend on the kind of goodies you provide to your players, and cheater numbers may easily vary by an order of magnitude, I daresay[63] that chances of you having a game with 100,000 simultaneous players and not having any

---

63 Yeah, sometimes I love a bit of ye olde English.

cheaters are negligible, pretty much regardless of what the exact game is that you're running.

THE BIG FAT HAIRY DIFFERENCE FROM E-COMMERCE

One thing to keep in mind is that game cheaters are very different from e-commerce fraudsters. With e-commerce, those who're trying to get around the system are either trying to angle the promotions or are outright fraudsters.[64] When speaking about games, the reasons behind cheating are much more diverse. For players, in addition to all the reasons to cheat described above, there are many others.

For example, as it has happened with "play chips" (see the *If You're Popular Enough, They Will Find Reasons to Cheat* section above), people cheat just to claim that they're better players than they really are. Or they cheat because they feel that the game rules are unfair (to them, that is). Or they cheat just because of the perception that "everybody else does it anyway," so they need to cheat to level the field. Or they try to save some time by using "bots" instead of "grinding" themselves. The possibilities are really endless here.

This, in turn, means that the line which separates "cheaters" from "honest players" is much more blurred with games than in e-commerce.

This, in turn, means that the line which separates "cheaters" from "honest players" is much more blurred with games than in e-commerce. Throw in the fact that e-commerce fraud is an outright crime and, say, using "bots" to avoid "grinding" is punishable at most by a ban on the site (which can be bypassed rather easily, at least unless you're paying for your game *and* the name on your credit cards is Rumpelstiltskin. For more discussion, see Vol. IV, chapter on Basic Security, and Vol. VIII), and you will realize—

> *Lots of people who would never ever cheat in e-commerce will easily cheat in online games.*

---

64 There are also people who want to use your site as a testing ground to improve their hacker skills or to brag about them after breaking you, as well as hacktivists, but fortunately, they're relatively few and far between.

While the number of "honest players" in online games still exceeds the number of "cheaters" by a wide margin, you cannot rely on the e-commerce experience, which usually goes along the lines of, "Oh, merely 0.3% of our customers are frauds."[65]

The second difference between e-commerce frauds and game cheaters is that due to much more significant interaction between players in games than in e-commerce—

> ### *Even a relatively small number of game cheaters can easily ruin the whole game ecosystem.*

As one example: if enough people are using bots to get an unfair advantage with your game (for example, to react to threats more quickly than a human can), your game will start to deteriorate—and in extreme cases can get to the point of being completely unplayable. In other words: dealing with cheaters is not all about money; it is about preserving the very substance of your game.

Dealing with cheaters is not all about money; it is about preserving the very substance of your game.

DEALING WITH CHEATERS

As noted above, cheaters are pretty much inevitable for any sizeable game. It is just a fact of life (just like "it is rainy outside today"). The real question, both in terms of rain and cheaters, always goes as follows: "Sure, it is pretty bad, but what can or should we do about it?" If it is raining—we're taking an umbrella; it won't protect us 100%, but with some luck (and if it is not also windy)—an umbrella can provide a more-or-less adequate protection from rain.

Pretty much the same goes when dealing with cheaters. While it is not realistic to obtain *100%* protection, it is generally possible to get *some* that is more-or-less adequate. In general, there are three things that can (and usually *should*) be done in this regard.

---

65   The number can vary significantly, but in e-commerce it is almost universally below 1% (and at ~1.5% of chargebacks, which include both frauds and honest mistakes, heavy penalties start to kick in; more in Volume VI's chapter on Payment Processing).

Gameplay

The first thing to think about is whether gameplay of your game encourages cheaters. This is a controversial point (after all, technicalities are not supposed to affect gameplay), but you need to analyze what your players will probably do to cheat. Try to put yourself in a cheater's shoes and think, *What would I do myself if I'd been paid for cheating the system?*[66]

Sometimes, such analysis can reveal that that cheating is going to be *that* easy that it will essentially kill the game; this tends to be especially import-ant in eSports-like gaming environments. And sometimes you can find that there is a gameplay change that would be minor for honest players, but which reduces the potential for cheating manifold.

BTW, there is a rather large camp of developers out there (usually coming from outside gamedev, and/or with an academic background), that says, "Hey, if the gameplay isn't bulletproof against cheating, you shouldn't even think about releasing it." I'm completely against this kind of attitude (in particular because I'm not even sure that there exists a single game that is indeed 100% bulletproof). What I am saying is that there *might* be a way to adjust gameplay a little so it doesn't aid and abet cheaters (and, as a nice side effect, often such an adjustment leads to the game rules being more straightforward).

You need to make sure that your *architecture* does *not* help cheaters.

Architecture

As a next step, you need to make sure that your *architecture* does *not* help cheaters. If it does, you will be in Really Big Trouble™ as soon as your game becomes popular. For example, if your game is a first-person shooter using Authoritative Clients, be prepared for all kinds of cheats up to "magic tele-ports"; these cheats can easily become bad enough to make your game barely playable. Then, in the best case, such cheats will cause you to start a series of extremely painful refactorings (see, for example, [Harton]), in the worst one, they may even kill your game completely.

---

66   Note that at this point we're speaking about abusing *gameplay* as such, without exploiting implementation loopholes etc. OTOH, certain technicalities (such as "it is not possible to have 100%-reliable identification of a player's device" and "it is not possible to provide a 100% guarantee that our Client wasn't modified") do need to be taken into consideration.

We'll look more at it later, starting with the *Authoritative Client: Pretty Much Hopeless Against Cheaters* section. <spoiler>Very briefly: for most games, we'll need to stick to Authoritative Server architectures.</spoiler>

Bot Fighting

And the last-but-certainly-not-least aspect of dealing with cheaters is direct cheater fighting. As a rule of thumb (and unless you're a stock exchange), it can usually be postponed until you deploy your game. As soon as your game is out of the door (and is alive and kicking), you need to start proactively looking for cheaters (more on it in Vol. VIII's chapters on Bot Fighting and Other Player Abuses), and deal with them as soon as you find them.

Details of direct fighting with cheaters will be discussed in Vol. VIII; for the time being, we just want to ensure that our architecture will allow us to perform such cheater fighting without rewriting the whole thing.

ATTACKS: THE REALLY BIG ADVANTAGE OF THE HOME TURF

When dealing with cheaters (in the realm of classical security, they are usually named "attackers"), it is very important to understand the fundamental differences between the two classes of the attack scenarios.

Home Game

In the first class of cheating or attack scenarios, the cheater or attacker tries to affect something that is under *your* direct control. For games, this "something" is usually your Server.

In such cases, you essentially have an inherent advantage from the very beginning; while attacks are always a possibility, for this first class of attacks, all are inevitably related to the bugs in your implementation. In other words—

In the first class of cheating or attack scenarios, the cheater or attacker tries to affect something which is under *your* direct control. For games, this "something" is usually your Server.

Whenever you have something that is under your control, you're generally more-or-less safe, save for implementation problems.

Of course, there are lots of bugs to be exploited, but you do have a fighting chance, and as soon as a specific bug is fixed, the attacker will need to find another bug, which is not that easy if you've done your job properly.

One example of such attacks happening "on your home turf" is attacking your Server, aiming to get some information such as "what is going on under fog of war," or even changing gameplay; while this is often possible, usually you do have a fighting chance against these attacks.

Road Game

The second class of attack scenarios is related to those cases where the attacker has your software[67] (such as your Client) under his full control, and can do whatever-he-wants with it. In these cases, things are *much* worse for you. In fact, whatever you do with your Client, the attacker is generally able to reverse engineer it and do whatever-they-want with your game from that point.

Examples of such attacks include such hacks as see-through-walls (a.k.a. wallhacks, or closely related lifting-fog-of-war hacks, a.k.a. maphacks) if your Client has this information, changing packet timestamps to whatever-attacker-wants (to abuse lag compensation), and all kinds of bots running on top of your Client.[68]

Sure, you can try to obfuscate your intentions (and your Client), but given enough effort (and we're not speaking about "the time comparable to lifetime of our sun"), *any* obfuscation can be broken. In terms of classical security, in this second class of attack scenarios, all you have at your disposal is so-called "Security by Obscurity," which (under traditional security models) is not considered security at all; while we will need to resort to "Security by Obscurity" in some cases,[69] we need to realize that—

Security by Obscurity

is the use of secrecy of the design or implementation to provide security. A system relying on security through obscurity may have theoretical or actual security vulnerabilities, but its owners or designers believe that if the flaws are not known, then attackers will be unlikely to find them.

—Wikipedia

---

67   In fact, the same logic applies even if the attacker has your hardware device.

68   N.B.: proxy bots are a bit different, though.

69   Notably for bot fighting and for preventing multiple accounts, where there are very few other ways of protection, if any.

> *"Security by Obscurity", while sometimes the only protection available at our disposal, cannot be relied on.*

To summarize the discussion above:

> **When speaking about cheaters, an advantage of "home turf" (having control over software or device) makes a huge difference. In particular, you cannot really protect something that you place into the attacker's hands.**

The situation in this regard is *that* bad that even if you could give each player a hardware device, these devices would also be hacked (to see the spectrum of attacks available on hardware, see [Skorobogatov]). In general, whatever-you-give-to-player should be considered hackable; the only thing we can do about it is increase the cost of hacking, but completely preventing the hacking is out of question.[70]

On the other hand, in general, security is *not* about making something completely unbreakable; instead, *the only aim for any security system out there is to increase the cost of breaking in*. Ideally, security aims to increase the cost of the attack above the value of the data within to make the attack economically unviable, but actually every bit of security counts. As a result I am a strong proponent of the view that while obscurity MUST NOT be used as a *replacement* for serious/"real" security,[71] obscurity still MAY be used to *complement* "real" security (and a special case of it is when "real" security doesn't exist at all, which is what we have when speaking about "Road Game" class of attacks).

---

70 In particular, Skorobogatov (the author being one of the top researchers in the field of hardware protection) says that "given enough time and resources any protection can be broken" (and he's speaking about breaking specialized hardware(!)).

71 The one that doesn't rely on hiding anything but the key.

PUBLISHED VS UNPUBLISHED ATTACKS

Our next consideration of cheating and attacks is the one related to the attack being published or not. While Rule #3 from [Pritchard] states that "cheaters actively try to keep developers from learning their cheats," this is not always the case.

Sometimes, cheaters do publish their attacks; the reasons for doing it vary. I've seen attacks published just to hit the site badly, to brag about being a Really Good Hacker™, to "level the field," and—probably the most frequently occurring one—to sell the attacking {tool|script| …} for money.

Published Attacks: Higher Impact, But Home-Turf Advantage Is Regained

Whatever the reason for publishing the attack, it will have quite a few effects on your game. On the one hand, it will make the impact of the attack significantly worse.

Whatever the reason for publishing the attack, it will have quite a few effects on your game. On the one hand, it will make the impact of the attack significantly worse. First, everybody interested in cheating can get the attack (sometimes for free or for as little as 0.001 bitcoin), and there will be quite a few people doing it. This, in turn, can cause serious changes in game experience for the other players (and this is your ultimate cheating-related nightmare). To add insult to injury, with such an attack, everybody will know that your game is cheatable with a few bucks, which doesn't really help build players' confidence; they will start seeing cheaters even when everything is fair and square.[72]

On the other hand, with published attacks you do regain some of the "Home Turf" advantage. Not that you can always completely disable the whole attack vector for this class of attacks, but whenever you're dealing with an attack-on-the-Client that is published, it is *you* who has a "Home Turf" advantage half of the time.

---

[72] Actually, your players will suspect cheating even without the cheat is being published, but publicized (and working) cheats will increase their suspicions by an order of magnitude.

In such cases, traditionally, the battle goes along the following lines:

▶ They get your Client and reverse engineer it. At this point, it is them who has the "Home Turf" advantage

▶ They publish the attack

▶ You {download|buy|…} the attack and reverse engineer the attacking code. At this point, it is *you* who plays it on the "Home Turf."

▶ You find a way to make your Client resilient to the attack.

▶ You publish your updated Client.

▶ Rinse and repeat…

Overall, as soon as you get your hands on the cheat, you can use all the same tools and techniques that-cheaters-are-usually-using-against-you, all the way down to IDA Pro and kernel-level debugging.

Essentially, this often becomes an exercise in "who is more persistent"—and with you being passionate about your game (and having no other options than to fight)—it is usually gamedevs who outlast each of the attacking teams (note that this doesn't prevent new attackers from appearing).

Unpublished Attacks

Unpublished attacks, while being much more difficult to deal with, present less risk of the Doomsday scenario of game-being-ruined-because-every-body-is-cheating. Not that you shouldn't care about unpublished attacks; what I want to say is just that they should usually be below published ones on your Anti-Cheating Team priority list.

A nasty variation (lying in between published attacks and unpublished ones) is attacks-that-are-published-in-closed-forums. This is usually done exactly to prevent you from obtaining the cheat and playing against it on your home field. Such attacks can be pretty annoying; however, if the closed-community-where-the-attack-is-published is small, it is not too bad (as the impact is limited). And if the community is large, you can (and usually *should*)

A nasty variation (lying in between published attacks and unpublished ones) is attacks-that-are-published-in-closed-forums.

infiltrate their ranks and get the copy, so, if your Anti-Cheating Team is doing their job well, it shouldn't be *too bad* either.

ATTACK TYPES

Now, let's discuss what types of attacks or cheats are most typical in a gaming environment, and what the impact of these attacks is if they're successful.

Legal Stuff and Problems Banning

Even before we start to discuss technical issues related to cheating and other attacks, we need to note that your ability to deal with cheaters starts not with technical protection, but with your Terms and Conditions.

Just recently I had a conversation with a guy from a Really Big Company™ who said that they have *huge* problems with banning cheaters because to ban the cheaters, they apparently need to prove that cheaters are cheating in a court of law (<ouch! />).

We'll briefly discuss related issues in Volume VII's chapter on Preparing to Launch,[73] but for now let's note that no technical protection will help you if your T&C is poorly written (and/or if the applicable law is on the cheater's side).

Game Cheats

With the annoying legal stuff out of the way, we can start discussing technical issues related to cheating. In this regard, we'll try to classify all the attacks into one of two broad categories: game-specific "Game Cheats" and much more well-known-besides-game-world "Classical Attacks."

First, let's take a look at Game Cheats; for the time being, we'll be looking at them from the point of view of the advantages they provide to the attacker; as soon as we can recognize the advantages, we'll be able to see the potential impact of the cheats on the game.

---

[73]   *Disclaimer: I am not a lawyer, and no legal advice will be provided.*

Game-Rule Violations

If your game is a soccer game and somebody is able to ensure that they score a goal regardless of the actual position of the ball (or is able to change ball trajectory without any players near the ball), you're in Big Trouble™. The same applies to any kind of fight (if the cheater is able to score a hit when shooting or hitting in the opposite direction, things go pretty badly), and to any other type of competitive game in general. Even not-exactly-competitive games are subject to manipulation in this regard (especially as competitiveness is often routinely introduced even in noncompetitive games such as social farming, for example, via different kinds of "leader boards" etc.).

Impact: Cheating-to-affect-gameplay will become known among the players pretty soon, and will damage the trustworthiness of your game (and of you, too); in extreme cases, your game can become completely unplayable because the number of cheaters is too high. Therefore, the impact of such an attack can be classified as "high" (and can easily become "extremely high," especially if the exploit is published).

Attack Vectors: Whether you can protect from this type of attack beyond "Security by Obscurity" depends heavily on your architecture. If your architecture gives the Client some kind of authority—it is sufficient to attack your Client, otherwise—they will need to go after your Servers (and the difference between protecting your Client and protecting your Server is the difference between playing away and playing home). See this chapter starting from the *Authoritative Client: Pretty Much Hopeless Against Cheaters* section for further discussion.

If your game is a soccer game and somebody is able to ensure that they score a goal regardless of actual things happening on the field, you're in Big Trouble™.

Information Exposure

> If you don't know a secret, you won't let it out.
> —Field operative folklore

Another common class of attacks is related to the game Client knowing more than it is supposed to be known by the player. And as soon as the Client knows something, this information can be extracted from the Client and shown to the cheater. Examples of such attacks include "see-through-walls"

As soon as the Client knows something, this information can be extracted from the Client and shown to the cheater.

(a.k.a. "wallhacks"), "lifted-fog-of-war" (a.k.a. "maphacks"), and "seeing-attributes-you're-not-supposed-to-see" (a.k.a. "ESP hacks").

Impact: These attacks tend to have a subtle impact on the game until they're known, but at the moment when the attack becomes published, the impact becomes high to very high.

Attack Vectors: The problem with information leak attacks is that what-ever-the-Client-knows is subject to the attack, with the attack happening on the attacker's "Home Turf." This means that any such information can (and will) be extracted sooner rather than later.

If your game implements something like "deterministic lockstep" (or, more generally, relies on all the Clients keeping the same Game World state because of feeding them identical inputs and the calculations being deterministic), your game is inherently vulnerable to information leaks, and in a bad way.

Moreover, even if you're using authoritative servers and classical publishing states with state updates coming from Server to the Client, you still need to be very careful to prevent your Client from knowing too much. In particular, you *should* implement so-called "Interest Management," as discussed in Chapter 3, and *should* make sure that this Interest Management works along the lines of "all the non-constant information is distributed to the Clients *only* on a need-to-know basis."

Reflex Augmentation

For those games that rely significantly on fast reflexes (think MMOFPS), one obvious advantage that cheaters try to obtain is to act as if their reflexes are better than their real reflexes. This includes such cheats as aimbots and triggerbots.

Impact: Unless the attack is popularized, the impact can be low, but if or when it is, it can become pretty high.

Attack Vectors: I know of three distinct attack vectors for reflex augmentation. The first goes along the lines of so-called aiming bots, a.k.a. aimbots, running on top of your Client and always hitting the target. To detect such

Client-based bots, you *do* have a fighting chance using antivirus-like (and VAC-like) scanning techniques.

Another attack vector is an aimbot implemented as a proxy. Such proxies sit between your Client and your Server, and can monitor and/or modify the traffic according to the needs of the cheater. One big problem with such proxy-based bots is that it is next-to-impossible to detect them. Fortunately, properly incremented encryption does protect against proxies reasonably well, though you need to keep in mind an unusual-except-for-games attack, which can be described as man-in-the-middle attack against attacker's own Client. This, in turn, calls for unusual protection measures such as running-your-own-CA and scrambling-your-certificate-within-your-executable. In general, encryption-related issues, as they apply to games, will be discussed in Vol. IV's chapter on Basic Security, and their applicability to cheating will be discussed in Vol. VIII.

The third attack vector for Reflex Augmentation is related to Lag Compensation. Lag Compensation will be discussed in Chapter 3, but for now let's note that for the cheater it is always possible to pretend that his lag is higher than it really is (and to drop this additional delay whenever he really needs it). This opens the door to improving the player's lag exactly when it is necessary (for example, *right before* the player shoots, saving a few frames' delay on the shot).

Abuses of Disconnect Handling

If the logic of your game happens to provide any kind of benefits to those who get disconnected, you can count on this logic to be abused. In extreme cases, your logic may even allow someone to "cheat death" by simply plugging out the Ethernet cable (or shutting down the Wi-Fi router) when the cheater realizes that he's about to die. Even if the benefit due to the disconnect is rather moderate and quite difficult to get advantage of (such as "disconnect on all-in," which was an industry standard in online poker fifteen years ago, and was pretty much dropped because of cheating), practice shows that it too will be abused.

Impact: Usually fairly low.

If the logic of your game happens to provide any kind of benefits to those who get disconnected, you can count on this logic to be abused.

Attack Vector: Well, disconnecting (plugging out the cable, shutting down the home router, etc.).

From what I've seen, the only way to deal with abuse of disconnect handling is to change your Game Logic to remove the benefit to those disconnecting. Any other attempts (such as "let's try to detect by the Client whether the Ethernet cable gets unplugged") tend to be bypassable way too easily (in particular, in case of Ethernet cable detection, it covers only plugging out the *immediate* cable, so even a simple $10 switch usually defeats such detection).

Grinding Bots

Grinding Bots (essentially automated players) are well known as a part of any popular-enough MMORPG (or any other game where the player's "experience" affects gameplay). As soon as you have "grinding" as a part of your game, there is an incentive to bypass the "grinding" and get the end result without spending hours on it.[74] For other games, reasons behind grinding bots are different, but they do exist pretty much regardless of the genre; when the spectrum of such bots goes from an MMORPG all the way to poker sites, you can expect pretty much everything else in between.

Abuse scenarios using grinding bots are endless.

Abuse scenarios using grinding bots are endless. Just as one example, if there are goodies associated with new accounts, bots may automatically register, play just enough to get those goodies, and then to pass these goodies along to a consolidation account; then the consolidation account can be used, say, to sell the stuff on eBay. BTW, if you think that this schema is too convoluted to work, don't count on it: I've seen that happening with my own eyes.

Impact: The impact of the grinding bots usually falls in a "low to medium" category depending on the bot being published or not.

Attack Vector: For bots (including grinding bots), there are two common attack vectors: Client-based bots and proxy bots. These bots (and methods to deal with them) are usually very similar to the bots discussed in the *Reflex Augmentation* section above.

---

74 While for a good game many people find that the "grinding" itself is fun, this doesn't mean that *all* players will agree with it.

Multiple Accounts

Whatever your game is about, there is usually enough motivation for players to have multiple accounts. From your side, reasons to disallow such multiple accounts are different and vary from enforcing bans to marketing and promotion-abuse considerations.

Impact: Fortunately, while multiple accounts are usually prohibited in T&C, and do affect gameplay in subtle ways, their impact on the game is usually very limited (that is, if you manage to convince your monetization guys that there is no 100% reliable way to identify a player's device, so they need to plan their promotions taking possible abuses into account).

Attack Vector: Protection from multiple accounts is mostly based on "Security by Obscurity" (except for paid accounts, for which you can use a credit-card number or the equivalent to identify your player, but even in this case protection can be bypassed for quite a while). As a result, completely preventing multiple accounts is not realistic,[75] but we can still make it a bit more complicated for the attacker (especially on non-jailbroken phones and consoles).

Some ways of detecting multiple accounts will be described in Vol. IV's chapter on Basic Security, but don't hold your breath over them—even a half-dedicated cheater will be able to cheat around your protections.

Classical Attacks

In addition to game-specific attacks, most of the attacks known in non-game space apply to games too. Here, we will discuss only a few of these attacks (those that are most popular against games).

DB Attacks

If your game is intended to last longer than one single game session (which is almost universal for MOGs), it needs some kind of persistence (usually implemented on top of a database). And if attackers can get access to your Server's

If attackers can get access to your Server's DB, they can do all kinds of nasty things.

---

75   Even less realistic than for other forms of "Security by Obscurity."

DB, they can do all kinds of nasty things. Not only can they steal (and optionally publish) all your players' passwords (though this can be mitigated by proper password hashing, see Vol. IV for details), they can also modify your database; for example, so that they have all the artifacts they want.

Impact: The impact of such a DB attack can be very high; in an extreme case, it can bring your whole game down for good.

Attack Vector: To get to your DB, the attacker usually needs to go after one of your Servers. And fortunately, whenever somebody attacks your Server, the attack happens on your home turf. Protecting Servers is a well-known field (which we'll discuss in Vols. IV, VIII, and IX), and Servers can be kept reasonably clean from malware too (that is, if you're careful enough). Not that you can *guarantee* that your Servers cannot be hacked, but such hacking can be made quite difficult (okay, let's make it *very difficult*), *and* you should be able to learn about the hack fairly quickly.

Stealing Your Source Code

Stealing source code (for example, via spearphishing) is a problem for any business, but it grows to be an *enormous* problem for games. In some cases, such source-code leaks become published (like in the case discussed in [Parkin]), but if it is a cheater who steals your code, he's likely to keep it to himself, so it is very difficult to say how often such occurrences happen.

Impact: As games (especially game Clients) rely heavily on Client-Side obfuscation, stolen source code will almost instantly defeat all such obfuscation, making your game wide open to a whole bunch of cheats.

The most common attack vector for stealing-your-code attacks is spearphishing (usually with a sprinkle of social engineering).

Attack Vector: The most common attack vector to enable stealing of the source code is spearphishing (usually with a sprinkle of social engineering). As it is extremely difficult to protect yourself from spearphishing attacks (even RSA has fallen to such an attack (see [Bright]), and RSA guys are usually light years ahead of any gamedev company security-wise), for large companies it is usually a good idea to mitigate the potential impact from one such attack.

Such mitigation can go at least in three directions:

▶ My favorite: limiting reliance on Client obfuscation. While obfuscation of the Client is known to be necessary for a few things in a game world, IMNSHO, it is very heavily overused. Moving authority to the Server-Side is possible for at least 99% of the things within your game, and limiting information-on-the-Client to "only-whatever-the-Client-needs-to-know-to-render" can be done for vast majority of the data too, and so on. Yes, it won't be possible to cover *everything*, but from what I've seen, authoritative Client-Side decisions and widely ignored Interest Management happen in *many* more situations than they should.

▶ Automated protocol obfuscation. With it in place, it will be significantly more difficult for the attacker to get through the different parts of your code. More on it in Vol. VIII.

▶ Limiting access to different parts of your source code to a need-to-know basis; more on it in Vol. III, chapter on Pre-Coding.

Password Phishing

One wide class of attacks aims at neither your Client nor your Server, but other players. And one way to target your players is so-called social-engineering attacks. These attacks have little to do with exploiting the technical side of your game, but instead are about exploiting the gullibility of your players.

In particular, phishing out a bunch of passwords is really easy: just set up a website promising "free gold" ("magical new weapon" or whatever-else-applicable-to-your-game) for your players, ask site visitors to login with their in-game login/passwords, and bingo! You've got a whole bunch of logins and passwords that can be used for any purpose (cheating included).

Impact: Fortunately, the impact of phished passwords on the game tends to be quite limited.

Attack Vector: All such attacks invariably get your player into the picture. And more often than not, the player becomes the weakest link in your security.

In the world of classical security, the best way to deal with this specific attack, which is quite dangerous in practice because of its simplicity, is using

2FA

is a method of computer access control in which a user is only granted access after successfully presenting several separate pieces of evidence to an authentication mechanism—typically at least two of the following categories: knowledge (something they know), possession (something they have), and inherence (something they are).

—Wikipedia

so-called 2-factor authentication (2FA). However, convincing your players to use 2FA (even as simple as Google Authenticator) is going to be an uphill battle. OTOH, if (at least for some player accounts) your game does handle really-valuable-things, and you just provide an *option* to use 2FA, it can improve things. (a) You'll get positive feedback from those security-conscious players, and (b) to those complaining, you will be able to say, "Hey, we did everything-we-could to prevent it; we even provided (and promoted) 2FA. Please don't blame us if you didn't use it." And BTW, I've seen 2FA used by a game that wasn't a stock exchange (worked like a charm, too). Implementing 2FA will be discussed in Vol. IX's chapter on Security, Take 2.

Keyloggers/Trojans/Backdoors on Another Player's Device

Another type of attack that targets your players, is placing a keylogger or some other kind of Trojan or backdoor onto player's device (PC or phone or…). Usually the aim of such an attack is to steal the user's password, but things such as "being able to know what the victim is up to" and "being able to make an action impersonating the victim" are not unheard of.

Impact: While this kind of attack is technically not our problem as gamedevs (we're not really in the picture), from the user's perspective it is ("hey, somebody has logged in as me and lost that Great Artifact I had, to somebody else—without me even knowing about it!"). As a result, this attack may need to be addressed, especially if the value of the things on the player's account is high enough. Fortunately, the impact of these attacks on the game ecosystem tends to be low.

Attack Vector: As a rule of thumb, we cannot possibly control the way the Trojan or backdoor gets onto a player's PC. However, we can mitigate its effects a little with the same 2FA used against password phishing; sure, it won't prevent "live" attacks (with the attacker seeing whatever-happens-on-the-player's-PC in real-time), but mounting these is significantly more complicated than just organizing Trojan-based password stealing, so 2FA does qualify as a way to mitigate the effects from Trojans.

Other than that, well, it *might* be possible to check for the most-commonly-used backdoors (detecting them is not that dissimilar from detecting bot software), but TBH, detecting a serious rootkit-based backdoor goes well beyond our humble capabilities as gamedevs. On the other hand, it doesn't mean that all attackers will use serious backdoors, so IMO the jury is out on the usefulness of this type of protection (and it can be implemented on top of antivirus-like and VAC-like protections fairly easily too).

DDoS

DDoS attacks are fairly easily to mount, so they're frequently mounted by disgruntled players to vent out their frustration. For DDoS, the battle really takes place simultaneously on the attacker's "Home Turf" and on your "Home Turf."

Impact: Fortunately, DDoS attacks, while painful, usually do not last long enough to cause too much trouble (that is, if they're organized by a disgruntled player or something). On the other hand, DDoS-based extortions (which seemed to subside for a few years) look on the rise now, and these *can* be nasty enough.

Attack Vector: There are many flavors of DDoS, but IMO the nastiest type of DDoS is the one that simply overloads your ISP's input channels, causing your ISP to filter your traffic out at its ingress filters (or even at its upstream ISP ingress filters) just to protect its other customers.

Dealing with large-scale DDoS attacks can be organized, but it requires preparation well in advance. More on it in Vol. VIII.

IMO the nastiest type of DDoS is the one that simply overloads your ISP's input channels, causing it to filter your traffic out at its ingress filters, just to protect its other customers.

MOG Attack Type Summary

Let's summarize the attacks mentioned above in Table 2.1:[76]

Attack	Impact	Attack Vector(s)	"Home Turf" Advantage	"Home Turf" Advantage if or when the attack is known	Where Protection Will be Discussed
You Are Not Allowed to Ban Me!	Very High	T&C /Legal	N/A	N/A	Vol. VIII
Cheats					
Game Rule Violations	High to Extremely High	For Authoritative Client: Client	Cheater's	Back and Forth	This chapter[77]
		For Authoritative Server: Server	Ours	N/A	Vol. IV, Vol. VIII
Information Leaks	Medium to Extremely High	For Deterministic lockstep: Client	Cheater's	Back and Forth	If "don't use it" qualifies as a protection, this chapter
		For Authoritative Server, and if Interest Management is properly implemented: None	N/A	N/A	Chapter 3
Reflex Augmentation	Low to Medium	Aiming Bots (Client)	Cheater's	Back and Forth	Vol. VIII
		Aiming Bots (Proxy)	If encryption is not implemented: Cheater's. If encryption is implemented: Ours	Same as for non-published attack	Vol. IV, Vol. VIII
		Lag Compensation (Client)	Cheater's	Back and Forth	Chapter 3

---

76 As usual, only typical values are provided, and your mileage may vary.

77 Well, the protection will be like "don't use authoritative clients," but it still qualifies as protection.

Attack	Impact	Attack Vector(s)	"Home Turf" Advantage	"Home Turf" Advantage if or when the attack is known	Where Protection Will be Discussed
Cheats					
Abuses of Disconnect Logic	Low	Connection	Cheater's	Still Cheater's	This chapter
Grinding Bots	Low to Medium	Client	Cheater's	Back and Forth	Vol. VIII
		Proxy	If encryption is not implemented: Cheater's. If encryption is implemented: Ours	Same as for non-published attack	Vol. IV, Vol. VIII
Multiple Accounts	Very Low	Client	Cheater's	Still Cheater's	Vol. IV
Classical Attacks					
DB Attacks	High to Extremely High	Server	Ours	N/A	Vol. VIII, Vol. IX
Stealing Your Source Code	Very High	Development Environment	Ours	N/A	Vol. VIII and Vol. III's chapter on Pre-Coding
Password Phishing	Low	Player	Cheater's (in spades)	Still Cheater's	Vol. VIII
Keyloggers / Trojans / Backdoors on Another Player's Device	Low	Player's Device	Cheater's	Still Cheater's	Vol. VIII
DDoS	Low	Server	None	N/A	Vol. VIII

As we can see from this table, only two of the attacks depend heavily on the architecture: Game Rule Violations and Information Leaks (in the context of Authoritative Clients and Deterministic Lockstep respectively). Let's take a closer look at the architectural approaches that affect these cheats.

AUTHORITATIVE CLIENT: PRETTY MUCH HOPELESS AGAINST CHEATERS (EXCEPT FOR CONSOLE-ONLY GAMES)

SPOF

A single point of failure (SPOF) is a part of a system that, if it fails, will stop the entire system from working

—*Wikipedia*

From time to time, a question arises in various forums: "Why bother with Servers, when we can have a SPOF-free, perfectly scalable system using P2P (as in 'peer-to-peer')?" Moreover, there are arguments out there that the Client-Server architectures are not scalable, and that the future lies with MOGs being P2P. To have something concrete to argue with, I will use [Skibinsky] as an example of such an argument.

With P2P, each Client performs its own calculations, which are then used to determine the state of the Game World. In one example, we could say that each player simulates her own character (and also some NPCs), and then simply sends results to all the other Clients (which simply apply these results to their copies of the Game World). This approach would even work, but only so long as there are no cheaters. However, as soon as there is even one player who wants to cheat, he can modify the Client; this is the point where things start to become ugly. In such architectures, the other Clients will simply apply the results-received-from-cheating-Client to their Game Worlds and our cheater is able to get all kinds of benefits (including but not limited to instant teleport, which is usually bad enough to kill the whole game).

As soon as there is even one player who wants to cheat, he can modify the Client; this is the point where things start to become ugly.

Strictly speaking, not every architecture that gives the Client this kind of authority is a P2P system; in practice, true P2P systems are relatively rare, and architectures electing one of the Clients to be a temporary Server are much more popular. Another variation includes the so-called non-Authoritative Server, with the Server merely forwarding the data between the Clients. Still, for the purposes of our current anti-cheating discussion, any kind of Authoritative Client is pretty much the same, so we'll consider all of them together for the time being.

From the point of view of "Game Rule Violation" type of attacks with an Authoritative Client, we're essentially operating on the attacker's "Home Turf," which makes us resort to "Security by Obscurity." This problem is a well-known one, and is widely acknowledged too; as a result, several techniques are proposed to address it; unfortunately, as we'll see below, at least as of 2017, none of them is really workable in practice.

Code Signing—Doesn't Really Work in a Hostile Environment (Except for Consoles)

The first technique commonly proposed to deal with cheaters in Authoritative Client architectures is code signing. At first glance it all sounds good: if we have our app signed, we can be reasonably sure that it performs as we wrote it.

As soon as end-user himself wants to break code signing — it becomes at best "Security by Obscurity"

However, the problem with the code signing of the game (as with any other code signing) is that as soon as the end-user *himself* wants to break code signing, it becomes at best "Security by Obscurity." This is a direct result of the fact that as soon as the user-who-checks-the-signature turns against us, we start operating on attacker's "Home Turf": in such a case,[78] all the root certificates (which are used to validate code signature) are under the control of the attacker, making them essentially useless. If the attacker can modify the root certificate, he can generate his own private/public key pair, use the public key to make his own root certificate, and then sign his-own-code with the private key.

Moreover, in such hostile environments, there is an even deeper question of "who is the one performing validation?" As soon as it is the code-controlled-by-user-himself performing that signature validation, he will find a way for the validation to succeed even if the signature has nothing to do with our private key.

BTW, [Skibinsky] also recognizes fundamental weaknesses of code signing, stating: "That still doesn't provide 100% security"; to be completely honest, I would go significantly further and say that, "When the user himself wants to bypass code signing, it provides only a marginal security improvement; that is, unless we're speaking of consoles."

The best protection in this field is certainly provided by consoles, and a console *does* provide a reasonable level of protection until it is jailbroken; in particular, consoles go to great lengths to disallow manipulating their root certificates (and their signature validation code as well). On the other hand, jailbreaks remain a Really Big Problem™ for consoles; in fact, *all* the major consoles are jailbroken—the only question is not *if* they're jailbroken, but *when* (IIRC, PS3 has lasted the longest, for about five years without jailbreak). On the third hand,[79] a great effort is made these days by console manufacturers to prevent jailbroken consoles from going online, which is essentially a shield-and-sword battle between hackers and console vendors; in practice, it might indeed help our MOG purposes: that is, if your game is console-*only*.

I know of a few successful games that essentially rely on code signing to prevent cheating in P2P-like architectures on consoles.[80] One prominent

---

78   Which is BTW quite unusual from a traditional security point of view.

79   You didn't know that rabbits have three hands, did you?

80   Actually, most of the time they're not really "P2P," but are more like "Authoritative Server running on one of the consoles"; however, from a cheating point of view, it is pretty much the same as P2P

example of such a game is *Halo: Reach*, and as far as I know, console-provided security did work reasonably well for them to prevent cheating.

However, restricting your game to consoles-only is often not really an option, especially for an MOG (and as soon as your game runs both on console and PC, PC is going to be the weakest link, and the one to be attacked).

Theoretical Protections

Besides the Code Signing and consoles, other anti-cheating measures were proposed in literature (in particular, in the very same [Skibinsky]); however, they're of a more theoretical nature, and I don't know of any successful game that relies on them to deal with cheats. Here goes a very cursory overview of these mostly theoretical techniques (with a very brief discussion of their weaknesses).

Cross-Checks—Undetectable Attacks, Taking Over the World, and Latencies

The first (mostly theoretical if applied to MOGs) technique to address inherent vulnerability of Authoritative Client systems to "Game Rule Violation" attacks is based on cross-checking of the calculations-made-by-our-potential-cheater by other peers. While the idea sounds nice, in this way there are several Big Problems™ too.

First, cross-checks cannot possibly detect a whole class of attacks where the cheating node merely re-orders the packets it receives (or pretends that it didn't receive some of the packets).

First, cross-checks cannot possibly detect a whole class of attacks where the cheating node merely re-orders the packets it receives (or pretends that it didn't receive some of the packets), doing it of course in a way to receive an advantage. If this is the only thing a cheater is doing, it will be able to pass all the cross-checks (that's by design, as packets do get delayed and dropped over the Internet routinely, and there is absolutely no way to double-check what was delivered and what wasn't).[81] This is one inherent and fundamental problem with cross-checking in distributed environments, though certainly not the only one.

---

81 While for any specific attacking pattern it *might* be possible to demonstrate that the attacker's packet loss or reorder statistics are out of the ordinary, doing it without knowledge of the attack specifics is extremely difficult (if possible at all).

We cannot expect MOG players to be as diligent as people running Bitcoin nodes, which enables attacks such as "Hey, let's install this new free cool mod with such and such features."

Next, we need to mention that the nodes performing cross-checks are themselves vulnerable to cheating. Note that even the Bitcoin system (which solves only a singular problem that is extremely narrow compared to general gaming) has an inherent 50% attack (i.e., if cheaters can control 50% of the network, they take it over), and Bitcoin performs cross-checks essentially over their whole network. With the inevitably selective nature of the cross-checks for MOGs (we simply cannot perform all the calculations on all the nodes due to performance limitations), things won't be any better for MOGs. Moreover, we cannot expect MOG players to be as diligent as people running Bitcoin nodes, which enables attacks such as "Hey, let's install this new free cool mod with such and such features" (effectively modifying all such Clients to run under the cheater's control. Bummer). In addition, the problem of "Taking Over the Game World" can be easily exacerbated by creating a caste of "trusted nodes" (in such cases, the attacker doesn't need to take over the whole world, but just build their own network of nodes that "trust" one another); for more discussion on "trusted" nodes, see *Trusted Nodes— Who Is the One We Trust?* subsection below.

And last but certainly not least, all these cross-checks will inevitably lead either to significant additional delays (which is unacceptable for the vast majority of games), or to cross-checks being performed not in real time, but "a bit later." The latter approach raises another Big Question™: "What shall we do with the game world when the cheater is caught?" Sure, we can ban the cheater for life (or more precisely, "until he opens a new email account and registers again"), but what should we do with the consequences of his cheating actions? This question, to the best of my knowledge, has no good generic answer: leaving cheater deeds within the world is at best unfair to the others (not to mention that a cheater may cheat in the interests of another player), and rolling the whole world back whenever the cheater is found is impractical (not to mention the frustration of all the players not affected by cheating, but losing significant time of their play).

I will stop short of saying that cross-checks can't possibly work for MOGs[82] and instead note that with cross-checks (a) there are many more

---

82   After all, they do work for distributed computing, though constraints for MOGs and distributed computing are very different.

problems than solutions, and (b) I don't know of a successful MOG that relies on cross-checks to address cheating.

Consensus (Actually, Majority Vote)— Even More Latencies

A further development of cross-checks is so-called consensus-based solutions. One example of such a system is Bitcoin, another one is a newer "Stellar Consensus Protocol" a.k.a. SCP [Joyce Kim]. Actually, both of these systems demonstrate the aforementioned latency problems; in short, they're damn slow. And while SCP claims to reach consensus in a mere 2-5 seconds (which indeed is a *huge* improvement over Bitcoin), this is still waaaaay tooooo loooong for a vast majority of the games out there.

Trusted Nodes—Who Is the One We Trust?

Yet another mostly theoretical technique more or less commonly proposed to address cheating in Authoritative Client architectures is a kind of "trust" system, with some of the nodes being trustworthy, and some being untrustworthy, and then only trustworthy nodes being used for calculations that affect our Game World.

While the idea looks attractive at first glance, there is a fundamental problem when trying to apply it to an MOG. The problem is simple: who are we going to trust?

In this regard, I don't know of any good strategy; instead, there are several questions for which I don't have good answers. Examples of these questions include:

Who are we going to trust?

> ▶ How to identify node if its owner wants to change the identity? Tying identification to device is impossible (except, maybe, for consoles; see above). Tying to easily changeable things such as IP or email is outright silly. And while it is possible to generate the key and store it on the device, and it will serve as a more-or-less reasonable identification as long

as the device is not hacked, such a key can be easily erased, so it won't prevent the owner from changing the identity.[83]

► If we cannot identify nodes when their owners want to change the node identity, how we're going to punish cheaters? And if we don't punish, what will prevent them from cheating again and again?

► What is the minimum number of organized cheaters necessary to "take over the world" (this number will inevitably be lower than the number in an absence of "trustworthy" nodes)?

IMO, the combination of these unanswered questions makes any "trusted node" approach fairly hopeless for a large-scale MOG based on Authoritative Client. In particular, there is no obvious way to prevent somebody from creating several dozens (or several-hundred, if necessary) of accounts, to make them trust one another, reaching "trusted node" level (the one allowed to perform calculations), and then to use these nodes (acting in sync) to run a game according to their own rules (outvoting and potentially banning any "honest" node whose calculations conflict with theirs). Moreover, this is actually a very high-risk scenario: imagine your game being overtaken by cheaters who can play their own game, while still using your software and your marketing assets and efforts; sounds like an Ultimate Nightmare™ for an MOG company.

Homomorphic Encryption—Doesn't Even Start to Fly

In theory, there is yet another technique, based on so-called homomorphic encryption. The theory behind it is very complicated and is well beyond the scope of this book, but the end result can be stated as follows: it is possible (both in theory and in practice) to build a system that uses other nodes in a completely non-transparent manner, so they're performing calculations without any ability to cheat (and even without an ability to read the data that they're processing). However, once again, while interesting in theory, this approach is not practical, at least not for MOGs: overheads incurred

---

83   In other words, such a key can only provide positive identification, not negative.

even by the latest greatest homomorphic systems are huge enough to prevent even using them for environments that are much less demanding performance-wise than games. And for games, it is a non-starter (at the very least, for the foreseeable future).

Authoritative Client MOG Summary

To summarize the discussion on Authoritative Client MOGs above: while Authoritative Client architectures (including both pure P2P and server-running-on-one-of-Clients) are known to work more-or-less okay for communities that can trust one another—

> *As of now, I don't see how an Authoritative Client MOG can provide reasonable protection from a dedicated cheater (except for console-only games).*

BTW, I am certainly not alone in this understanding: the movement against Authoritative Clients (and toward Authoritative Servers) is gaining more and more traction within the industry (see, for example, [Sweeney] and [Fiedler, What every programmer needs to know about game networking], just to name a few).

The movement against Authoritative Clients (and toward Authoritative Servers) is gaining more and more traction within the industry.

While in theory there might be games that can be protected using Authoritative Clients (as in, "I don't have formal proof that such games can't possibly exist"), think more than twice when choosing to rely on Authoritative Clients beyond consoles. Oh, and make sure to re-read the *If You're Popular Enough, They Will Find Reasons to Cheat* section above.

DETERMINISTIC LOCKSTEP: NO GAME-RULES VIOLATIONS, BUT WIDE-OPEN TO INFORMATION LEAKS

Another rather popular idea for multiplayer games (especially for real-time strategies) is to make sure that all the Clients have an *exactly* identical state. This is achieved by (a) having all the code for all the Clients being *exactly* the same *and* deterministic, (b) having *exactly* the same initial state, and (c) feeding *exactly* the same inputs to all the Clients. For more discussion on Deterministic Lockstep specifics, see the all-time classics of [Terrano and Bettner] and [Fiedler, Deterministic Lockstep].

BTW, let's note that Deterministic Lockstep as such does not prevent us from having an Authoritative Server: at least in theory, we could run the Authoritative Server that is identical to any of the Clients (and will take its data as authoritative to figure out who won). On the other hand, such a Deterministic-Lockstep-with-Authoritative-Server is rarely used in practice; IMO, it mainly happens for two reasons. (a) For quite a few games it is okay to merely poll several Clients at the end of the "game event" (such as RTS battle), and unless at least half of the players is cheating, it is trivial to find out the real winner just by figuring out the majority (on the other hand, if the battle is a match between two parties, it is not possible to completely rule out that *one whole party* cheats). (b) As achieving 100% cross-platform determinism is next-to-impossible, this Deterministic-Lockstep-with-Authoritative-Server approach doesn't fly well for Clients running on non-PC platforms (including consoles).

Going back to our current anti-cheating analysis, we can see that Deterministic Lockstep (whether with Authoritative Server or not) does prevent the modifying-gameplay kind of cheating pretty well (especially if an Authoritative Server is present, or if the possibility of 50%+ of cheaters can be ruled out), which is, obviously, a Good Thing™.

The problem is that with Deterministic Lockstep, all the Clients are bound to keep the *whole* state of the Game World.

However, the grass is not all that green on the Deterministic Lockstep side. The problem is that with Deterministic Lockstep, all the Clients are bound to keep the *whole* state of the Game World. This means that a dedicated cheater can easily extract the state of Game World from the Client, and can easily implement all those see-through-walls and lifted-fog-of-war cheats (a.k.a. wallhacks and maphacks).

In addition, Deterministic Lockstep has some purely technical problems (ranging from difficulties with achieving 100%-deterministic behavior across different platforms to having to wait for the slowest-guy-at-the-moment). These problems have lead Glenn Fiedler to write, "I recommend using deterministic lockstep over the internet for 2-4 player games only."

On the other hand, there is still one very popular case for Deterministic Lockstep (especially among indie gamedevs)—it is Real-Time Strategy (RTS) games. Still, unless proven absolutely hopeless for a specific game, I very clearly prefer "classical" Authoritative Servers (i.e. Authoritative Servers that replicate their state to Clients, and not Deterministic-Lockstep-with-Authoritative-Server) even for RTS; actually, the only argument against Authoritative Servers for RTS is traffic, but it *seems* to be solvable; see discussion in Chapter 3 on ways to optimize RTS traffic. And with traffic problems out of the picture, Authoritative Servers very clearly win over Deterministic Lockstep for several significant reasons:

▶ With classical Authoritative Servers, the slowest player no longer holds everybody else up. This becomes a clear prerequisite if you want to have Game Worlds with more than 5-10 players.

▶ With classical Authoritative Servers, whomever lost connection can still reconnect in a finite time (and for Deterministic Lockstep, this problem was very unpleasant, in particular, with earlier versions of *Heroes of the Storm*[84]).

▶ With classical Authoritative Servers, there is an option to utilize all of the advantages of UDP (using it for eventually consistent state sync and reducing observable latencies more than is possible to achieve with reliable UDP; more on it in Vol. IV's chapter on Network Programming). While *usually* RTS is relatively insensitive to latencies, improving latencies never hurts.

---

84   Later, they fixed it via creating snapshots, but snapshots are a Big Headache™.

As Authoritative Servers can do Interest Management, they greatly reduce any potential for maphacks or wallhacks.

▶ With classical Authoritative Servers, you can allow players with Clients on different platforms to play in the same Game World (with Deterministic Lockstep, doing it requires cross-platform determinism, which is next-to-impossible in practice; see more discussion on it in Vol. II's chapter on (Re)Actors).

And most importantly: *as Authoritative Servers can do Interest Management, they greatly reduce any potential for maphacks or wallhacks.* The idea behind Interest Management is simple: with an Authoritative Server, all the game-decision logic resides on the Server, and the Client is essentially just drawing Server-Side state. As a result, information sent to the Client can be limited to (give or take) whatever-can-be-seen-on-the-screen. While the Client usually needs to have a bit more information than fits on screen (to allow for movements or scrolls or…), it is still very far from it keeping the whole Game World. For more discussion on Interest Management, see Chapter 3.

With all this in mind, and taking into account that those wallhacks and maphacks tend to hit exactly-those-RTS-they-are-targeting in a pretty bad way, I tend to say that Deterministic Lockstep (at least in the context of over-the-Internet games aiming for more than a few players) should be used only as a last resort, i.e., if all the attempts to reduce traffic by other means (which will be discussed in Chapter 3) fail; and, assuming that you did a good job of optimizing traffic, this IMHO should be very unlikely.

AUTHORITATIVE SERVER: AS CHEATER-PROOF AS THEY GET

With all these problems plaguing Authoritative Clients and Deterministic Lockstep architectures, it is not really surprising that in recent years the "Authoritative Server" approach gets more and more popular. Moreover, IMNSHO, it the only really viable MOG architecture for *most* of the games out there.

In the usual approach to Authoritative Servers for a virtual world game, Clients usually have a 3D engine, but this 3D engine is used purely for rendering and not for decision-making. On the other hand, all the player inputs (not "object coordinates resulting from movements," but more or less "player keypresses and mouseclicks themselves") are sent to the Server, and it is the Server that moves the players (and other stuff) around; it is also the Server that makes all the decisions about collisions, hits, etc. Moreover, with an Authoritative Server, it is the Server that makes all the changes in its own copy of the game world (and the Server's copy is an authoritative copy of the game world, which is then replicated to the Clients to be rendered).

With an Authoritative Server, it is the Server that moves the players (and other stuff) around; it is also the Server that makes all the decisions about collisions, hits, etc.

Among other things, it means that for Virtual World games[85] with an Authoritative Server, it is the Server (and not the Clients) that needs to implement the physics engine (though 3D rendering engines still reside on the Clients).

On the other hand, for fast-paced games, the delays of going-to-Server-and-back-to-Client with every keystroke are often not acceptable. In such cases, the Client often implements some kind of "Client-Side Prediction," essentially applying its own inputs to its own copy of the Game World; this Client-Side Prediction may lead to moving the PC around, and in some cases, it may even show hits based on its own understanding of the Game World. On the other hand, with Client-Side Prediction, the Client's copy of the Game World is not authoritative, so if the vision of the Server and the vision of the Client become different, it is the Server's copy that is always "right." Therefore, all effects of the decisions made by Client-Side Prediction are always transient; moreover, the effects of these decisions do not leave the Client, so that any cheating of anybody-but-yourself becomes unfeasible. For more discussion on Client-Side Prediction for fast-paced games based on Authoritative Servers, see Chapter 3.

From the point of view of preventing cheaters from affecting your gameplay, Authoritative Servers are the best thing you can have. If you have enough checks on the Server-Side, you always can enforce game rules with relative ease. And while when using Client-Side Prediction, temporary disagreements between Clients and Server are possible, it is always clear how to resolve the conflict (as noted above, it is Server that always "wins").

---

85   Such as RPGs and FPSs.

It is worth noting that merely using an Authoritative Server doesn't necessarily imply security against cheaters; Authoritative Servers merely *provide the means* to make your game secure, and you will need to do quite a few things on top of Authoritative Servers to utilize these means and make your game reasonably cheater-proof (Interest Management, discussed in Chapter 3, being just one of these things).

Authoritative Servers: Scalability Is Imperfect But Workable

> There is only one objection against this theory,
> and it is that the theory is wrong.
>
> —C.N. Parkinson

Before committing to Authoritative Servers, let's consider one common argument pushed by opponents of using-Authoritative-Servers-for-gaming; this is the (mis-)argument that Client-Server systems are not scalable. In particular, such an argument is presented by [Skibinsky], but this is by far not the only source of such allegations. Leaving aside outright ridiculous statements such as "one of the fundamental weaknesses of the C/S architecture is its dependency on a single physical channel to the datacenter"[86] and "all packets have to arrive from clients to a single router," let's concentrate on those arguments worth discussion.

O(n)

Big O notation is a mathematical notation that describes the limiting behavior of a function when the argument tends towards a particular value or infinity.

—*Wikipedia*

The most important line of the argument of alleged non-scalability of Client-Server games revolves around the "$O(P^2)$ traffic estimate." The idea behind the argument goes as follows: first, let's consider a game world with P players within; now let's consider each player making some kind of change every N seconds, and let's assume that this change needs to be communicated to all the P-1 of the other players. Hence (they argue), for P players in the world, we need to push $O(P^2)$ bytes of traffic per second, making Client-Server architectures non-scalable.

---

[86]   Oh, really? TBH, I have yet to see even a half-decent datacenter without multi-homing.

If $O(P^2)$ would indeed be the case, then we'd indeed have quite significant scalability problems. Fortunately, in practice this $O(P^2)$ estimate doesn't really stand; let's take a closer look.

Fortunately, in practice this $O(P^2)$ estimate doesn't really stand.

First, let's note that in the real world the number of people we're directly interacting with has no relation to the number of people in the world. In virtual Game Worlds, it is normally the same thing—the number of people (or other entities) players are interacting with is limited not by the world population, but by our immediate vicinity, which in most cases has nothing to do with the world size. This is the point where the $T=O(P^2)$ estimate falls apart (assuming reasonable implementation), and is replaced with $T=O(P)*C$, where C is the constant representing the size of this "immediate vicinity."[87] From this point on, the estimate is no longer $T=O(P^2)$, but just $T=O(P)$ (with mathematicians among us sighing in relief).

In fact, this technique is well-known for MOG developers under the name "Interest Management"[88] and will be discussed in Chapter 3.

Second, if $T=O(P^2)$ is the case, it would mean that limits on the bandwidth of individual users would be hit pretty soon, so that even if somebody designs a world with everybody-to-everybody direct interaction all of the time, it still won't run regardless of architecture (i.e., it won't run in Client-Server, but it won't run in P2P either).

These theoretical exercises are also supported by practical experiences; while the dependency of traffic from the world size is usually a bit worse than simple $T=O(P)$, given reasonable implementation, it is never as bad as $T=O(P^2)$. In other words—

> *In a properly implemented Client-Server game,*
> *for a large enough world population P,*
> *traffic T is much closer to O(P) than to O(P²).*

---

87 In [Skibinsky], this effect is referred to as *immediate action-reaction manifold*, and it is relied on to ensure P2P scalability, though for some reason it is mentioned only in the P2P context.

88 Yes, the very same one that helps deal with cheating.

It means that both your income I *and* your expenses E grow more or less proportionally to number of players P.

This observation has one very important practical consequence: as soon as T is close to O(P), it means that your traffic is roughly proportional to world population P, which means that your expenses E are also proportional to P. On the other hand, within certain non-so-implausible assumptions, your income I is also more or less proportional to P. As long as this stands, it means that both your income I *and* your expenses E grow more or less proportionally to P; this in turn means that if you were making money with 10,000 players, you will still make money (and even more of it) with 1 million players.

An Example Calculation

To bring all the big-O notation above a bit more down to earth and to demonstrate these effects from a more practical perspective, let's consider the following example:

Let's consider a game where you can interact directly with at most only C=100 other players, regardless of the world size and regardless of the world population P. Of course, architecting and implementing your game to ensure a limit on C requires that you implement Interest Management, but doing so is perfectly feasible for most of the games out there.

Let's take the traffic estimate per player-interacting-with-another-player, from [Skibinsky], i.e., as ~15 bytes/sec (in practice, your mileage will vary, but if you're doing things right, it usually won't be off by more than an order of magnitude, so we can take it as a rather reasonable estimate). Let's also assume that your monetization efforts are making you $0.05/month. And let's further assume that your Servers are residing in the datacenter,[89] and that pricing is around $2,000 for an unmetered 10 Gbit/s uplink, around $300/month for an 1 Gbit/s uplink, and around $30/month for a 100 Mbit/s uplink (these sample prices are taken for the same datacenter of the same large hosting ISP at the beginning of 2017).

At the same time, with your monetization you'll be making around $500/month, which means that your traffic costs are not too bad.

Therefore, when you have 10,000 simultaneous players, you'll have traffic of at most 15 bytes/sec/interaction * 10,000 players * 100 interactions/player ~= 1.5e7 bytes/sec ~= 0.015GByte/s ~= 0.13 Gbit/s; this will cost you around

---

89   And not in your office; see Vol. VII's chapter on Preparing for Launch for discussion.

$40/month. At the same time, with your monetization you'll be making around $500/month, which means that your traffic costs are not too bad.[90]

When you grow to 1 million simultaneous players, then your traffic per user will increase. As noted above, T won't grow as $T \sim P^2$, but there will be a modest increase in per-user traffic because while each part of traffic T' (with sum of all T's being T) can in most cases be optimized to plain $T' \sim P$; in practice usually you're too lazy (or have too little time) to optimize all of them. For the purpose of our example, let's assume that your per-player traffic has grown five-fold (you should be rather lazy—or busy—to get to 5x per-user traffic increase, but, well, it can happen). As a result, when you grow to 1 million simultaneous players, your traffic will grow 500-fold, bringing it to 65 Gbit/s, costing you $13,000/month. While this may sound like a lot of money, we should note that at the same time, with your $0.05/player/month monetization and a million players, you'll be making $50,000/month, which is still much more than enough to cover traffic bills (and note that if it ever becomes a problem, you still have that about-5x-times overhead, most of which can be recovered given sufficient development time).

Summary: Authoritative Server Is Not Ideal, But Is the Only Thing Workable

Let's summarize our findings about the three different approaches in the following table:

	Scalability	Resilience to Game-Rule Violation	Resilience to Information Leak
Authoritative Client	Up to "Very Good"	Poor	It depends
Deterministic Lockstep	Very Good	Good	Poor
Authoritative Server	Acceptable	Good	Good

---

90   Don't rush to buy that house in the Bahamas, though—while traffic costs can indeed be negligible, other costs, especially advertisement costs to keep new players coming, are usually not.

Given our discussion above in the *Dealing with Cheaters* section, having poor resilience to Game-Rule Violation cheating is a show-stopper for most of the MOGs out there. And as noted above, this point of view seems to be supported by MOG developers around the world. As for Deterministic Lockstep, the combined effects of inherent Information Leak and less-than-10 max players per Game World effectively rule it out for most of the games out there.

For most of the games out there, this leaves us with the only workable solution: an Authoritative Server. While there are some exceptions to this rule (in particular, console-only games that can work with Authoritative Clients, and some of the RTS that may warrant Deterministic Lockstep), as a Big Fat Rule of Thumb™, Authoritative Servers are *the* way to go.

THINK POSITIVE!
OR, MAYBE THERE'S STILL HOPE...

- Maybe there's still hope?
- Nope!
　　—Garfield the cat

While you're destined to spend a large chunk of your time fighting cheaters, *and* zero cheating is a utopia for any game with more than a thousand players, you still *may* keep your cheaters in check *and* prevent them from affecting the ecosystem of your game too much.

After reading about all the cheater-related problems discussed above, you may get the impression that cheaters will inevitably gain the upper hand against you. However, this is not the case. While you're destined to spend a large chunk of your time fighting cheaters, *and* zero cheating is a utopia for any game with more than a thousand players, you still *may* keep your cheaters in check *and* prevent them from affecting the ecosystem of your game too much.

One thing that tends to help us greatly in this regard is based on the following observation:

> *"You don't have to run faster than the bear to get away. You just have to run faster than the guy next to you."* —Jim Butcher

For our anti-cheating fight, it can be paraphrased as:

> *"You don't have to be 100% cheat-proof to save your game from cheaters. You just have to do better than the guy next to you." —No Bugs Hare*

The economy of cheats—especially of those commercially available ones—dictates that if there are two targets, one being very juicy but very well-protected, and another being moderately juicy but poorly protected, commercial cheaters are clearly going for the latter (and yes, I've seen it first-hand in real life). After all, it is nothing personal, just business.

Every Bit Counts: Multi-Layer Protection

One all-important consequence of the reasoning above, is—

> *On the anti-cheating front, every bit counts.*

As we cannot possibly create a bulletproof way to win the battle with cheaters, and as the more cheating-proof we are, the less the chance that we'll be singled out for the attack, it makes perfect sense to add more and more defenses, trying to catch cheaters from many different angles (at least as long as these additional defenses don't cause observable collateral damage to players).

It makes perfect sense to add more and more defenses, trying to catch cheaters from many different angles.

BTW, there is one more interesting observation that supports the multilayer defense approach. If the attacker comes in, breaks your defense, and only then do you start to think how to patch that hole, then the next time he will be very motivated to break in (and will likely succeed). On the other hand, if your defense has five or so layers he needs to penetrate, then after breaking one or two (and without any positive feedback that he managed to achieve something), he is very likely to lose all drive and faith in his abilities (or the feeling that he's going in the right direction).

In other words—

> ### *Don't* feed the cheater's ego,
> ### and ***don't*** provide feedback to him.

A short real-world story in this regard: Once upon a time, there was a cheater who had almost broken a communication protocol for a large game (and who shared it in a relevant forum, asking for some minor help to complete the break); while the game had a (near-)perfect Authoritative Server (so that it could not be manipulated from the outside by illegal means), there was still the possibility that people would start writing grinding bots.

As a side note: the attack was quite ingenious by the standards of that time (the guy replaced root certificate within the Client, and then mounted a MITM attack against his own Client to get to the protocol).

In response, gamedevs made five separate layers of protection (each of which was sufficient to prevent the attack from happening), and deployed all of them *simultaneously*. Not only has the attacker never been heard about, but for several years *there were no known protocol-level breaking attempts at all*. As a result, I think this story qualifies as pretty good (though inherently anecdotal) kinda-evidence to support the case for multilayer protection, and with several protection layers deployed at the same time.

MITM

a man-in-the-middle attack (often abbreviated MITM), is an attack where the attacker secretly relays and possibly alters the communication between two parties who believe they are directly communicating with each other.

—Wikipedia

BOTTOM LINE FOR CHAPTER 2: YES, IT IS GOING TO BE AN AUTHORITATIVE SERVER

Summarizing from Chapter 2:

▶ Cheating is One Big Problem™ for MOGs

▶ Players will cheat even if you're sure they have zero reason to

▶ Game-Rules Violations is one of the big potential problems for your game

▶ P2P and other Authoritative Client-based architectures provide very poor protection against Gameplay Cheating

▶ Deterministic Lockstep has inherent weakness to Information Leak cheats, and a bunch of other limitations making it unsuitable for MOGs

▶ Despite some claims to the contrary, Authoritative Servers can be made scalable

▶ Given the balance of pros and cons, Authoritative Servers look like the best option as of now; some (including myself) will even argue that in most cases it is the only viable option. While exceptions are theoretically possible, they are quite unlikely.

As a result—

> *For the rest of this book, we will discuss Authoritative Servers and **only** Authoritative Servers.*

The two possible exceptions where you might deviate from the Authoritative Server model are the following:

▶ Console-only games with multiplayer capability. In this case, a rather popular (and apparently working) solution is to use one of the consoles as an "elected" Authoritative Server. While I am not a big fan of this approach, it might fly (and has been seen to fly for real-world games too). BTW, most of the stuff within this book will still apply to such MOGs (with one of the consoles acting as an elected Authoritative Server).

▶ RTS games with only-a-few-players within the same Game World. Some of these games *might* require a Deterministic Lockstep to deal with all those thousands of simultaneously moving units. Still, I'd rather not write Authoritative Servers off, at least until you (a) read Chapter 3 on known ways to compress these units, and (b) experiment with such compression yourself (as it applies to your specific game). If you manage to limit your traffic while staying within Authoritative Server model, you'll be able to get quite a few benefits from it.

Phew. I hope that I managed to convince you to use Authoritative Servers for your next MOG; while there can be some rather narrow exceptions, I am pretty sure that for the vast majority of the games out there, it is *the* way to do it.

Bibliography

Bright, Peter. 2011. *Spearphishing + zero-day: RSA hack not "extremely sophisticated"*. http://arstechnica.com/security/2011/04/spearphishing-0-day-rsa-hack-not-extremely-sophisticated/.

Fiedler, Glenn. 2014. *Deterministic Lockstep*. http://gafferongames.com/networked-physics/deterministic-lockstep/.

—. 2010. *What every programmer needs to know about game networking*. http://gafferongames.com/networking-for-game-programmers/what-every-programmer-needs-to-know-about-game-networking/.

Harton, Eugen. 2016. *Once A Cheater Always A Cheater: Gotta Catch 'Em All*. http://www.gdcvault.com/play/1023193/Once-A-Cheater-Always-A.

Kim, Joyce. 2015. *Stellar Consensus Protocol: Proof and Code*. https://www.stellar.org/blog/stellar-consensus-protocol-proof-code/.

Parkin, Simon. 2016. *Catching up with the guy who stole Half-Life 2's source code, 10 years later*. http://arstechnica.com/gaming/2016/06/what-drove-one-half-life-2-super-fan-to-hack-into-valves-servers/.

Pritchard, Matthew. 2000. *How to Hurt the Hackers: The Scoop on Internet Cheating and How You Can Combat It.* http://www.gamasutra.com/view/feature/3149/how_to_hurt_the_hackers_the_scoop_.php.

Skibinsky, Max. 2005. "The Quest for Holy Scale." In *Massively Multiplayer Game Development 2*, 339-373.

Skorobogatov, Sergey. 2011. *"Hardware Security of Semiconductor Chips: Progress and Lessons".*
http://www.cl.cam.ac.uk/~sps32/NCL_2011.pdf.

Sweeney, Tim. 2009. *Unreal Networking Architecture.*
https://docs.unrealengine.com/udk/Three/NetworkingOverview.html.

Terrano, Mark, and Paul Bettner. 2001. *1500 Archers on a 28.8: Network Programming in Age of Empires and Beyond.* http://www.gamasutra.com/view/feature/131503/1500_archers_on_a_288_network_.php.

CHAPTER 3.
COMMUNICATIONS

Now, after all the preliminaries, we're finally ready to discuss what MOGs are all about—communications. However, please don't expect me to discuss much of the lava-hot "UDP vs. TCP" topic—we're not there yet (most of this question, along with the ways to mitigate their respective issues, will be discussed in detail in Volume IV's chapter on Network Programming). For now, we need to understand the *principles* behind the MOG operation; mapping them to specific technologies is a related but different story, and we'll follow up with the discussion in Vol. IV.

CLIENT-2-SERVER AND SERVER-2-CLIENT COMMUNICATIONS

As we discussed at length in Chapter 2, throughout this book we'll be speaking about Authoritative Servers. While much of the same logic will apply to scenarios when the Server app runs on one of the player's computers (consoles, etc.), we'll still call it a communication between the "Client" and the "Server."

In this regard, several different types of communication arise (see, for example, [Aldridge]):

State Sync is synchronization or replication of the current state of the Game World from our Authoritative Server to the Client.

▶ **Player Inputs,** going from Client to Server. These are inputs such as player clicks and controller inputs—plain and simple. *NB: As discussed in Chapter 2, with Authoritative Servers, we cannot process inputs and make game-related decisions on the Client—and should instead feed them (pretty much as mouse and/or keyboard clicks) to the Server.*

▶ **State Sync,** going from Server to Client.[91] State Sync is synchronization or replication of the current state of the Game World from our Authoritative Server to the Client. We'll name the state that is synchronized over the network "Publishable State" (and as we'll see below, it will usually be different from both the Server State and Client State). Note that achieving this eventually synchronized copy of the current Publishable State on the Client in a way that is efficient both latency-wise and traffic-wise is not trivial (and we'll discuss it in the *"Reference Base" for Unreliable Communications* section below), but for now we just need to assume that it is usually possible.

▶ **Transient Events,** going from Server to Client. These include things such as "there is a bullet hit at this point," and are usually implemented on top of some kind of broadcasted or multicast messages.[92] The main difference from "Publishable State" sync is that Transient Events make sense only "right now" and, if they're lost, there is no point sending

---

91   Also known as "state replication."

92   As Interest Management can and sometimes *should* apply to Transient Events, it can be some kind of "filtered broadcast"; see below.

them again, which makes them an ideal case for an unreliable message delivery (or an unreliable RPC call).

▶ **Forwarded Inputs,** going from Server to Client. These are essentially "hints" to allow Client-Side Prediction to account for movements of other players better, and may be either inputs of other Clients, or (more often) derivatives-made-by-Server-from-other-player-inputs. The rough idea goes along the lines of "if certain movement is already indicated by the player's input, but is not really visible yet within the Publishable State, then to make the Client-rendered-representation more precise, it may be beneficial to use other players' inputs to improve Client-Side Prediction."

  ▪ On the other hand, this additional information is ripe for Information Leak cheats, so, as a rule of thumb, I'm against Forwarded Inputs (though I still admit that keeping players happy usually outweighs anti-cheating considerations). More discussion on Forwarded Inputs will follow in the *Forwarded Inputs* section below.

RTT, INPUT LAG, AND HOW TO MITIGATE THEM

For the time being, we'll concentrate on the two most obvious things—Player Inputs and State Sync. In other words, we'll be speaking about the Client sending Player Inputs to the Server, and receiving back updates-to-the-Game-World-State.

Data-Flow Diagram, Take 1

Note that if your game is fast-paced (think MMOFPS or to a lesser extent first-person MMORPG), the approach described with regard to the Take 1 Diagram, won't allow you to produce a game that doesn't feel "sluggish" (it will work, but won't feel responsive when run over the Internet). However, please keep reading, as we need it as a starting point for our further discussion that will lead us to schemas suitable for fast-paced games.

First, let's take a look at a very simple data-flow diagram for a typical not-so-fast MOG:

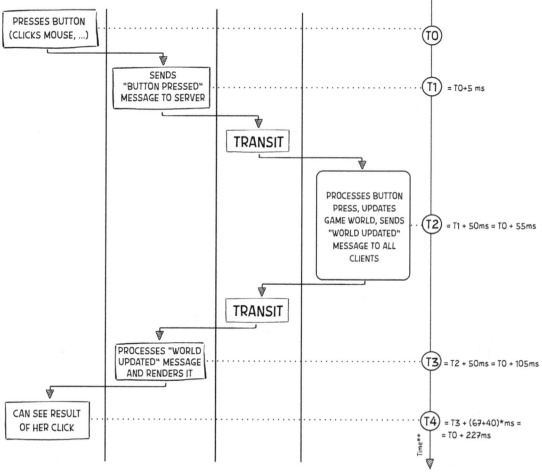

NOT REALLY PRACTICAL FOR FAST-PACED GAMES: SEE FIG 3.3 AND FIG 3.4 FOR FURTHER IMPROVEMENTS

fig 3.1

*67ms for rendering lag, and 40 ms for display lag

**all times are for example purposes only, YMMV greatly

Despite the visual simplicity of this diagram, there are still a few things to be mentioned:

1. All the specific delay numbers on the right side are for example purposes only. Your Mileage May Vary, and it may vary greatly. Still, the numbers do represent a realistic (and even "quite typical") case.

2. It may seem that the Client here is pretty "dumb." And yes, it indeed is; most of the Game Logic in this picture resides on the Server-Side.

   a. On the other hand, in most of the games there are some player actions that cause Client-only changes (and don't cause any changes to the Server-Side game world). These actions can and should be kept to the Client. These are mostly UI things (like "show and hide HUD," and usually things such as "look up"), but for certain games this logic can become rather elaborate. Oh, and don't forget stuff such as purchases, etc. If you keep them in-game (see Vol. II for further discussion), it will require quite a few dialogs with associated Client-Side logic (such as "select an item" and "enter payment details", etc.), and these dialogs are usually also purely Client-Side until the moment when the player decides to go ahead with the purchase.

For fast-paced games, there is one big problem with the flow shown in this diagram, and the name of the problem is "latency."

3. Last, but certainly not least: for fast-paced games, there is one big problem with the flow shown on this diagram, and the name of the problem is "latency." It is obvious that for this simplistic data flow, the delay between the player pressing a button and her seeing the results of herself pressing the button (which is known as "input lag"[93]), will be at least so-called round-trip-time (RTT) between the Client and the Server (which is shown as 100ms for Fig 3.1; see the *RTT* section below for more discussion regarding typical RTTs out there). In practice, though, there is quite a bit added to the RTT, and for our example on Fig 3.1, 100ms RTT resulted in 227 overall delay. And if this delay exceeds typical human expectations, the game starts to feel "laggy," all the way down to "outright unplayable." Let's take a closer look at these all-important input lags.

---

93 IMO a misnomer, but I don't want to invent my own terminology where not absolutely necessary.

If your game is slow- or medium-paced (including casino-like games such as poker), you can safely skip to the *Game World States and Reducing Traffic* section.

Input Lag: The Worst Nightmare of an MOG Developer

Note: if your game is slow- or medium-paced (including casino-like games such as poker), you can safely skip to the *Game-World States and Reducing Traffic* section.

As noted above, for MOGs the most critical concern is related to the relation between two times: input lag and related user expectations. Let's consider both in detail.

Input Lag: User Expectations

First, let's take a look at user expectations and, of course, user expectations are highly subjective by definition. However, there are some common observations that can be obtained in this regard. As a starting point, let's quote [Wikipedia, Input Lag]—

> *"Testing has found that overall 'input lag' (from controller input to display response) times of approximately 200 ms are distracting to the user."*

Let's take this magic number of 200ms as a starting point for our analysis. And, give or take, it is also corroborated in several other sources. In [Aldridge], numbers between 100ms and 300ms are mentioned as critical for the gameplay of *Halo: Reach*—though it is unclear whether it is about just network lag or overall input lag. [West] notices that 10/60th seconds = 167ms feels "quite responsive," but says that 200ms "is too long to wait for a gun to fire." The ballpark number of 200ms is also consistent with other independent observations on human reaction time. For example, [Lipps, Galecki and Ashton-Miller], based on a study of reaction times of sprinters competing in the Beijing Olympics, state that, "At the 99.9% confidence level, neither men nor women can react in 100 ms, but they can react in as little as 109 ms and 121 ms"; while it is not exactly the same as noticing the lag, it still gives us the same order of magnitude, and (keeping in mind that these numbers are for top sprinters in the world) seems to confirm that the 200ms number is probably not too far off. In a completely different setting [Human Benchmark], after measuring over 40 million reaction-time clicks for Internet users, an average reaction time of 279 milliseconds (with the median at 268 ms) was observed, which is also pretty close to the magic number of 200ms.[94]

On the other hand, we should note that for competitive purposes (like MMOFPS or MOBA), each and every millisecond does count, but as long as our MOG (a) stays below 100-200ms, *and* (b) delays are consistent for different players, we should be fine.

On the third hand <wink />, let's note that strictly speaking the number is not universally 200ms, that estimates by different people will vary, and that the tolerance does vary across different genres. Still, even for the most time-critical games, a number below 100-150ms is usually considered "good enough" and for any real-time interaction a lag of 300ms will be felt easily by lots of your players (though whether it will feel "bad" is a different story). To be more specific, for the remaining part of this chapter let's consider two sample games: one is OurRPG with an input lag tolerance of 300ms (let's assume it doesn't have fights and is more about social interactions, which make gameplay less critical to delays), and another game is OurFPS with input lag tolerance of 150ms.

Let's also note that these 150-300ms of input-lag tolerance is just a fact of life (closely related to human psychology or physiology, etc.) so that we cannot really do much about it.

Input Lag: How Much We Have Left for MOG

The first problem we have is that there are several things eating at this 150-300ms original lag allocation (even without our MOG code kicking in). This includes lag introduced by game controller, lag introduced by rendering engine (which depends on many things, including the size of the render-ahead queue), and display lag (mostly introduced by LCD monitors).

These 150-300ms of input lag tolerance is just a fact of life (closely related to human psychology or physiology etc.) so that we cannot really do much about it.

---

94   Especially as their measurements *seem* to include input+display lags, though not RTT.

Typical mouse lag is 3-6ms [Pasini], less for gaming mice. For the purpose of our discussion, let's account for any game-controller lag as 5ms.

Typical rendering engine lags vary between 50ms and 150ms. 50ms (=3 frames at 60fps) is rather tricky to obtain, and is not that common, but is still possible. A more common number (for 60fps games) is 67ms (4 frames at 60fps), and 100-133ms is not uncommon either (see [Leadbetter]).

Typical display lag (not to be confused with pixel-response time, which is much lower and is heavily advertised, but it is not the one that usually kills the game) as of 2017 starts from 10ms, has a median of around 40ms, and goes all the way to 100ms (see [DisplayLag.com]).[95]

It means that out of the original 150-300ms, we need to subtract a number from 65ms to 255ms. Which, in turn, implies that for quite a few players out there, the game is lagging even before an MOG and network lag has kicked in.

To be more specific, let's note that we cannot really control such things as mouse lag and display lag; we also cannot realistically say "hey guys, to play our game you *must* get the Absolutely Best Monitor," so at least we should aim for a median player with a median monitor. Therefore, we should assume that out of our 150-300 ms, we need to subtract around 95ms (5ms for a game controller or mouse, 50 for a rendering engine, and 40 for a median monitor).

Now let's take a look at the lag introduced by a rendering engine. Here, we *can* make a difference. Moreover, I am arguing that—

> *For MOGs, rendering latencies are even more important than for single-player games.*

The difference between 100ms and 50ms for a single-player game won't feel the same as the difference between 200ms and 150ms for an MOG.

The point here is that for a single-player game, if we'd manage to get overall input lag say below 100ms, it won't be that much of an improvement for the player, as this number is below the typical human ability to notice things. However, for an MOG, where we're much closer to the magic 150-300ms because of RTTs, effects of the reduced latency will be significantly more pronounced. In other words, the difference between 100ms and 50ms for a

---

95   As of the beginning of 2016.

single-player game won't feel the same as the difference between 200ms and 150ms for an MOG.

For the purpose of our example calculation, let's assume that we've managed to get or make a rendering engine with a reasonably good 50ms latency. This (as mentioned above) means that we've already eaten 95ms out of our 150-300ms initial allocation. And even if everything else works lightning fast, we need to have RTT<55ms for OurFPS, and RTT<205ms for OurRPG. While it might look pretty good to us, these numbers are still not telling the complete truth (and we'll see why, in a moment).

Accounting for Packet Losses and Jitter

At first glance, it *seems* that our calculations above show that we can get away with a simplistic diagram from Fig. 3.1, even for some of fast-paced fps-based games.

Well, actually, we cannot, at least not yet: there is one more important network-related complication that we need to take into account. To get the data from Client to Server, we need to send it over the Internet, and sending data over the Internet has its own peculiarities with regard to delays.

Internet is Packet-Based, and Packets Can Be Lost

First, let's talk a little bit about the mechanics of the Internet (only those that we need to deal with at the moment). I'm not going to go into any detail or discussions here (we'll discuss these things in Vol. IV's chapter on Network Programming); for the time being, let's just take it as an axiom that—

> *When data is transmitted across the Internet,*
> *it always travels within packets, and each*
> *of these packets can be delayed or lost.*

This stands regardless of the exact protocol used (i.e. whether we're working on top of TCP, UDP, or something more exotic such as GRE). While TCP handles packet loss internally (retransmitting packets when necessary), such

For TCP, the overhead is 40+ bytes per packet; for UDP it is usually 28 bytes per packet (that's not accounting for Ethernet headers).

losses invariably cause delays; in other words, TCP just trades packet delays for losses.

In addition, let's take as another axiom that—

> ### Each of these packets has some overhead.

For TCP, the overhead is 40+ bytes per packet; for UDP it is usually 28 bytes per packet (that's not accounting for Ethernet headers, which add their own overhead). For our current purposes, exact numbers don't matter too much; let's just note that for small updates they're substantial.

Now let's see how these observations affect our game data flow.

Cutting Overhead

The first factor we need to deal with is that for a fast-paced game, sending out a world update in response to each and every input is not feasible. This (at least in part) is related to the per-packet overhead we've mentioned above. If we need to send out an update that some PC has started moving (which can be as small as 8 bytes), adding overhead of 28-40 bytes on top of it (which would make 350-500% overhead) doesn't look good.

That's at least one of the reasons why game simulation is usually run within a pretty much classical "game loop," but with rendering being replaced with sending out updates:[96]

```
while(true) {
  TIMESTAMP begin = current_time();
  process_input();

  update();
    //update() normally includes all the world simulation,
    // including NPC movements, etc.

  post_updates_to_clients();
    //here, we're effectively combining all the world updates
    // which occurred during current 'network tick'
```

---

[96]   For a discussion on game loops, see Vol. II's chapter on (Re)Actors.

```
  // into as few packets as possible,
  // effectively cutting overhead

TIMESTAMP elapsed = current_time()-begin;
if(elapsed<NETWORK_TICK)
  sleep(NETWORK_TICK-elapsed);
}
```

With this approach, we're processing all the updates to the "game world" one "network tick" at a time. The size of the "network tick" varies from one game to another, but 50ms per tick (i.e., 20 network ticks/second) is not an uncommon number (though YMMV may vary significantly(!)).

Note that on the Server-Side (and unlike for a usual Client-Side game loop from Vol. II) the choice of different handling for time steps is limited, and that on the Server-Side it is usually pretty close to the code variation above (the one waiting for the remainder of time until the next "tick"). Moreover, more often than not, it is written in an event-driven style along the following lines:

```
void GameWorld::process_event(const Event& event) {
  //here 'event' contains ALL the client inputs
  // that came in but are not processed yet

  process_input(event);
  update();
  post_updates_to_clients();

  post_timer_event_to_myself(SLEEP_UNTIL,
                             event.started+NETWORK_TICK);
}
```

(for an extensive discussion on event-driven programming, see Vol. II's chapter on (Re)Actors).

For the purposes of our example, let's assume that we have a "network tick" of 1/20s (=50ms), so that we're adding 0 to 50 ms (depending on when the player's input came in relative to the "network tick" start) of additional latency; let's denote it as (0:50)ms. Then our remaining allocation of latency for OurFPS becomes (5:55)ms, and for OurRPG, (155:205)ms.

If we stay within the simplistic schema shown in Fig. 3.1, then each lost packet will mean visible (and unpleasant) effects on the player's screen: everything will stop for a moment, and then "jump" to the correct position when the next packet arrives.

Client-Side and Server-Side Buffering on Receipt

So far it looks good, but we still haven't dealt with the packet losses and sporadic delays (also known as "jitter").

If we stay within the simplistic schema shown on Fig. 3.1, then each lost (or substantially delayed) packet coming from the Server to the Client will mean visible (and unpleasant) effects on the player's screen: everything will stop for a moment, and then "jump" to the correct position when the next packet arrives.

To deal with it we need to introduce a buffer on the Client-Side (let's name it "buffer-on-receipt") by simply delaying "normal" incoming packets for some predefined delay time dt. This is done with a single aim in mind: if one of the packets gets delayed (for time $\tau < dt$), we will be able to act "as if" it was not delayed at all (simply reducing dt for this packet). It can be illustrated by the following diagram:

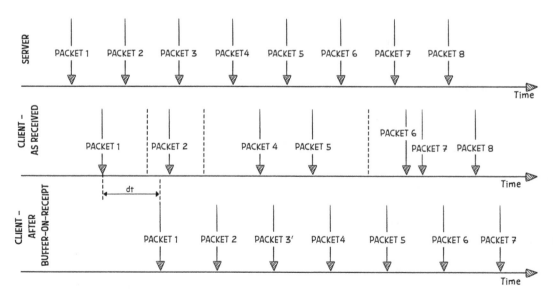

fig 3.2

The "Server" timeline shows packets as they were sent by the Server; if we're doing a good job on the Server-Side, they will come at regular intervals. However, the picture on the Client-Side (middle timeline) will be *very* different.[97] As we can see, some packets can get lost (such as Packet 3) and delays can vary greatly (representing "jitter"); dashed lines within this timeline represent expected positions of delayed packets.[98]

The third timeline ("after Buffer-on-Receipt" one) shows how delays and packet loss can be handled by our Buffer-on-Receipt. Handling delays is quite obvious here; what is more interesting is the handling of packet loss. Here we do not have any information from Packet 3 (as it was lost in transit); however, by the time we need to emit Packet 3 from our Buffer-on-Receipt, we already have Packet 4—so we can interpolate the data from Packet 2 and data from Packet 4 to get an "approximated" Packet 3' (and replace the lost Packet 3); see also the *Client-Side Interpolation* section below.

The delay *dt* we need to introduce with this buffer-on-receipt depends on many factors, but even with the most aggressive UDP-based state-sync algorithms (the ones that allow us to reconstruct the whole state on each network tick), the minimum we can do is have a buffer of one network tick to account for one-lost-packet-in-a-row.[99] In practice, the buffer of around 1-3 "network ticks" is usually desirable.

On the other hand, it should be noted that this Client-Side buffer-on-receipt *may* be somewhat reduced due to the overlap between our buffer-on-receipt and the render-ahead buffering used by the rendering engine (see Vol. V's chapter on Graphics 101 for a brief discussion of buffering techniques by graphics engines). It would be incorrect, however, to say that you can simply subtract the time of render-ahead buffer by the rendering engine (by default 3 frames=50ms for DirectX) from the time that we need to add for RTT purposes. Overall, this is one of those things that you'll need to find out yourself for your specific game.

As by the time we need to emit Packet 3 from our Buffer-on-Receipt, we already have Packet 4—we can interpolate the data from Packet 2 and data from Packet 4 to get an "approximated" Packet 3' (and replace the lost Packet 3).

---

97 N.B.: In practice, the second timeline will usually be shifted *much* more to the right than shown in Fig 3.2, but for the purpose of our discussion, Fig 3.2 will do.

98 Actually, determining these expected positions for the packets is not really trivial; the task is very similar to the problem normally solved by Phase-Locked Loops in hardware.

99 In theory, it is possible to bypass this restriction, but in most cases it won't be practical because of correlations between packet losses.

In addition to the Client-Side buffer-on-receipt (which accounts for loss or jitter of packets sent by Server to Client), there is often another (Server-Side) buffer-on-receipt that is needed to account for jitter of the packets sent by the Client to the Server (these packets usually contain player inputs).

For the purpose of our example, let's assume that we have a "network tick" of 1/20s (=50ms), and that we have both Client-Side and Server-Side buffers-on-receipt delaying by a very aggressive 1 network tick. It means that we've already run out of our latency allocation for OurFPS (our remaining time is (-45:-95)ms; i.e., we're 95ms *behind* for OurFPS even *before* RTT kicks in), but still have (55:105)ms left for RTT for OurRPG.

As soon as we said that we're no longer doing things "as soon as they arrive from the Server-Side," we're pretty much bound to perform some kind of time sync between Server and Client.

Time Synchronization

As soon as we say that we're no longer doing things "as soon as they arrive from the Server-Side," we're pretty much bound to perform some kind of time sync between the Server and the Client. First, as our Server is authoritative, we're speaking about synchronizing time on our Client with the sequence of the packets coming from the Server, at least so we can say when we expect the next packet. Also, we'll assume that all Server packets are timestamped.[100] Now we're ready to discuss different time sync-algorithms that allow us to get the Client time synced with the Server.

Overall, there are several approaches, and no single one is ideal. We'll briefly discuss each.

Sync-Once

The simplest idea is to sync the time between the Client and the Server once (at the beginning of the game session or game event or…) and then rely on both the Client and the Server clock running at pretty much the same speed.

One way to implement simple one-time time sync is described in [Simpson], and it works. On the other hand, I am not a big fan of one-time time synchronization (this or any other) for two quite big reasons:

---

100   Actually, if they're sent at well-known intervals (as they normally are), simple packet number (which can also be seen as a "tick stamp") will do.

▶ If it is off once, we don't have any chance to fix it (in spite of all the information we're continuously obtaining). And if the Internet happened to behave really weirdly during the original time sync (which is bound to happen from time to time, at least for some of your players because they got unlucky), it can lead to pretty nasty desynchronizations.

▶ As typical PC/Server clock precision (actually, precision of the quartz crystal the PC is using) can easily be at 20ppm (20 parts per million, or 2e-5), it means that we can get a discrepancy of 1 frame (1/60sec) within as little as 400 seconds (~=7.5 minutes).[101] While not exactly fatal for most games out there, it indicates that we can indeed run into certain time-sync issues, causing unnecessary pain for our players.

If it is off once, we don't have any chance to fix it.

One additional thing to remember about Sync-Once (and actually, any other time-sync algorithm) is that I *strongly* suggest implementing time sync using *the same communications means* as the communications you're normally using. I.e., if your normal game protocol uses TCP, don't implement time sync over UDP and vice versa; also using NTP as such (or SNTP), in spite of NTP/SNTP lying on top of UDP is not desirable as routers can handle it very differently from ordinary UDP. The latter is not *that strict* a requirement (after all, time sync is time sync, give or take), but doing it otherwise tends to cause certain subtle issues (first, it can easily affect firewalled players, but my *feeling* is that time sync itself can also be affected).[102]

NTP

is a networking protocol for clock synchronization between computer systems over packet-switched, variable-latency data networks.

—Wikipedia

Sync-Once with Subsequent Adjustments

It is possible to improve Sync-Once time sync by adjusting time sync after initial synchronization.

For example: if we see that the time-stamped Server-Side packet came *significantly earlier* than we'd expected, it may indicate either that the RTT has changed (for example, due to a route change), or that Server time is currently

---

101 That's for the worst case of the difference between the Server and the Client quartz crystals being 40ppm.

102 In particular, because packet delays on the way forward and the way back can be different for different protocols.

ahead of Client time. And if Server-Side packets start to arrive *consistently* later,[103] it may indicate that the Client time moved ahead (or again, an RTT has changed). And to distinguish between an RTT change and time-sync drift, we could make the Server include into the packet fields such as number-of-last-received-packet-from-this-Client and time-since-last-received-packet-from-this-Client. Combined, this information will allow us to adjust time sync, and also to measure changes in RTT.

Alternatively, we can just re-initiate time sync (similar to that Sync-Once) at some frequency (like "once per minute"). It has its own dangers (in particular, answering the question "what to do if the discrepancy on second measurement is very large?" is not that easy), but overall it might work.

Overall, I tend to like such Sync-Once-with-Subsequent-Adjustments (especially the first subtype described above, the one with gradual re-adjust-ment) better than simple Sync-Once.

Overall, I tend to like such Sync-Once-with-Subsequent-Adjustments (especially the first subtype described above, the one with gradual re-adjustment) better than simple Sync-Once.

NTP-Like Protocol

Another option is to use NTP-like protocol using your Server as a kinda-NTP source. Though, if going this way, do *not* use real NTP; syncing your Client system-wide time to your Server, instead of just syncing your intra-game time, is not what your players will appreciate.

Also, while NTP as such is known to be very reliable (and addresses both problems of sync-once), implementing full-scale NTP just for game purposes is IMO serious overkill.

PLL

is a control system that generates an output signal whose phase is related to the phase of an input signal. While there are several differing types, it is easy to initially visualize as an electronic circuit consisting of a variable frequency oscillator and a phase detector.

—Wikipedia

Phase-Locked Loop (PLL)

Last, but not least, another algorithm that is directly related to time sync (while being pretty much unused by games[104]) is so-called Phase-Locked Loop (PLL). Strictly speaking, PLL doesn't really synchronize time; what it is doing is creating a clock that is synchronized (both frequency-wise and phase-wise) with an incoming signal (in our case, with packets coming from

---

103   As in "arriving later five times in a row."

104   Disclosure: I didn't use PLLs in this context, but I had a great experience with them elsewhere.

the Server, as shown on Fig 3.2). However, very often such a clock-synchronized-with-incoming-signal is exactly what we need. This is especially true when speaking about our buffers-on-receipt, as such a clock will answer the question of "when to expect the next packet" in nearly-the-best-possible-way.

PLLs are used all over the place in electronics (you can count on at least several of them running within your PC and another few in your phone right now), and they *are* the best (by far) way to synchronize to incoming signals with a more-or-less-known frequency, but for some reason they're neglected in software.

Note that PLL as such won't account for RTT (though it will re-adjust when RTT is changed); however, PLL can be aided with RTT information (for example, using the same fields in the packet as we discussed in the context of Subsequent Adjustments to Sync-Once) to achieve a real time-sync solution (that is, *if* you need it).

Note that PLL as such won't account for RTT; however, PLL can be aided with RTT information to achieve a real time-sync solution.

As for implementing PLL itself in software, it is *much* easier than it might seem at first glance. Essentially, it consists of a phase detector (which says by-how-much our prediction-of-the-next-Server packet went wrong, which is basically the difference between *predicted_time* and *arrival_time*), integrator (can be as simple as "multiply current integrator value by $k<1$ and add new value" on each oscillation), and a variable-frequency oscillator (which can be implemented by simply using the current output of the integrator to calculate the period of the next oscillation, which in turn will be implicitly based on the Client's system clock frequency, but this is exactly the point). That's pretty much it (and the output of our oscillator will be the *predicted_time*). On the other hand, be prepared to play with numbers quite a bit to get it working (it is not rocket science, but for the first time it can take quite a bit of effort); in particular, (a) make sure that your k is very close to 1 (though it *must* be strictly <1), (b) make sure that the output of your integrator can't change your oscillation period by a factor of more than 1e-4 or so,[105] and (c) make sure that with zero input from the integrator, your oscillator generates "normal" (="expected") frequency of your Server packets.

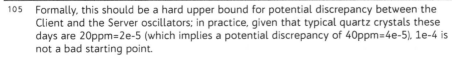

105   Formally, this should be a hard upper bound for potential discrepancy between the Client and the Server oscillators; in practice, given that typical quartz crystals these days are 20ppm=2e-5 (which implies a potential discrepancy of 40ppm=4e-5), 1e-4 is not a bad starting point.

TL;DR on Time Sync

Overall, time sync between the Client and Server is quite easy to implement "somehow" (and it will work), though implementing it in a reliable way (the one that won't fail even when the network of your player behaves really weirdly) can be rather challenging. As a result, you may need to experiment with your time sync in your "public beta" quite a bit (and I cannot predict in advance which of the time-sync methods will work for your game).

On TCP

Above we've discussed how the picture looks if we send IP (or UDP) packets ourselves. If we're using TCP, things are rather different.

I don't want to get onto a flamewar-ridden minefield of "TCP vs UDP" right now (we'll do it in Vol. IV's chapter on Network Programming), but will just mention two things that are relevant to our discussions in this chapter:

▶ Without packet loss, TCP can be made to have the same latencies as UDP. If we're using TCP_NODELAY for our TCP connection *and* there is no packet loss, TCP will behave very similarly to UDP (there will be differences, but they will be pretty much negligible in most usage scenarios).

▶ In the presence of packet loss, however, TCP loses badly to UDP, latency-wise. If we're using TCP stream under significant packet loss, two things happen that are bad for latency:

- The first is that as TCP is a stream, all the packets following the lost one will be delayed (in spite of being already available on the receiving side) until the lost packet is retransmitted and received (this is known as "Head-of-Line blocking").

- The second thing that happens at this point is that the lost packet is normally retransmitted only after 200ms' time.[106]

---

106   Strictly speaking, an RFC says it should be a minimum of 1 second, but in practice these days it is more like 200ms. On the other hand, there are exceptions, and it *may* be retransmitted earlier, but usually we shouldn't rely on it. For more discussion on TCP retransmit timeouts (RTOs), see Vol. IV's chapter on Network Programming.

- Moreover, if there are two packets lost in a row, the additional delay grows 3x (to ~600ms), and if there are three packets lost in a row, 7x (to ~1.5 sec). BTW, if we have 5% packet loss for a game sending 20 packets/second, three packets in a row will get lost every 5 minutes or so. For more detailed discussion, see Vol. IV.

- Combined, it means that the entire communication will probably get stuck for hundreds of milliseconds on a regular basis (once per several minutes).

As a result, for Server-to-Client connections over TCP, we're speaking about retransmit delays of the order of hundreds of milliseconds, which in turn will usually force us to have our own buffer-on-receipt delays of the order of half-a-second or more, which is substantially higher than the buffer of 1-2 network ticks we need for UDP-based connectivity.

These delays-in-case-of-packet-loss are one of the big reasons TCP is not popular (to put it mildly) among the developers of fast-paced games (and for good reason[107]). On the other hand, using TCP for Server-2-Server communications is a very different story (in particular, because packet loss within a single Datacenter should happen only once in a blue moon).

Using TCP for Server-2-Server communications is a very different story (in particular because packet loss within a single Datacenter should happen only once in a blue moon).

Input Lag: Taking a Bit Back

One trick that *may* be used to reduce a *feeling* of "input lag" by the player a little bit is introducing Client-Side animations. If, immediately after the button press, the Client starts some animation (or makes some sound, etc.), while at the same time (i.e., at the beginning of the animation, or even before it) the Client sends the request to the Server-Side, then from the player's perspective the length of the animation is "subtracted" from the "input lag." For example, if in a shooter game you'll add a 50ms trigger-pulling animation (while sending the shot right after the button press), then, from a player's perspective, the "Input Lag" will start 50ms later, so, in a sense, we *reduce* perceived lag

107   Though see discussion on UDP-over-TCP in Vol. IV.

by these 50ms. Adding tracers to the shoots is known to create a feeling that bullets travel with limited speed, buying back another few frames (however, tracers are more controversial, at least at close distances).

While the capabilities of such tricks are limited, when dealing with Input Lag, every bit counts, so you should consider if they are possible for your game.

Taking such trickery into account (and assuming that we got 50 ms "back" as a result) means that we're a bit better (but still behind) for for OurFPS with (5:-45)ms (that's before accounting for RTT(!)); for OurRPG, let's assume that we've found similar animations, so that we have (105:155)ms left for RTT.

Data-Flow Diagram, Take 2: Fast-Paced Game Specifics

> Note: If your game is fast-paced (think MMOFPS), the approach described with regard to the Take 2 Diagram is still likely to feel "laggy." However, please keep reading, as we will discuss the remaining problems, and the ways to deal with them, in Take 3 (which is in turn based on Take 2).

The considerations discussed above (game loop, Client-Side buffer-on-receipt, Server-Side buffer-on-receipt, and "taking back" animations) lead us to Fig 3.3:

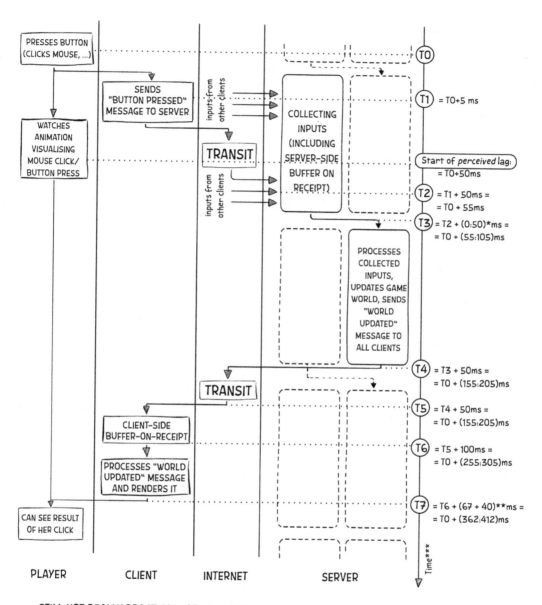

PRESSES BUTTON
(CLICKS MOUSE, ...)

SENDS
"BUTTON PRESSED"
MESSAGE TO SERVER

WATCHES
ANIMATION
VISUALISING
MOUSE CLICK/
BUTTON PRESS

TRANSIT

inputs from other clients

inputs from other clients

COLLECTING
INPUTS
(INCLUDING
SERVER-SIDE
BUFFER ON
RECEIPT)

PROCESSES
COLLECTED
INPUTS,
UPDATES GAME
WORLD, SENDS
"WORLD
UPDATED"
MESSAGE TO
ALL CLIENTS

TRANSIT

CLIENT-SIDE
BUFFER-ON-RECEIPT

PROCESSES "WORLD
UPDATED" MESSAGE
AND RENDERS IT

CAN SEE RESULT
OF HER CLICK

$T0$

$T1$ = T0+5 ms

Start of *perceived* lag:
= T0+50ms

$T2$ = T1 + 50ms =
= T0 + 55ms

$T3$ = T2 + (0:50)*ms =
= T0 + (55:105)ms

$T4$ = T3 + 50ms =
= T0 + (155:205)ms

$T5$ = T4 + 50ms =
= T0 + (155:205)ms

$T6$ = T5 + 100ms =
= T0 + (255:305)ms

$T7$ = T6 + (67 + 40)**ms =
= T0 + (362:412)ms

Time***

PLAYER   CLIENT   INTERNET   SERVER

STILL NOT REALLY PRACTICAL FOR FAST-PACED GAMES: SEE FIG 3.4 FOR FURTHER IMPROVEMENTS

fig 3.3

*0:50 means "from 0 to 50", and is based on 50-ms network tick

**ms for rendering lag, and 40 ms for display lag

***all times are for example purposes only, YMMV greatly

One additional problem with the diagram Fig 3.3 is that we effectively have our visual frame rate equal to "network tick"; in our example, it means that we'll be rendering at 20fps instead of 60fps, which is certainly not the best thing visually.

As noted above, it is already behind for OurFPS, even before we start to account for RTT (!).

BTW, one additional problem with Fig 3.3 is that we effectively have our visual frame rate equal to "network tick"; as "network ticks" are often kept significantly lower than 60 per second (in our examples, it was 20 per second), it means that we'll be rendering at 20fps instead of 60fps, which is certainly not the best thing visually.

On the other hand, for OurRPG, we still have that (105:155)ms of time reserve to account for RTT. Let's see whether it is able to stand against real-world RTTs.

RTT

Now let's take a look at that RTT monster, which often appears at night, in our worst nightmares, and is eating ~~all the cookies we've hid under the pillow~~ all that's left of our input lag allowance.[108]

First, let's note that while RTT (="Round-Trip Time") depends greatly on the player's ISP (and especially on the "last mile" connection), even in a very ideal case, there are hard limits on "how low you can go with regards to RTT." Very roughly, for RTT and, depending on the player's location, you can expect the ballpark numbers shown in Table 3.1 (assuming the very best ISPs, etc. Getting worse is easy; getting significantly better is usually not exactly realistic):

---

108   To make things worse, this monster is usually quietly hiding behind the curtain of LAN until you start to test with real-world RTTs.

Player Connection	RTT (not accounting for "last mile")
On the same-city "ring" or "Internet Exchange" as server (see [Wikipedia, Internet Exchanges], but keep in mind that going out of the same city will increase RTT)	~10-20ms
Inter-city, cities separated by distance D	At the very least, $2*D/c_{fib}$ (c_{fib} being speed of light within optical fiber, roughly $c_{vacuum}/1.5$, or ~2e8 m/s). Practically, add around 20-50ms depending on the country.
Trans-US (NY to SF)	At the very least (limited by c_{fib}) ~42 ms; in practice at least 80 ms.
Trans-Atlantic (NY to London)	At the very least (limited by c_{fib}) ~56 ms [Grigorik]; in practice at least 80 ms.
Trans-Pacific (LA to Tokyo)	At the very least (limited by c_{fib}) ~90 ms, in practice at least 120ms.
A Really Long One (NY to Sydney)	At the very least (limited by c_{fib}) ~160 ms [Grigorik]; in practice at least 200 ms.

In addition, you need to account for a player's "last mile," as described in Table 3.2:

Additional "last-mile" RTT…	
..added by player's "last mile": cable	[Grigorik] reports ~25ms. My own experience for games is about 15-20ms[109]
..added by player's "last mile": (A)DSL	[Grigorik] reports ~45ms. My own experience for games is more like 20-30ms[109]
..added by player's Wi-Fi	~2-5ms (assuming immediate connection to Wi-Fi router, without repeaters or wireless access points)
..added by player's concurrent download	Anywhere from 0 to 1000ms and more

Two things to keep in mind in this regard:

► If your Server is sitting with a good ISP (which it should), it will be pretty close to the backbone, latency-wise. This means that in most of the "reasonably good" cases, a real player's latency will be one number from Table 3.1, plus one or more numbers from Table 3.2 (as the Server's "last mile" latency can be written off as negligible); it is still necessary to double-check it (for example, by pinging from another Server).

If your Server is sitting with a good ISP (which it should), it will be pretty close to the backbone latency-wise.

---

109   The difference can be attributed to downloads that tend to cause longer RTTs; also gamers tend to invest in better connectivity.

▶ The numbers above are for hardware Servers sitting within datacenters. Virtualized servers within the cloud tend to have higher RTTs (see Vol. VII for further discussion), with occasional delays (when your cloud neighbor suddenly starts to eat more CPU or bandwidth or...) easily going into the multiple-hundreds-of-ms range. BTW, speaking of clouds: in quite a few places, you can get cloud without virtualization, usually referred to as "bare-metal cloud" or something similar; this kind of cloud will eliminate these additional delays. For more discussion on cloud vs. traditional rented Servers, see Volume VII's chapter on Preparing for Launch.

LAN RTT vs Internet RTT

LAN-based games (with typical wired LAN having RTTs below 1 ms, and even Wi-Fi normally being below-5ms range) can't really be compared to MOGs, latency-wise. If your MOG needs comparable-to-LAN RTT to be playable—sorry, it won't happen (but see below about the Client-Side prediction that may be able to alleviate the problem in many cases, though at the cost of significant complications).

CDN

A content delivery network or content distribution network (CDN) is a globally distributed network of proxy servers deployed in multiple data centers.

—Wikipedia

On CDNs and Geo Server Distribution

One may say "hey, as we need to improve latency, let's just use CDN—problem solved." Unfortunately, it is not that easy. Those traditional CDNs that are used to improve latencies for web sites don't work for reducing game latency.[110] The reason is that traditional CDN is all about caching the data closer to the end-user (which indeed improves latency; that is, as soon as the request can be served from the cache, without going to the Server). However, for games (and especially for fast-paced ones), the data still needs to go the whole way from the Client to the Server, which eliminates any latency benefits from the CDN.

---

110   CDNs still may be used (and often *are*) for tasks such as game-content distribution, but the game itself is usually out of the question.

Similar-to-CDN latency improvement, however, can be (and often *is*) achieved by distributing your game servers so that each of your customers has a Server more-or-less nearby. More on it in the *Back to Input Lag* section below.

RTT and Players

While we're on the subject of RTT, let's mention three things that your support folks will certainly need to tell to your players with regard to RTT and latency (and sooner rather than later):

1. No, better bandwidth doesn't necessarily mean better latency (you will need to tell it to your players to answer questions such as "how come that *exactly* as soon as I've got a better 100Mbit/s connection, your servers started to lag on me? Are you guys punishing players with good connections?")

2. It is easy to show whatever-number-we-want in the Client as a "current latency" number, but comparisons of the numbers reported by different games are perfectly pointless (this actually is a Big Fat Argument™ to avoid showing any latency numbers at all, though publishing the number is still a GDD-level decision).

3. When saying "it was much better yesterday," are you sure that nobody in your household is running a huge download?

No, better bandwidth doesn't necessarily mean better latency.

Back to Input Lag

From Table 3.1 and Table 3.2, we can see that in the very best case (when both your Server and your Client are connected to the very same intra-city ring or exchange, everything is top-notch, last mile is a non-overloaded cable, no concurrent downloads running in the vicinity of the Client while playing, etc.), we're looking at 35-45ms RTT. Which means that—

> *For FPS-like games, and without special trickery, we're out of luck even if all the players are on the same city exchange.*

Within the same (large) country, the best-possible RTT goes up to around 80-100ms.

Within the same (large) country, the best-possible RTT goes up to around 80-100ms. Which means that with a simple diagram from Fig 3.3 we still *might* be able to handle OurRPG; that is, if you restrict your players to one country (creating something like "US Server," though in fact it will be a whole Datacenter full of Servers). Actually, country-specific Datacenters are very common, and are not *that* difficult to implement and maintain, but they still restrict the flexibility of your players (and also can have adverse effects on "player critical mass," as defined in Chapter 1). While it might happen that you won't have a choice in this matter, it is still important to understand all the implications of such a decision.

Single-continent Datacenters (with RTTs in the range of 100-120ms) are close cousins of country-specific ones, and are also frequently used for fast-paced games. Even with special stuff such as Client-Side Prediction, for fast-paced games such as MMOFPS, you *may* easily end up with per-continent or per-country Datacenters. On the other hand, for single-continent Datacenters, even for OurRPG, we're already starting to hit the "being sluggish" threshold, so even for non-FPS games we may need some further trickery (as described below).

Purely geographically, for the US the best Datacenter location for a time-critical game would be somewhere in Arkansas. More realistically (and taking into account real-world cables), if trying to cover the whole US with one single datacenter, I would seriously consider Dallas or Chicago; such a choice would limit the maximum RTT while making the games a bit more fair.

If you want a worldwide game, then maximum-possible RTT goes up to 220+ms, making even OurRPG feel sluggish without the special stuff discussed later. Worse, there will also be a significant difference for different players. While simple data flow shown on Fig 3.3 might still fly for a relatively slow-paced worldwide RPG (think *Sims*), worldwide MMOFPS and MOBAs based on it are usually out of the question.

All these observations lead us to the next iteration of our flow diagram, which introduces substantial (and non-trivial) processing on the Client Side.

Data-Flow Diagram, Take 3: Client-Side Prediction and Interpolation

So far, with Fig 3.3 we have two annoying problems: one is excessive lag, and the other is low Client-Side frame rate. The latter problem occurs because if implementing your game exactly as shown on Fig. 3.3, client-frame rate is stuck at the network tick rate, and as the typical network tick rate is 20 ticks/second, you'll end up with the Client-Side rendering at 20fps, which is quite a problem visually.

To deal with these problems, we need to introduce some processing on the Client-Side. I won't go into too much detail here, giving only a basic description of the algorithms involved; for further discussion, please refer to the excellent series on the subject by Gabriel Gambetta [Gambetta, Fast-Paced Multiplayer]; while he approaches the subject from a slightly different perspective, all techniques discussed are the same.

Client-Side Interpolation

The first thing we can do is related to the Client-Side buffer-on-receipt (the one we introduced for Take 2 and Fig 3.3). To make sure that we don't render at the "network tick" rate (but render at 60fps instead), we can (and should) interpolate the data between the "current network tick" and "previous network tick" within our buffer-on-receipt.

For example, if our "network ticks" go at a rather typical 20 ticks/second, we can get our Client-Side rendering run at 60fps—simply creating two out of three rendered frames via such Client-Side Interpolation.

This does make movement visually smoother and we'll get back our 60fps rendering rate, and without any increase to traffic. Such Client-Side Interpolation is quite a trivial thing and doesn't lead to any substantial complications. On the negative side, while it does make movement smoother, it doesn't help improve input lag.

The next thing we can do is go beyond interpolation and to do some extrapolation.

Client-Side Extrapolation, a.k.a. Dead Reckoning

The next thing we can do is go beyond interpolation and do some extrapolation. In other words, if we add velocities to our Game World state,[111] then—in case we don't have the next update yet because the packet was delayed—we can extrapolate the object movement to see where it would move if nothing unexpected happens.

The simplest form of such extrapolation can be done by a simple calculation of x1=x0+v0, but can also be more complicated, taking into account, for example, acceleration. This is also known as "dead reckoning," though the latter term is used in several similar, but slightly different, cases, so I'll keep using the term "extrapolation" for the specific logic described above.

The benefit of such extrapolation is that we can be more optimistic in our buffering, and not account for the worst-case when three packets are lost (extrapolating instead in such rare cases). In practice it often means (as usual, YMMV) that we can reduce the "stutter" in case of packet loss, which is especially important for our very aggressive buffer-on-receipt being just one single "network tick."

Running into the Wall, and Server Reconciliation

> I can hear the sound of a brick wall in distress.
> —Super Rock from *The Furchester Hotel*

What if while we're extrapolating NPC's movement, he runs into the wall?

On the flip side, unlike interpolation, extrapolation causes significant complications. The first set of complications is related to internal inconsistencies. What if while we're extrapolating NPC's movement, he runs into the wall? If this can realistically happen within our extrapolation, causing visible negative effects, we need to take it into account when extrapolating and detect when our extrapolated NPC collides, and maybe even start an appropriate animation. How far we want to go this way depends (see also the *Client-Side Prediction* section below), but it *may* be necessary.

---

111   These velocities can either be transferred as part of the "World Update" message or calculated on the Client-Side.

The second set of extrapolation-related issues is related to so-called "Server Reconciliation." It happens when the update comes from the Server, but our extrapolated position on the Client is different from the Server's.

BTW, this difference can happen even if we've faithfully replicated 100% of the Server-Side logic on the Client Side just because we didn't have enough information at the point of our extrapolation. For example, if one of the other players has pressed "jump" and this action has reached the Server, on our Client-Side we won't know about it for at least another 100ms or so, and therefore our perfectly faithful extrapolation will lead to different results than the Server's.

When such a conflicting update comes in to the Client, this is the point when we need to "reconcile" our Client-Side vision of the Game World with the Server-Side vision. And as our Server is authoritative and "always right," it is not that much of a reconciliation in a traditional sense, but "we need to make the Client world look as we're told by the Server."

On the other hand, if we implement Server Reconciliation as a simple fix of coordinates whenever we get the authoritative Server message, then we'll have a very unpleasant visual "jump" of the object between the "current" and "new" positions.

To avoid this, one common approach (instead of jumping your object to the received position) is to start a new prediction (based on new coordinates) while continuing to run the "current" prediction (based on currently displayed coordinates), and to display a "blended" position for the "blending period" (with the "blended" position moving from the "current" prediction to the "new" prediction over the tick). For example:

displayed_position(dt) = current_predicted_position(dt) * (1-alpha(dt))

+ new_predicted_position(dt) * alpha(dt),

where alpha(t) = dt/BLENDING_PERIOD, and 0 <= dt < BLENDING_PERIOD.

Other ways to reconcile include splines or Bezier curves, and also variations of blending (including so-called *projective velocity blending*, which as [Murphy] suggests tends to cause the least problems when predicting fast-moving objects). For a solid overview of these reconciliation techniques (and of other issues related to physics-based predictions in general), make sure to take a look at [Murphy].[112]

Client-Side Prediction

The idea here is to start moving the player's own PC as soon as the player has pressed the button, eliminating this "sluggish" feeling for PC movements.

With Client-Side Interpolation and Client-Side Extrapolation, we can reduce stutter a bit (and also pump the rendering frame rate up to 60fps <phew />). However, even after these improvements, it is likely that the game will still feel "sluggish" (our calculations above show that even OurRPG is likely to feel "laggy" if its servers are used beyond one single country).

To improve things further, it is common to use "Client-Side Prediction." The idea here is to start moving the player's own PC as soon as the player has pressed the button, completely eliminating this "sluggish" feeling for PC movements. Indeed, within the Client we do know what the PC is doing, and can show it; and if we're careful enough, our prediction will be almost-the-same as the server authoritative calculation, at least until the PC is hit by something that has suddenly changed trajectory (or came out of nowhere) within these 300ms or so.

Implementation-wise, Client-Side Prediction can be implemented, for example, via duplicating a part of the Server-Side Game Logic[113] on the Client. It should be noted that for the purposes of Client-Side prediction, we do *not* really need 100% cross-platform determinism between the Client and the Server (see more discussion on cross-platform determinism in Vol. II's chapter on (Re)Actors), and "almost-the-same" behavior of the Client and the Server is fine (as any small discrepancies, such as those resulting from different rounding etc. will be fixed as part of the "reconciliation" process that will follow shortly—again, within at most 300ms or so).

If you're going to dive into the depths of Client-Side Prediction, make sure to read both [Gambetta, Fast-Paced Multiplayer (Part II): Client-Side

---

112   Note, though, that I don't interpret [Murphy] as suggesting *transferring* quaternions over the network (and that I still insist on using Euler angles—or compressed quaternions—for *data transfer*, as discussed in the *Before Compression: Minimizing Data* section below); using quaternions for *calculations* is a different story, which I have no problems with.

113   Including simulation.

Prediction and Server Reconciliation] and [Fiedler, State Synchronization]:[114] both provide a more in-depth analysis than I can fit here (or am qualified to perform).

Client-Side Prediction: Dealing with Discrepancies

On the negative side, Client-Side Prediction may cause serious discrepancies between the "Game World as seen by the Server" and the "Game World as seen and shown by the Client" (i.e., between Server State and Client State). While this effect is very similar to the "reconciliation problem" that we've discussed for "Client-Side Extrapolation," for Client-Side Prediction the discrepancy is usually more severe than for mere Client-Side Extrapolation. The reasons for this increased discrepancy for Client-Side Prediction are twofold:

> On the negative side, Client-Side Prediction may cause quite serious discrepancies between "Game World as seen by Server" and "Game World as seen and shown by Client" (i.e., between Server State and Client State).

▶ First, it happens due to a significantly larger time gap between the Client-Side Prediction and obtaining authoritative data from the Server-Side.

▶ Second, with Client-Side Prediction, other players are adding their inputs, which affect the Server but are usually not accounted for by Client-Side Prediction.

■ This effect, however, can be mitigated by the Server forwarding other players' inputs to all the Clients, so the Client can predict better (for more details, see the *Forwarded Inputs* section below, including a discussion on the increased risk of Information Leak cheats).

A few things to keep in mind when implementing Client-Side Prediction:

▶ Most of the time, you'll need to keep a list of "outstanding" (not confirmed by the Server yet) input actions, and re-apply them after receiving every authoritative update; otherwise, unpleasant visual effects can arise (see [Gambetta, Fast-Paced Multiplayer (Part II):

---

114 While [Fiedler, *State Synchronization*] is in fact about distributed authority schemas (which I argue against because of cheating, see the *On Distributed Authority* section below), most of the discussion there is actually also directly applicable to Client-Side Prediction.

Client-Side Prediction and Server Reconciliation] for further discussion of this phenomenon).

▶ As noted in [Fiedler, State Synchronization], in some cases you *may* need to add more information (such as velocities) to your Publishable State to enable Client-Side Prediction.

▶ The problem of PC-running-into-the-wall (once again, in a manner similar to Client-Side Extrapolation, but with more severe effects due to a larger time gap) usually needs to be addressed.

▶ To make it even more complicated, inter-player interactions can be not as well-predicted as we might want, so making irreversible decisions (like "the opponent is dead because I hit him and his health dropped below zero") purely on the Client-Side is usually not the best idea (what if he managed to drink a healing potion that you don't know about yet, as the packet from the Server telling you about it is still en route?). In such cases, it is usually better to keep the opponent alive on the Client-Side for a few extra milliseconds, and to start the ragdoll animation only when the Server does say he's really dead; otherwise, visual effects like when he was starting to fall down but then sprang back to life (because Client-Side Prediction and Server-Side authoritative version worked a bit differently) can be very annoying.

On Distributed Authority

One thing that should be mentioned in regard to Client-Side Prediction is that on the way of implementing it, there is a very dangerous pitfall. As soon as we implement Client-Side Prediction, we have a (non-authoritative) simulation on the Client Side; and as soon as we have simulation on the Client-Side, there may be the desire to make "a tiny bit of it" authoritative.

> *Such systems, with a distributed authority between the Client and the Server, should be avoided.*

The problem with such systems is that as soon as you move even a tiny bit of authority to the Client, it becomes very easy to add more and more authority there. Eventually you will get a working game, but, as lots of decisions are made on the Client-Side, it won't stand any chance against cheaters even in the medium run.

I don't want to go into the dangers of Authoritative Clients here once again (there was a long discussion on it in Chapter 2). Let's just note that there was more than one major game that ran into severe cheating problems because of such a distributed-authority approach; moreover, one of the companies behind these games is currently in their second year of rewriting, trying to move all the Client-Side decision-making to the Server-Side (where it belonged in the first place).

Take-3 Diagram

Adding these three Client-side Improvements (Client-Side Interpolation, Client-Side Extrapolation, and Client-Side Prediction) gets us to Fig 3.4:

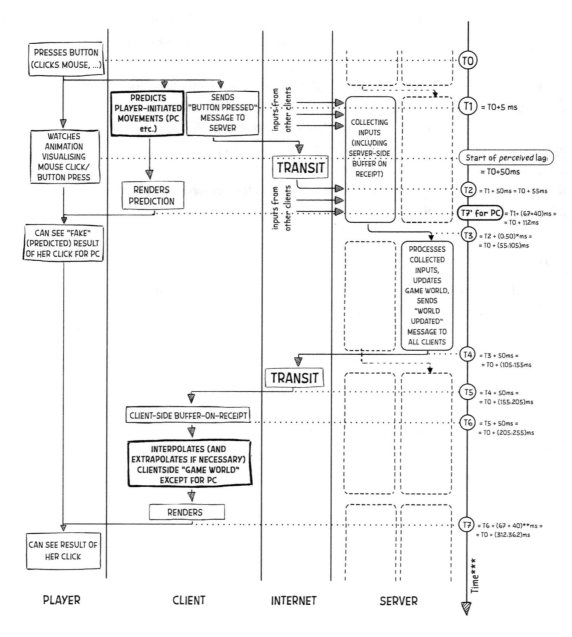

PRESSES BUTTON
(CLICKS MOUSE, …)

PREDICTS
PLAYER-INITIATED
MOVEMENTS (PC
etc.)

SENDS
"BUTTON PRESSED"
MESSAGE TO
SERVER

inputs from
other clients

COLLECTING
INPUTS
(INCLUDING
SERVER-SIDE
BUFFER ON
RECEIPT)

(T0)

(T1) = T0+5 ms

WATCHES
ANIMATION
VISUALISING
MOUSE CLICK/
BUTTON PRESS

TRANSIT

Start of *perceived* lag:
= T0+50ms

RENDERS
PREDICTION

inputs from
other clients

(T2) = T1 + 50ms = T0 + 55ms

(T7' for PC) = T1+ (67+40)ms =
= T0 + 112ms

CAN SEE "FAKE"
(PREDICTED) RESULT
OF HER CLICK FOR PC

(T3) = T2 + (0:50)*ms =
= T0 + (55:105)ms

PROCESSES
COLLECTED
INPUTS,
UPDATES
GAME WORLD,
SENDS
"WORLD
UPDATED"
MESSAGE TO
ALL CLIENTS

(T4) = T3 + 50ms =
= T0 + (105:155ms

TRANSIT

(T5) = T4 + 50ms =
= T0 + (155:205)ms

CLIENT-SIDE BUFFER–ON–RECEIPT

(T6) = T5 + 50ms =
= T0 + (205:255)ms

INTERPOLATES (AND
EXTRAPOLATES IF NECESSARY)
CLIENTSIDE "GAME WORLD"
EXCEPT FOR PC

RENDERS

(T7) = T6 + (67 + 40)**ms =
= T0 + (312:362)ms

CAN SEE RESULT OF
HER CLICK

Time***

PLAYER   CLIENT   INTERNET   SERVER

fig 3.4

*0:50 means "from 0 to 50", and is based on 50-ms network tick

**67ms for rendering lag, and 40 ms for display lag

***all times are for example purposes only, YMMV greatly

As we can see, the processing of the authoritative data coming from the Server is still quite slow. But the main improvement in perceived responsiveness for those-actions-initiated-by-the player (and it is these actions that cause the "laggish" feeling, as timing of the actions by others is not that obvious for the player) comes from the Client-Side Prediction and the rendering of this prediction. Client-Side Prediction is processed purely on the Client-Side, from receiving controller input, through Client-Side Prediction, and goes directly into rendering, without going to the Server at all, which (as you might have expected) helps latency a *lot* (resulting in T7 for PC being around T0+112ms, which is, for the example above, ~200 ms better than T7 for non-PCs). Of course, it is just a "prediction" (and in a sense is "fake"), but if it is 99% correct 99.99% of the time (and in the remaining cases the difference is not too great), it *feels* okay for the player, and this *feeling* is exactly what our players want us to achieve.

With Fig 3.4 (and especially Client-Side Prediction) we've managed to get quite an improvement, at least for those actions initiated by PC; at 112ms lag, the game won't feel too sluggish. But can we say that with these numbers everything is now good? Well, sort of, but not exactly. The remaining problem is that there is still a significant (and unavoidable) lag between any update-made-by-Server and the moment when our player will see it. This (as [Gambetta, Fast-Paced Multiplayer (Part IV): Headshot! (AKA Lag Compensation)] aptly puts it) is similar to living in a world where the speed of light is slow, so we see what's going on with a perceivable delay.

In turn, for some really fast-paced games (think shooters), it leads to unpleasant scenarios when I'm, as a player, making a perfect shoot from a laser weapon, but I'm missing because when my shot reaches the Server, I'll be late by about 100ms or so (and the target will move by that time). And this is the point where we're getting into the realm of controversy, known as Lag Compensation.

Lag Compensation— Potential for Cheating vs. Player Happiness

Three Client-Side improvements we've discussed above are very common for fast-paced games (in spite of implementation complexities) and are also known to work very well. The next bunch of improvements, known as Lag Compensation, is more controversial.

There are at least two distinct forms of Lag Compensation (probably more). The first is known as "Server Rewind."

Server Rewind

The classical form of Server Rewind is aimed to fix the problem outlined above, the one where a player is making a perfect shot and missing because his "press button" message reach the Server only later, when the target has already moved.

The idea behind Server Rewind is that the Server (keeping an authoritative copy of everything) can reconstruct the world at any moment, so when the Server receives your packet saying you're shooting at the moment T (and all the other data such as the angle at which you're aiming etc.), the server can "rewind" the world back to that moment T of your shot and make a judgment whether you hit or missed based on that information. This can be used to compensate for the delay, and therefore make players' "clean shots" much better.

On the other hand, "Server Rewind" may easily lead to a different player, who already managed to hide behind the wall, being shot anyway. In a sense, we're trading one perception-lag-related problem ("not hitting from an obviously 'clean shot'") for a different perception-lag-related problem ("being hit when already safe"). However, as this second problem *tends* to cause less annoyance for players, Server Rewind is usually a reasonable thing to make your players happy.

Subtracting Client RTT on the Server-Side

In [Aldridge], a different type of Lag Compensation is described. In *Halo: Reach*, they had an "Armor Lock" and the problem was that whatever they were doing, the moment when the "Armor Lock" was starting to protect the player who invoked it wasn't exactly the moment that the players were expecting (which led to lots of player complaints in public beta).

To deal with it, the best solution they found was changing game mechanics on the Server-Side: instead of the delay-between-button-is-pressed-and-armor-lock-applied being exactly 3 frames—on the Server-Side, they made it "3*frame_time - this_player_RTT" so that the player herself started to experience protection exactly when she was expecting it (after 3 frames of animation on her Client); this approach, while being inconsistent in the Server space, has made players happy, and this is ultimately what really matters.

This approach, while being inconsistent in the Server space, has made players happy—and this is ultimately what really matters.

Lag Compensation Is Inherently Open to Cheating...

The whole Lag Compensation thing can be seen as a clean win for everybody. However, there is an all-important consideration that you need to think about *well before* starting to implement any kind of Lag Compensation. It is that—

> *All kinds of Lag Compensation are*
> *inherently open to cheating.*[115]

With Server Rewind, if I can send my timestamp to the Server and the Server implicitly trusts it, I am able to cheat the Server, making the shot a bit later while pretending it was made a bit earlier. With subtracting Client RTT, cheating is trickier, but it is possible to *simulate* higher RTT while the cheater doesn't need it—and then to get an almost-instant reaction when he happens to need it.

For example, if our game is a Good-Bad-Ugly-style shootout and I am the Bad Guy cheating, I can write a bot that will introduce an additional delay for my packets all the time (imitating higher RTT) and then, when I press "shoot," it can remove that additional delay. This will effectively lead to me having an

---

[115] In other words, Lag Compensation *is* a clear win for everybody, cheaters included.

edge (equal to that additional delay) in a shootout; and as the whole point of the shootout is about reflexes, it can have a pretty negative effect on the gameplay. Moreover, such a delay can be implemented on a separate proxy box (which is inherently undetectable by any anti-cheating software), i.e., without any risk to me as a cheater. Note that even encrypting traffic (which protects from most proxy bots) is not efficient against this kind of cheating, simply because packets can be delayed without decrypting them.[116]

In other words, Lag Compensation can be used to compensate not only for Network Lag, but also for Player Lag (poor player reflexes), as they're pretty much indistinguishable from the Server's point of view (which leads to such Artificial Lag attacks being pretty much undetectable).

Note that in this respect, Lag Compensation is very different from the three Client-Side improvements discussed above: as Client-Side Interpolation/Extrapolation/Prediction do not make the Server trust the Client, they're inherently invulnerable to this kind of abuse.

That's exactly why Lag Compensation is controversial, and I suggest avoiding it for as long as you can.

…OTOH, Player Happiness Is Much More Important

On the other hand—

> *If it takes Lag Compensation to make your players happy, go for it! Unhappy players will kill your game **much** earlier than any cheaters.*

Living in the real world, we often have to make some compromises. And allowing the potential to cheat to make honest players happy is one of those compromises that *may* become necessary in the real world (at least for fast-paced games such as FPS).

---

116 It is worth noting that encryption still makes sense in this case. If the game traffic is not encrypted, the "shoot" command (activating removal of the additional delay) can also be automatically detected on the proxy; otherwise, the cheater would need to have some kind of additional notification to the proxy box, but it can also be done relatively easily in hardware.

When permitting Lag Compensation, just make sure to:

▶ Double-check that nothing but Lag Compensation will do to keep your players happy. In practice, it is only very fast-paced games (FPS) that tend to need Lag Compensation; if you're trying to do it for an RPG, think twice about whether you have already tried everything else (especially Client-Side Prediction).

▶ Keep that lag-related potential cheating in mind, and try to mitigate it. In particular, too great swings of timestamps and RTTs should be detected and packets with such swings should be ignored. Jitter of around 20ms happens all the time; 100ms does happen occasionally, but jitters of 300+ms are probably too much (and ten seconds is clearly out of the question). Not that I'm saying that they cannot happen (and I certainly do *not* mean to ban such a player), but I'd say that ignoring packets with such large jitters (or adjusting the jitter to the nearest allowed value) will be the prudent thing to do.

Double-check that nothing but Lag Compensation will do to keep your players happy.

■ Also, let's note that (especially for a shooter game) there are tons of other cheats you'll need to deal with (starting from aiming bots), so that you're pretty much deemed to enter into a bot-fighting mode anyway. And as soon as you deal with bots, chances are that you've also dealt with most of the Lag Compensation attacks. We'll discuss dealing with bots in Volume VIII's chapter on Bot Fighting, but very shortly, to make the lives of bot writers more difficult, you'll need *both* to encrypt your traffic[117] (to prevent proxy bots) *and* protect the integrity of your Client while it is running, and as soon as you've done these two things, you've also already curbed (though not 100% prevented) quite a bunch of Lag Compensation attacks.

And as soon as you deal with bots, chances are that you've also dealt with most of the Lag Compensation attacks.

---

117 This includes protection from a man-in-the-middle attack mounted by a player against himself, which is very unusual for classical security.

▶ Implement Lag Compensation on a per-action basis, monitoring the impact of your changes on the players. And while we're at it, make sure to watch the GDC presentation [Aldridge]; it is a goldmine of real-world experience in the field.

For FPS-like games, Lag Compensation *is* likely necessary to make your players happy. And if it happens that Lag Compensation is necessary to achieve player happiness, well, we don't have any other options than to do Lag Compensation, whether we like it or not.

Overall, the whole reasoning above can be generalized into the following statement (which stands pretty much across the board)—

> **If** *some feature-that-may-be-abused-by-cheaters* **is** *necessary to make your players happy, do it, but* **only after** *you've run out of non-cheatable ways to achieve the same effect.*

There Are So Many Options! Which Ones Do I Need?

With all these options on the table, an obvious question is "hey, what exactly do I need for my game?" Well, this is a Big Question™ with no good answer until you try it for your specific game (over a real link and/or over a latency simulator). Still, there are some observations that may serve as a reasonable starting point for your analysis:

If your game is slow-paced or medium-paced (i.e., actions are in terms of "seconds"), chances are that you'll be fine with the simplest dataflow.

1. if your game is slow-paced or medium-paced (i.e. actions are in terms of "seconds"), chances are that you'll be fine with the simplest dataflow (the one shown on Fig 3.1).

2. If your game is more fast-paced (think MMORPG or MMOFPS), you'll likely need either the dataflow in Fig 3.3, or the one in Fig 3.4

   a. In this case, it is often better to start with the simpler one from Fig 3.3 and add things (such as Client-Side Interpolation, Client-Side Extrapolation, Client-Side Prediction) gradually to see if you've already got the feel you want without going into too many complications.

b. If after adding all the "Client-Side" stuff, you still have issues (which you shouldn't, except for FPS), you may need to consider Lag Compensation, but beware of cheaters!

c. For further optimizations, you may need to go beyond the techniques described in this book (and/or combine them in unusual ways); however, going further is usually quite game-specific, so it is difficult to generalize it. In any case, what can be said for sure is that you certainly need to know about the techniques discussed in this chapter (and also to "feel" how they work) before trying to invent something else.

GAME-WORLD STATES AND REDUCING TRAFFIC

By this point, we've finished describing data flows that may apply to your game, and can now go one level deeper, looking into the specifics of those messages going between the Client and the Server. First, let's take a close look at the message that tends to cause most of the trouble (and tends to eat the most bandwidth). This is the "World Update" message from Fig. 3.1, and Fig. 3.3, and Fig 3.4. In turn, it is closely related to the concept of a Publishable World State.

Server-Side, Publishable, and Client-Side Game-World States

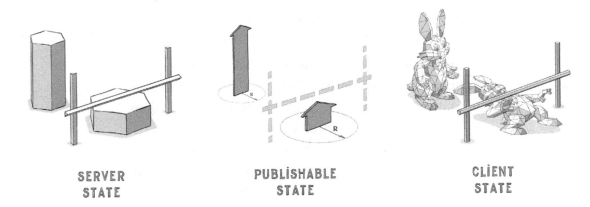

SERVER
STATE

PUBLISHABLE
STATE

CLIENT
STATE

Among aspiring simulation-based game developers, there is often a misunderstanding about the Game World State, which results in the question "why do we need to care about different States for our Game World and not have only one state, so that the Server-Side State is the same as the Client-Side One?" This kind of question is especially common when your development workflow is Client-Driven (as defined in Chapter 1).

The answer is: "Well, depending on your game, you *might* be able to have the same state as Client-Side, Server-Side, and even Publishable, but for quite a few games, you won't."

Limit on Bandwidth

The problem here is purely technical, but very annoying—it is the problem of bandwidth. As of 2017—

> *If your game is using more than 1Mbit/s/player, you're in Deep Trouble™.*

Most of the serious multiplayer games out there are using between 1kbit/s (think social games[118]) to 200kbit/s (think first-person 3D simulations) per simultaneous player. Going further down, while desirable (due to reduced traffic costs etc.), is usually not strictly required.

On the other hand, if your game uses *over* 500-1000 kbit/s/simultaneous_ player, you'll find yourself in pretty hot water. The main problem you'll face will be that for quite a few of your players, with more traffic than that you'll overload their "last mile,"[119] which in turn tends to bring latencies and/or packet loss to the point where the game becomes outright unplayable. While there are lots of ISPs saying that they're providing speeds of "up to 100Mbit/s," (a) most of your players won't be paying for this kind of bandwidth (at the beginning of 2017, over half of all broadband connections in the world are still (A)DSL), (b) those 10Mbit/s your player may have are usually of the "up to" kind (="will never be observed other than on paper"), and (c) there is usually lots of traffic competing with your game (from downloads and torrents within the same household to downloads and torrents by neighbors; see more on the mechanics of oversubscription in Vol. IV's chapter on Network Programming).

As a result, I'd say that 200kbit/s is the traffic you should aim for, even in 2017, and even if your game is a simulation. Note that for mobile games (or, more formally, for those games intended to be played over a mobile connection), your allowance is usually significantly lower—I'd say in the range of 20-50kbit/s, and the lower, the better.

Note that for mobile games, your allowance is usually significantly lower—I'd say in the range of 20-50kbit/s, and the lower—the better.

Additional Reasons to Optimize Bandwidth

In addition, let's keep in mind that sometimes reducing the Server packet size *may* help even if the Client's "last mile" overload is caused by a concurrent download, as there are some routers out there configured to give preference to smaller packets; we'll have a cursory discussion of certain aspects of over-the-Internet packet prioritization in Vol. IV's chapter on Network Programming.

---

118 For asynchronous games, "simultaneous player" is a bit of misnomer, but at our current level of abstraction, it will do.

119 Roughly, the connection from home router to ISP; see more discussion in Vol. IV's chapter on Network Programming.

One further potential reason to minimize bandwidth is that traffic can be rather expensive—depending on your monetization, that is. While traffic prices have steadily decreased for at least the last twenty years or so—as of the beginning of 2017, you can get unmetered 1Gbit/s for around $300/month, and unmetered 10Gbit/s for around $2,000/month—it is still far from being free. To put it into perspective: if you can monetize $0.05/month per player, with each player eating 200kbit/s bandwidth (and 20% of your players playing at your peak time) over a 1Gbit/s link, you'll be able to run around 1Gbit/s /200 kbit/s/simultaneous_player * 5 active_players/simultaneous_player = 250,000 active_players, paying $2,000/month for traffic (i.e., $0.008/active_player/month), but making $0.05*250,000 = $12,500/month in monetization.

As we can see, it is all about the amount you can monetize per player; if your monetization team can squeeze $1/active_player/month, you won't have much to worry about, but if you're coming closer to $0.01/active_player/month (which can easily happen if the vast majority of your players are free, and the percentage of free players is growing each day), you can find yourself under significant pressure to optimize your traffic costs. Or, looking at it from a different perspective, by reducing your traffic costs, you may be able to get a significant business advantage and/or tap into games that are not feasible to monetize otherwise.

Let's keep in mind that for quite a few games, the cost of renting Servers to run the game can easily overshadow traffic costs.

On the other hand, let's keep in mind that for quite a few games, the costs of renting Servers to run the game can easily overshadow traffic costs; with a more-or-less "typical" simulation game running 1,000 simultaneous_players/Server,[120] 5 active_players/simultaneous_player, and $200/Server/month, our per-player Server costs can get into $0.04/active_player/month (so reducing traffic costs of $0.008/active_player/month won't help much). However, this balance can change significantly if you decide to pay for "Premium"/"Real-Time" traffic (instead of the usual "Best Effort" one that is used by default), or if you're using cloud services, which can easily charge 10x more for the same traffic; we'll discuss different types of traffic (actually, different types of SLA) a bit in Vol. VII's chapter on Preparing for Launch.

---

120   A "workhorse" 1-Unit/2-Socket one.

Triangles and Bandwidth

I hope that I've managed to convince you that the number of "a few hundred kbit/s/simultaneous_player" is the maximum you can afford these days. Now we can get to the second part of our exercise and observe that—

> *If trying to push information about 3D triangles from the Server to the Client, we'll be orders of magnitude over 1Mbit/s limit.*

Let's consider a very simplistic scene from a 3D game with just five moving characters in the vicinity, represented with 10K triangles each;[121] then, even without other items (weapons, items, environment, etc.), we're speaking about 50,000 triangles (and for our order-of-magnitude-estimate purposes, we can assume that the number of vertexes is about the same). As all five of our characters are moving, so are all the vertexes; this means that on each "network tick" we'll need to transfer five characters/scene * 10,000 vertexes/character * 30 bit/vertex[122] ~= 1.5Mbit/scene, and with a typical 20 "network ticks" per second, we'll get to 30Mbit/second/scene, which is well over our 1Mbit/s limit, and this is for a very simplistic scene. <ouch! />

As we'll see below, with a separate Publishable State, we could reduce such a simple scene to about 100 bit/character/network_tick, and the entire traffic to around 100 bit/character/network_tick * five characters/scene * 20 network_ticks/second = 10Kbit/second/scene; this is a 3,000x improvement over transferring triangles or vertexes.

---

121   And this is not much by today's standards.
122   That's even if we're using fixed-point representations, as discussed below; usual floating-point representations will take up to 10x more.

Three Different States of MOG

Now, let's see how to achieve this 3,000x improvement. Let's note that the analysis below is made for a 3D-simulation game (specifically, for OurRPG); for some games (especially social ones), the different States described below can be merged together, and it can even happen that you'll have all three States that are the same. Still, IMO it is beneficial to consider all three States as separate before deciding to merge them; in particular, it will allow you to see any potential drawbacks of such a merge.

Client-Side State

Let's consider an example MMORPG game, OurRPG. Let's assume that our players can move within some 3D world; they can talk, fight, gain experience, and so on. Physics-wise, let's assume that we want to have rigid body physics and ragdoll animations, but our fights are very simple and don't really simulate physics and instead have animated fight movements (think "Skyrim").

If we have our game as a single-player, the only thing we'd need would be a Client-Side State, complete with all the meshes (with thousands of triangles per character), textures, and so on.

Server-Side State

Now, as we're speaking about MOGs with an Authoritative Server, we need a Server-Side State. And one thing we can notice about this Server-Side State is that it doesn't need to be as detailed as the Client-Side State.

In particular, as we don't need to render anything on the Server Side, we usually can (and *should*) drop all the textures on the Server-Side, and use more low-poly 3D models on the Server Side.

Actually, to keep the number of our Servers within reason, we need to leave only the absolute minimum of processing on the Server Side, and achieving this "absolute minimum" can be defined as "dropping everything that doesn't affect gameplay." In practice, for most classical RPGs (those without karate-like fights where limb positions are essential for gameplay), you can get away with simulating each of your PCs and NPCs as a box

IMO it is beneficial to consider all three States as separate before deciding to merge them; in particular, it will allow you to see any potential drawbacks of such a merge.

In practice, for most classical RPGs you can get away with simulating each of your PCs and NPCs as a box (parallelepiped), or as a prism (hexagonal or octagonal one).

(parallelepiped), or as a prism (say, a hexagonal or octagonal one). Cylinders are also possible, though if you're using classical polygon-based 3D simulation on the Server Side, you'll essentially end up with simulating a prism anyway. In addition, models of your Server-Side rooms can (and *should*) also be simplified greatly: while you do need to know that there is a wall there with a lever to be pulled in the middle, in most cases you don't need to know the exact shape of the lever.

In extreme (I'd say "very fortunate") cases, you won't even need 3D on the Server Side at all. While this is certainly not guaranteed, I suggest you start your analysis by checking if you can get away with a 2D Server-Side simulation. Even if you figure out that you do need 3D, such analysis can still help you drop quite a few things that are unnecessary on the Server Side.

For OurRPG, however, we do need 3D on the Server-Side (well, we want to simulate rigid body stuff and ragdolls, not to mention multilevel houses). On the other hand, we don't need more than a hexagonal prism (with additional attributes such as "attacking or crouching or..." and things such as "animation frame number") to represent our PCs/NPCs; when it comes to rigid objects simulated on the Server-Side, they also can be represented using only a few dozen triangles each.

When we need to simulate ragdoll on the Server-Side, we won't even try to simulate movements of all the limbs. What we will do is calculate movement of the center of mass of the dying character. While for some games this may happen to result in too-unrealistic movements, for other games we might be able to get away with it (and doing it this way will save lots of CPU power on the Server-Side), so this is what we'll try first. If a simple center of mass won't work, we might go a bit further and implement something along the lines of the logic described in [Aldridge], but still, sending all the ragdoll simulation across the network won't be necessary.

This polygon reduction will in turn lead to a drastic reduction in the size of our Server-Side State compared to the classical Client-Side State (the one we'll need to render the game), and to a drastic reduction in CPU cycles needed to simulate it, too.

Publishable State

Now, as we've got Server-Side State and Client-Side State, we need to pass the data from the Server-Side to the Client-Side. To do so, we'll use another state—let's name it Publishable State.

The most important thing about the Publishable State is that it usually *should* be even simpler than the Server-Side State. Whenever we *can* make Publishable State smaller, we *should* (see the reasoning about reducing bandwidth above).

And as a Big Fat Rule of Thumb™, quite a few simplifications are possible for the Publishable State. For example, for OurRPG we can do the following:

▶ To represent PCs/NPCs, we usually can (and therefore *should*) throw away all the meshes and use only a tuple of (x,y,z,x-y-angle, animation-state,animation-frame).[123],[124]

- In addition to the tuple required for rendering, there are likely to be dozens of fields such as "inventory," "relationships with the others," and so on; whether they need to be published depends on your Client-Side logic.

- By default (and until proven that you need a specific field for the Client-Side), avoid publishing these things. The smaller your Publishable State is, the better.

- In some cases, however, you may need them. For example, if your game allows you to steal something from PC/NPC, then your client's UI will likely want to show other characters' inventory to find out what can be stolen. This information about the other characters' inventory *may* be obtained by requesting your Server, or *may* be published. In the latter case, it becomes a part of the Publishable State.

To represent PCs/NPCs, we usually can (and therefore *should*) throw away all the meshes and use only a tuple of (x,y,z,x-y-angle,animation-state,animation-frame).

---

123 Actually, we can also use this representation for Server-Side, but it may or may not be convenient there. On the other hand, removing meshes is an almost-must for Publishable State.

124 Whether we need velocities to be published is not that obvious; see the *Dead Reckoning as Compression* section below.

▷ Note that making inventory publishable won't have *too great* an effect on the update size, as it is possible to optimize it via delta compression (see the *Delta Compression* subsection below); on the other hand, it will increase traffic during initializations/transitions.

▷ On the other hand, keep in mind that publishing such information *may* facilitate "Information Leak" attacks on your Client, so if requesting the Server at the point of "trying to steal" doesn't feel too sluggish, it is better to do it this way.

- Even if you need such rarely changing fields as a part of your Publishable State, you usually *should* separate them from the frequently changed ones (for example, into separate publishable trees). As fast-paced updates have different timing requirements from slow-paced ones, it *may* easily lead to different synchronization policies (for example, at the UDP-level), and it is simpler to express these policies when you have separate top-level trees. For example, inventory is updated rarely, and is usually quite tolerant to delays of the order of 200ms or so; as a result, it is usually unwise to be too aggressive with re-sending it (and as a result, it is usually okay to use a reliable UDP channel to transfer it, waiting for retransmit-on-200ms-timeout if the packet is lost). On the other hand, coordinates and other rendering-related stuff does need to be updated in real time, so you should be quite aggressive with re-sending them (usually they're re-sent on each network tick until the Server gets confirmation from the Client; more on it in the *"Reference Base" for Unreliable Communications* section below).

► To represent rigid objects, we again *should* throw away all the meshes and use only a (x,y,z,x-y-angle,x-z-angle,y-z-angle) tuple.

As we can see, there are quite a few ways to simplify the Publishable State, even comparing it to the Server-Side State. From a minimizing-bandwidth point of view, the most important simplification occurs when we're dropping meshes (triangles or vertexes) in favor of transferring coordinates (and rotations) of the whole characters and whole objects. This usually provides a tremendous savings in traffic.

One more thing that needs to be routinely handled as part of the Publishable State is chat. Going against the common practice of implementing chat as one of the "transient events" (which are in turn usually implemented on top of "broadcasted messages"), I usually argue for implementing chat as part of the Publishable State (usually a slow-paced part of it). My rationale goes as follows: *the player should not feel the difference if she was disconnected and instantly reconnected (and even less of a difference if just one packet got lost).* As a player, I *hate* situations when I've been disconnected-then-reconnected-in-half-a-second and cannot see that-all-important-ping even in my chat history. In other words, while I am disconnected, my PC proxy in the Game World is still connected, so at least there should be a way to learn about what happened while I was away. To achieve this (IMO Very Desirable) behavior of the chat history being an actual attribute of the Game World (opposed to a "transient event," which depends on my connectivity at the moment), the simplest way is to implement chat as part of the Publishable State.

As soon as we've defined our Publishable State and got it on the Server-Side, we need some magic to synchronize it with the Client-Side. The most obvious way would be to just send all those updates to the Publishable State over TCP, and it will even work for a prototype. However, when packet loss is present, UDP-based eventually consistent synchronization is known to allow *much* better latencies than TCP-based ones; we'll discuss one such

Going against the common practice of implementing chat as one of the "transient events," I usually argue for implementing chat as part of the Publishable State.

UDP-based protocol in the *"Reference Base" for Unreliable Communications* section below.

Why Not Keep Them the Same?

Now let's go back to the question of why not to use the very same Client-Side State as the Server-Side State and the Publishable State? While it was already essentially answered before, this question is asked so frequently (by first-time MOG developers, that is) that I feel obligated to re-iterate the answer (while throwing in a few more details):

▶ Depending on your game, you *may* be able to keep all three States the same.

▶ However, for a 3D simulation, it will likely lead to:

   ▪ Greatly increased Server-Side CPU load (and therefore, running costs for the Servers).

   ▪ Greatly increased traffic (up to the point of being completely unplayable for most Internet players).

      • This includes traffic becoming $O(N^2)$, and it will kill larger Game Worlds (as with States being identical, all the movements need to be transferred to all the Clients).

   ▪ Information Leak attacks. As soon as we postulate that all three States are identical, we essentially allow the hacker to extract all the information and provide "wallhacks" or "maphacks."

▶ The separation of different States is *not* limited to 3D simulations, and some of the considerations above can easily apply to other genres. For example, for Real-Time Strategies (RTS), all the considerations listed for 3D games (except, maybe CPU load) still apply.

For some of the non-simulation and non-RTS games (such as social games or blackjack), the difference between Publishable/Server-Side/Client-Side States can be much less pronounced, and in many cases the Server-Side State *may* be the same as the Publishable State (though the Client-Side State will often still be different).

Non-Sim Games and Summary

For some of the non-simulation and non-RTS games (such as social games or blackjack), the difference between Publishable or Server-Side or Client-Side States can be much less pronounced, and in many cases the Server-Side State *may* be the same as the Publishable State (though the Client-Side State will often still be different).

For example, let's consider a blackjack game with the Server-Side State being the same as the Publishable State. In such a case, whenever a card is dealt for a blackjack game, it can be represented as an update of the Server-Side State to reflect that the card is already dealt; as the Publishable State is the same as the Server-Side State, the update to this Server-Side or Publishable State will be pushed to the Client. However, all the animation of the card being dealt is usually still processed purely on the Client-Side (instead of simulating the card flying over the table on the Server-Side, and transferring coordinates changing at 20 network ticks/second).[125]

Now, we can try to generalize our findings over the whole spectrum of MOGs (from social ones to MMOFPS), making two very generic (though still quite practical) observations. First, whatever our game is, the following inequation should stand—

$$\textit{Publishable State} \le \textit{Server-Side State} \le \textit{Client-Side State}^{126}$$

The second observation is—

$$\textit{We \textbf{should} work hard on reducing the size of the Publishable State.}$$

---

125 Information *that* there should be animation can either be derived from the change of the Publishable State on the Client-Side or sent as a Transient Event from the Server-Side.

126 We're speaking about their respective sizes, of course.

Publishable State: Delivery, Updates, Interest Management, and Compression

After we decide what the Publishable State should represent (and know how to update it on the Server-Side), we can go further forward. The next question we face is "how to deliver this Publishable State (including updates) from the Server to the Client?"

How to deliver this Publishable State (including updates) from the Server to the Client?

Of course, the most obvious way of doing it would be to just transfer the whole Publishable State once (when the Client is connected), and then transfer updates whenever the update of the Game World occurs (which may be "each network tick" for quite a few simulation-based games out there).

However, very often we can do better than that traffic-wise. And as reducing traffic is a Good Thing™, both for reducing Server costs and players' latencies, let's take a closer look at these optimizations.

Interest Management: Traffic Optimization *and* Preventing Cheating

The very first thing to optimize traffic (and to help against cheaters) is so-called Interest Management. Interest Management deals with sending each Client only those updates that the Client needs to render the scene. Interest Management is extremely important for quite a few games out there both because of improving traffic and reducing the potential for Information Leak attacks.

Let's consider OurRPG mentioned above, and the Publishable State that needs to transfer 50 bytes/network-tick/character. Now let's assume that OurRPG is a big world with 10,000 players. Transferring all the data about all the PCs to all the players would mean transferring 10,000characters * 50bytes/tick/character * 20ticks/second = 10MBytes/second to each player, and 100GBytes/second ~= 1TBit/s total (and that's with our Publishable State being reasonably optimal; i.e., without transferring meshes). That's an enormous amount of data even for 2017, and while there are datacenters out there able to serve this kind of traffic, it is going to be Damn Expensive; even

Mathematically speaking, without Interest Management, the amount of data our servers will need to send (to all players combined) is O(N²). Interest Management reduces this number to O(N).

O(n)

Big O notation is a mathematical notation that describes the limiting behavior of a function when the argument tends towards a particular value or infinity.

—*Wikipedia*

worse, 10Mbytes/second (~=100Mbit/s) will be way too much for most of our potential players. Bummer.

On the other hand, if we notice that out of those 10,000 players, at any given moment each player can see at most twenty other players (which is the case most of the time for most of the more-or-less realistic scenes), then we can implement so-called "Interest Management." With Interest Management, we can send each Client only those updates-that-are-of-interest-to-this-particular-Client (in other words, sending only those things that are needed for rendering). Then, we need to send only 20characters * 50bytes/tick/character * 20ticks/second = 20KByte/second to each player (200MBytes/second total, which is going to cost roughly $1,000/month), *much* better.

Mathematically speaking, without Interest Management, the amount of data our servers will need to send (to all players combined), is O(N²). Interest Management (if properly implemented) reduces this estimate to O(N). The same thing from a different perspective can be stated as—

> *Interest Management normally allows for a capping on the amount of traffic sent to each player, regardless of the total number of players in the game.*

Note that when choosing you Interest Management algorithm, you need to think about worst-case scenarios when a large chunk of your players gathers in the same place (what about that royal wedding or presidential inauguration ceremony that everybody will want to attend?). From a traffic perspective, this can be really unpleasant, and you do need to think about how to handle it well in advance. If going beyond the most obvious (and BTW working pretty well) solution of "we don't have any big events, so it won't be a problem," things may become complicated (and if your game is a 3D one, the same scenarios can easily raise the number of triangles to be rendered on the Client-Side beyond any reasonable limits, bringing any graphics card to its knees). One of the ways to deal with it is to limit the number of trans-ferred-characters to a constant limit (ensuring that O(N) thing), and when this limit is exceeded, to render the rest as a "generic crowd" simulated purely by the Client-Side and wandering around by some simple rules (and the same "generic crowd" people can be rendered as really low-poly models to deal with the number-of-polygons issue).

Implementing Interest Management

In practice, implementations of Interest Management can vary significantly. In the simplest form, we can send only information of those characters that are currently within a certain radius from the PC (or even "send updates only to players within the same "zone"—whatever "zone" means). However, these are certainly not the only ways to shoe this horse; for a list of different Interest Management approaches with CPU-used and amount-of-information-sent comparison, see [Boulanger, Kienzle and Verbrugge].

An interesting variation of Interest Management, described in [Baryshnikov], includes changing LOD depending on the distance from the PC; in other words, a more-distant-from-the-PC object would have less information sent (this can include such things as "fewer of the properties sent" and/or "updates for such objects sent less frequently" and/or "acceptable level of precision loss due to lossy compression/dead reckoning being higher").

LOD

In computer graphics, accounting for Level of detail involves decreasing the complexity of a 3D object representation as it moves away from the viewer or according to other metrics such as object importance, viewpoint-relative speed or position.

—*Wikipedia*

Grid-Based Interest Management

To implement Interest Management in an efficient manner, we need to solve the task "find the objects that are at least somewhat close to the given player" very efficiently. Otherwise, we'd need to scan the whole list of the objects belonging to the same large area served by the same Game World Server — and do it for each Client, which would lead us to $O(N_{objects} * N_{players})$ operations for each simulated frame; with more-or-less typical number of objects per Game World Server being in the tens of thousands and number of Clients being in the hundreds, it quickly becomes extremely inefficient.

On the positive side, let's note that the quick algorithm of looking for those "somewhat close" objects doesn't need to be precise, and *may* contain extra objects that will be filtered out later (however, it *should* contain *all* the objects that are potentially close). In other words, we're actually looking for *candidates* to be sent to the Client (with *candidates* potentially subject to the further filtering).

To implement such a preliminary quick search, it is common to cover our 2D or 3D map with a "grid,"[127] and to maintain the position-within-the-grid for all our objects (including players). Then, to get all the "candidates" for a specific Client, we could get the grid cell of the respective player, and then we could get all the objects belonging to this-grid-cell-plus-adjacent-grid-cells as our *candidates*; if we optimize our data structures, this can be done very quickly. From this point on, we can either use this list of *candidates* directly (it would correspond to "Square Tile" algorithm from [Boulanger, Kienzle and Verbrugge]), or can filter it further to the extent we want.

Interest Management as a Way to Prevent Information-Leak Cheating

In more complicated implementations, we can take into account walls, etc., not transferring objects that are behind the wall from the player, or are covered by "fog of war." As a very nice side effect, such an approach also helps to address "see-through-walls" cheating, a.k.a. wallhack (as well as lifting-fog-of-war, a.k.a. maphack, and reading other player attributes, a.k.a. ESP cheat). In extreme cases, it is theoretically possible to even use frustum-based interest management (more in the *On Frustum-Based Interest Management* section below).

This also leads us to a second big advantage of Interest Management—

> *Interest Management (if properly implemented)* **may** *allow you to address Information-Leak cheats.*

The logic here is simple: if the Client doesn't receive information on what is going on in "fog-of-war" areas or behind the wall, then no possible hacking of the Client will allow to reveal this information, making this kind of attack pretty much hopeless.

---

127   The size of the cell in the "grid" should be comparable to "area of interest" of the player.

An extreme case of this class of cheats would be for an (incredibly stupid) poker site, which has pocket-card data as part of a Publishable State and doesn't implement any Interest Management. It would mean that such an implementation will send pocket cards to all the Clients (and then the Clients won't show other players' cards until the flag show_all_cards is sent from the server). *Don't do this.* If you do implement it this way, the Client will be hacked very soon, with pocket cards revealed to cheaters from the beginning of the hand (which will ruin your whole game very quickly). Interest Management (or, even better, excluding pocket cards from the Publishable State altogether, with, say, point-to-point delivery of pocket cards) is *an absolute must* for this kind of game. More or less the same stands for quite a few real-time strategies out there, where lifting "fog of war," a.k.a. maphack, would give way too much of an unfair advantage.

An extreme case of this class of cheats would be for an (incredibly stupid) poker site that has pocket cards data as a part of the Publishable State and doesn't implement any Interest Management.

On Frustum-Based Interest Management

As we'll discuss in Vol. V's chapter on Graphics 101, frustum is a pyramid within our 3D Game world that includes all the stuff our player can see at the current moment. And the idea behind the frustum-based Interest Management is that, as we cannot see beyond the frustum, we don't need to transfer information about the objects outside the frustum (which in theory should both reduce the amount of traffic sent and deal with relevant cheats).

Frustum

In 3D computer graphics, the view frustum… is the region of space in the modeled world that may appear on the screen; it is the field of view of the notional camera

—*Wikipedia*

In spite of being theoretically attractive, using frustum for Interest Management is problematic because of two issues: First, most of the time it doesn't help much traffic-wise; on the other hand, for a wide range of games, frustum-based Interest Management could still be potentially very important to prevent Information Leak cheats(!), so we might want to keep it regardless of traffic. However, unfortunately there is a second problem with frustum-based Interest management—the problem of sharp turns.

If our PC makes a sharp turn, then (assuming that we're using frustum-based Interest Management) we will need to provide information about the turn to the Server, which will then need to feed us a lot of information (about all the objects that got into the frustum because of the turn); and the delay between a player pressing the button and getting a response from the Server will be at least one RTT. Therefore, if your PC is rotating with a constant angle velocity, and makes a full turn in two seconds, these 100ms of delay will amount to an angle of 18 degrees, which we'll need to have as a "reserve" in addition to our current frustum just in case your PC is going to turn. It might seem a rather mild requirement, but we need to keep in mind that in case of any occasional delay above this "reserve," we'll face a pretty bad choice of "should we start to stutter" or "should we continue the turn, showing the Game World without dynamic objects." In addition, if the number of objects is high, sending all those objects that came into view because of the sharp turn, it may also lead to the need to transfer a few hundred kilobytes of information all of a sudden—and this will take additional time (if the player has a pretty decent 10Mbit/s connection, transferring 100KBytes still takes 100ms. Ouch!).

In certain cases, the problem of sharp turns can be mitigated by one or more of the following tricks: (a) adding inertia to turns, and (b) using distance-based Interest Management for close objects and frustum-based for distant objects (as mentioned in [Glazer and Madhav, p. 257]). By adding inertia to turns, we'll be able to buy some more time after the turn has started (and the Server has started to transfer the necessary data toward the Client) and before the Client needs to show those previously unknown objects. Using distance-based Interest Management for close objects, we'll be able to show the scene without stuttering and with most-important close-to-us objects, even if a delay has occurred.

One real-world example of kinda-frustum-based Interest Management was described in [Aldridge]. In *Halo: Reach*, they didn't completely filter out items positioned outside the frustum, but rather reduced their priority. And given the success of *Halo: Reach*, there should be something right about this approach.

Before Compression: Minimizing Data

One thing that needs to be mentioned even before we start to compress (and *long before* we start to transfer) our Publishable State is that most of the time we can (and *should*) minimize the amount of data we want to include in our Publishable State.[128] Way too often it happens that we're publishing data fields in exactly the same form as they are available on the Server-Side, and this form is usually redundant, leading to unnecessary data being transferred over the network. A few common rules of thumb for data minimization:

Most of the time we can (and *should*) minimize the amount of data we want to include in our Publishable State.

1. *Don't* transfer doubles; while double operations are cheap (at least on x86/x64), transferring them is not. In 99% of cases, transferring a float instead of a double won't lead to any noticeable change in rendering (while reducing traffic 2x). On the other hand, see below regarding how to improve it further by using fixed-point numerics.

2. *Do* think about replacing floats with fixed-point numerics (actually, an integer with an understanding of where the point is or, more precisely, what the multiplier is to be used to convert from Server-State data to a Publishable State and vice versa).

   a. One pretty bad example of a float being obviously too much is transferring an angle for an RPG. Most of the time, having the angle transferred as a 2-byte fixed-point value will cover all your rendering needs with an ample reserve (16 bits will allow to represent angles with a precision of 0.005 degree). If you're working with bits (for example, working with a bit-stream, or packing the whole rotation as described below), a mere 10 bits (which is 3x less than the usual 4-byte float) will give you the precision of 0.35 degree, which is usually sufficient for rendering purposes.

   b. For coordinates, calculations are more complicated, but as long as we need a fixed spatial resolution (and for rendering, this is exactly what we need most of the time), fixed-point

---

128   Strictly speaking, we may consider data minimization as a lossy Compression Technique—but it is *so* important that I prefer to discuss it separately.

encodings are inherently more efficient than floating-point ones, as we don't need to transfer the exponent for fixed-point. In addition, with standard floats it is more difficult to use a non-standard number of bits. For example, if we have a 10,000m-by-10,000m RPG world, and want to have positioning with a precision of 1cm, then we need 1e6 possible values for each coordinate. With fixed-point numerics, we can encode each coordinate with 20 bits, for 40 bits (5 bytes) total. With floats, it will take 2*32 bits = 8 bytes (that's while having comparable spatial resolution(!)), or 60% more (and if we transfer doubles, it would go up to 16 bytes, over 3x loss compared to fixed-point encoding).

c. Yet another case for transferring fixed-point numerics is all kinds of currencies (actually, for most-of-the-currencies-out-there it is cents that should be transferred, and the rest should be just interpretation, with conversion to dollars performed on the Client-Side right before displaying it)

3. *Do* convert your rotations (which are usually represented as quaternions or rotation matrices within your 3D/physics engines; see also Vol. V's chapter on Graphics 101), into Euler angles or some kind of "compressed quaternions" (see, for example, [Zarb-Adami], [Fiedler, Snapshot Compression], or [Glazer and Madhav, p. 129-130]) for your Publishable State.

a. The problem with transferring full quaternions or matrices is two-fold:

i. They're redundant, which means that they're large;

ii. Probably even more importantly, they're redundant, which means that the rounding of them becomes problematic (that's because after the severe rounding, their normalization is likely to be off, causing all kinds of trouble[129]).

After the severe rounding, their normalization is likely to be off, causing all kinds of trouble.

---

129 Sure, you can re-normalize both quaternions and rotation matrices after the rounding or after the transfer, but, well, what's the point of transferring redundant information just to throw it away?

b. Both Euler angles and "compressed quaternions" remove this redundancy, allowing for much better resilience to rounding (as was mentioned in particular in [McShaffry and Graham, Chapter 14, p.471], and also observed in the real world). For example, if using Euler angles, if we need to represent rotation of a rigid body object with a precision of 0.35 degrees (which can be coded with a mere 10 bits, as discussed above), we'll be able to fit it into 30 bits (or 4 bytes). Comparing it to transferring a float-based rotation matrix consisting of 9*4=36 bytes, we're speaking about a 9x difference, and if comparing to float-based quaternions (4*4=16 bytes), it is a 4x difference. Not too little gain for two transforms, if you ask me (note that transforms to and from Euler representation or compressed-quaternions needs to be done *only* for data sent over the network and *not* for each and every mesh triangle within our Server-Side—or Vivec forbid—Client-Side engines). With a compressed-quaternion representation, compared to Euler-angle representation, we're significantly reducing conversion complexity (that is, if your internal representation is quaternion-based), at the cost of slightly worse errors due to rounding (for a detailed analysis, see [Zarb-Adami]). Overall, which of these different compressed representations to use is up to you; the most important thing is to use *not-too-redundant* representations for the purpose of the network transfer.

c. In some cases, you might run into problems with rounding of the angles or rotations of the aligned surfaces (for example, rounding the angle of the tablecloth separately from the angle of the table can lead to pretty bad misalignments). If this happens, one of the ways to deal with it (besides the obvious "don't round these specific angles") is to encode rotation of the object relative to its parent in the scene graph (i.e., each child in the scene graph will have its rotation defined in relation to its parent). In more extreme cases, you

Scene Graph

A scene graph is a general data structure commonly used by vector-based graphics editing applications and modern computer games, which arranges the logical and often (but not necessarily) spatial representation of a graphical scene.

—*Wikipedia*

may need to encode angles of some children in relation to a specific *face (or edge)* of the parent; this is usually sufficient to guarantee that at least that specific face will be well aligned with the child.

Compression

By this point, we have our Publishable State with a proper Interest Management, and have already minimized it to eliminate unnecessary stuff[130]— but still want to reduce our traffic. As a next step, we'll need to use some "Compression Techniques."

---

130   This includes eliminating unnecessary-for-rendering lower "noisy" bits in coordinates and angles, as described above.

What Exactly Is "Compression"?

Note that we'll interpret "Compression" much more broadly than usual ZIP or JPEG compression (and our Compression will use quite a few tricks that are not typically used for generic compression), but on the other hand all of our "Compression Techniques" will still follow exactly the same pattern:

1. Take some data on the source side of things (Server-Side in our case).

2. "Compress" it into some kind of "compressed data."

3. Transfer the compressed data over the Internet.

4. "Decompress" it back on the receiving side (with or without data loss; see on "lossless" vs. "lossy" compression below).

5. Get more-or-less-the-same data on the target side of things.

We'll interpret "Compression" much more broadly than the usual ZIP or JPEG compression (and our Compression will use quite a few tricks that are not typically used for generic compression).

Also let's note that some of the techniques described below, while being well-known, are usually not named "Compression"; still, I think naming them "Compression Techniques" (as a kind of "umbrella" term) makes a lot of sense and provides quite a useful classification.

To make our Compression practical and limited (in particular, to avoid using a Game World State for Compression), let's define more strictly what our "Compression Techniques" are allowed (and, more importantly, not allowed) to do:

1. Our "Compression Techniques" are allowed to use a "reference base" to reduce the amount of data sent.

   a. Of course, this "reference base" *should* be something already known to *both* sender *and* receiver. In particular, it may be a buffer representing the data within the reliable stream (like in case of LZ77 or deflate), or may be "some previously synchronized snapshot of the Publishable State." We'll discuss "reference bases" (both for reliable streams and for unreliable packets) in more detail below.

Our "Compression Techniques" are allowed to know about the nature of the specific fields we're transferring.

Lossy compression

Lossy compression (irreversible compression) is the class of data encoding methods that uses inexact approximations (or partial data discarding) to represent the content.

—Wikipedia

2. Our "Compression Techniques" are allowed to know about the nature of specific fields we're transferring; these specifics can be described, for example, in IDL (see the *Example: Encoding* section below for IDL-related examples).

   a. Just as one example, if we have two fields, one of which is a coordinate, and another one is velocity along the same coordinate, this relation *may* be used by our "Compression Technique."

   b. "Compression Techniques" are allowed to rely on game-specific constants, as long as they're game-wide.

      i. For example, if we know that for OurRPG the usual pattern when the user presses the "forward" button is "linear acceleration of A m/s^2 until speed reaches V, then constant speed V," we *are* allowed to use this knowledge (as well as A and V constants) to reduce traffic.

3. "Compression Techniques" are *not* allowed to use anything else. In other words, we won't consider things like Client-Side-Extrapolation-which-takes-into-account-running-into-the-wall, as "Compression" (doing it would require "Compression" to know wall positions, and we want to keep our "Compression" within certain practical limits).

4. "Compression Techniques" can be either "lossless" or "lossy." However, if our Compression is "lossy," we *must* be able to put some limits on the maximum possible "loss" (for example, if our compression transfers "x" coordinate in a lossy manner, so that the *client_x may* differ from *server_x*, we *must* be able to limit the maximum possible (*server_x — client_x*)). In the sections below, all the Compression Techniques are lossless unless stated otherwise.

On "Reference Bases" for Compression

The concept that we name "reference base" is extremely important for achieving good compression. There are lots of algorithms out there that rely on it—from game-specific "Delta Compression" and "Dead Reckoning" to classical "LZ77." Moreover, it is reference-based algorithms that tend to save the most bandwidth (for example, within *deflate* it is LZ77—and not Huffman coding—which usually provides most of the savings).

In general, I know of two types of "reference bases" in the game context. The first refers to some previous state (or "current state"). In this case, the sender, instead of saying that "NPC coordinate is X," can say something like the "NPC coordinate didn't change in this tick," or the "NPC coordinate changed by dX." This kind of "reference base" is typical for Delta Compression and Dead Reckoning.

The second type of "reference base" refers to a portion of a stream that was recently communicated between the parties. For example, whenever an LZ77 compressor notices that a significant portion of the stream is being repeated, it can replace it with a (much shorter) sequence that is understood as "jump N bytes back from current position, and use M bytes from that point."

"Reference Base" for Unreliable Communications
Low-Latency Compressible State Sync

Most of the commonly available compression algorithms out there aim to work with reliable communications and reliable streams (such as TCP or ordered reliable UDP). However, as it was mentioned above (and as we'll discuss in more detail in Vol. IV's chapter on Network Programming), such reliable streams inherently suffer from Head-of-Line Blocking, and Head-of-Line Blocking is really bad for our latencies.

To remove Head-of-Line Blocking (while keeping compression), it *is* apparently possible to have a "reference base" that is known to both Client and Server, even in the case of unreliable communications.

One way of enabling compression over unreliable low-latency communications is described, for example, in [Fiedler, Snapshot Compression]; for the

To remove Head-of-Line Blocking (while keeping compression), it *is* apparently possible to have a "reference base" which is known to both Client and Server, even in case of unreliable communications.

purposes of this book, let's name it "Low-Latency Compressible State Sync". Essentially, it can be described as follows:

▶ Every packet going from the Server to the Client[131] contains its number (can be tick number).

▶ There are packets going in the opposite direction (from Client to Server; can be the same packets that carry player inputs), and they contain an acknowledgement, which is essentially the "number of the last packet received by the Client."

▶ For each of the Clients, the Server keeps a "list of recent packets acknowledged by Client."

▶ Whenever the Server sends a packet, it MAY use *both* of the following as a reference base:

  ▪ All the packets that are on the list-of-recent-acknowledged-packets for this specific Client. Note that a reference to previous packets is rarely used, but still *might* allow for LZ77-like algorithms (more on it in the *Compression Using Acknowledged Packets* section below).

  ▪ All the Game World States that were immediately produced from these recently-acknowledged-packets. This is the most common option used in practice.

▶ In any case, for such packets the Server *must* specify which of the packets (or states) it refers to. In other words, our Server will be saying "this is PACKET #Y, WHICH REFERS TO THE STATE CREATED BY PACKET #X, and using all the Delta Compression and Dead Reckoning COMPARED TO THE STATE CREATED BY PACKET #X." As we know for sure that the Client has already received that exact PACKET #X (which should be enough to reconstruct the state), we can be reasonably sure that on receiving our new PACKET #Y, our Client will be able to reconstruct the whole Publishable Game World State (as of moment #Y) correctly.

---

131 Actually, the same thing will work in any direction, but we'll stick to the most common scenario to keep the description a bit more specific.

▶ Bingo! We have our reference base (enabling delta compression, dead reckoning, LZ77-like algorithms, etc.) over an unreliable connection.

Fig 3.5 shows one possible interaction between the Server and the Client while using the protocol described above:

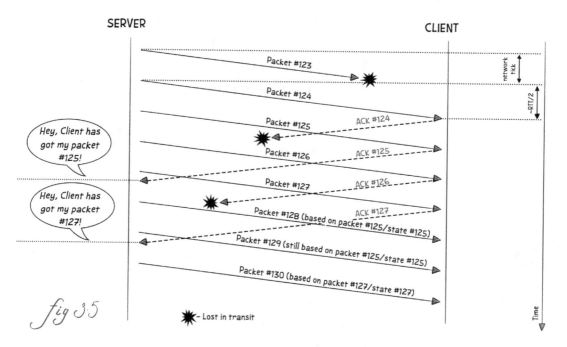

fig 3.5

One note: the approach described above means that PACKET #Y can be easily *different* for different Clients (in an extreme case, it can be different for each Client). However, as for MOGs we're bound to use unicast anyway (more on it in Vol. IV), so this isn't *too* bad.

Another note is that with this protocol, we do *not* guarantee delivery of each-and-every packet (and that's a Good Thing™, as otherwise we'd waste lots of time and bandwidth). Instead, what we're doing is guaranteeing eventual state synchronization even when some packets are lost.

Advantage of Low-Latency Compressible State Sync over TCP and Reliable UDP

One all-important property of the Low-Latency Compressible State Sync algorithm described above, is that, while enabling compression, it does *not* introduce Head-of-Line blocking, so if the packet is lost – this algorithm allows to avoid associated stutter and delays. In contrast, if we're using *any* compression which relies on a non-acknowledged-yet state (such as "current" state), or on a non-acknowledged packet – we are bound to have Head-of-Line blocking, there is no way around it <sad-face />.

Or, from a slightly different perspective:

> **Latency-wise, Low-Latency Compressible State Sync usually beats Reliable UDP[132] which in turn beats TCP.**

Delta Compression

With the definitions in place, let's start discussing the various flavors of Compression.

Arguably the most well-known Compression Technique used for MOGs is so-called "Delta Compression." Actually, there are two subtly different things known under this name in the context of games.

Actually, there are two subtly different things known under the name of "Delta Compression" in the context of games

Two Flavors of Delta Compression

The first flavor of "delta compression" (let's name it "Whole-Field Delta Compression") is about skipping those fields that didn't change compared to the "reference base" (often, you're just transferring one single bit, saying "the next field or bunch of fields didn't change" instead). This kind of "Delta Compression" is an extremely common technique (known at the very least since *Quake*) that is applicable to any type of field, whether it is numerical or not. This, in turn, allows publishing such rarely changing things as players' inventories (though see note in the *Publishable State* section above about

---

132   At least those systems which use Reliable UDP to construct any kind of reliable stream

completely omitting inventory from the Publishable State, or about making it available on demand; while not always possible, this is generally preferable).

The second flavor of "Delta Compression" (let's name it "Incremental Delta Compression") is a close cousin of the first, but is still a bit different. The idea here is to deal with situations when a numerical field does change compared to the "reference base" (so skipping the field completely is not really an option), but instead of transferring new value of the field, we transfer a *difference* between the "new value" and "old value."[133] For example, if the field is an x coordinate, and has had an "old value" of 293.87, the "new value" is likely to be 293.88, and is unlikely to be zero, so the spectrum of differences becomes strongly skewed toward values with a smaller absolute value, which in turn enables further optimizations. The gain here can be obtained by either simply using fewer bits to encode the difference, or to play around with variable-length encodings such as VLQ, or to rely on running another layer of compression (such as Huffman coding or arithmetic coding; see the *Classical Compression* subsection below), which will generally encode more-frequently-occurring-symbols (in this case, those closer to zero) with less bits.

Let's note that if we want it, this "Incremental Delta Compression" can also be made "lossy." In particular, we *may* round the delta transferred, as long as we're sure that pre-defined loss limits are not exceeded. Note that the ensuring of loss limits usually requires the Server to keep track of the current value on the Client Side (more strictly, the last-value-acknowledged-by-the-Client-Side), so that rounding errors, while accumulating, still remain below the loss limit.

VLQ

A variable-length quantity (VLQ) is a universal code that uses an arbitrary number of binary octets (eight-bit bytes) to represent an arbitrarily large integer.

—Wikipedia

Delta Compression—Generalization to Arbitrary Trees

Besides these two common flavors of Delta Compression, let's note that Delta Compression can be further generalized into updates of arbitrary trees; in this case, "arbitrary tree" is a tree as defined in graph theory and, in practice, can include such things as programming-structures-including-other-structures-and-so-on, and scene graphs. Let's consider this arbitrary tree as a root node, and any node can contain some data plus some child nodes.

Tree (graph theory)

In mathematics, and more specifically in graph theory, a tree is an undirected graph in which any two vertices are connected by exactly one path.

—Wikipedia

---

133   For audiophiles among us, this is pretty much what (A)DPCM is doing for audio signals.

In fact, basic logic of applying Delta Compression to such a tree is pretty simple: if nothing in the parent node is modified, then we can send only one bit indicating that the whole subtree-starting-with-this-node wasn't modified, that's it.

Things, however, start to become interesting if we want to consider a case of partial desynchronization, which happens when the Client is a valid Client that was synced at some time in the past, but since that point has lost some of the updates, and rolling forward of these updates is not desirable for whatever reason. Apparently, this problem of partial desynchronization is solvable (not only has it been solved in practice for a game with hundreds of simultaneous players, but it also allows for quite a few elegant solutions on top of it, saving quite a bit of traffic while providing interactivity). Moreover, there is more than one solution for this problem; unfortunately, these solutions are rather complicated, so for the time being I'll omit them from this book (please give me a shout if you need them, though).

Delta Compression of Arbitrary Trees— Collecting Updates "On the Fly"

When using Delta Compression for arbitrary trees, it may make sense to provide an API that will get the "delta" by writing it right as the tree is modified.

When using Delta Compression for arbitrary trees (and especially scenarios when within this tree we have a sequence or list or vector that is manipulated by Game Logic), it may make sense to provide an API that will get the "delta" not by calculating it by comparing two Game World States but rather by writing the "delta" right as the tree is modified.

For example, if one of our Game World State nodes is a "Chat" node, containing a list of the ten most recent chat messages,[134] then two typical operations will be "insert to the end of list" and "remove from the beginning of the list." While comparing two lists ("new" and "old" ones) to find out the "delta" is technically possible in the case when generic operations are allowed over the list, it is quite difficult (and time-consuming).

On the other hand, if instead of the usual

`push_back(Container& c, T& t)` function,

---

[134]   As was noted above, I feel that in those-games-that-show-chat-history-indefinitely, chat should be implemented via Game World State rather than via Transient Events.

we'll provide an alternative API such as

```
push_back(Container& c, T& t, CurrentUpdate& u),
```

we'll be able to collect all the updates made to the object *c* (storing them within the object *u*) not as an afterthought, but while our object *c* is being updated (and then send them to Clients based solely on object *u*, without spending time to calculate the difference between the trees).

In practice, from what I've seen, traditional "calculate the difference between two states" works best for the frequently-updated-but-simple fields (such as coordinates or velocities), and "updates on the fly" tend to work better for rarely-updated-but-complicated structures (such as inventory lists, chat, and so on). As always, YMMV.

Dead Reckoning As Compression

Another big chunk of simulation-related Compression Techniques is known as "Dead Reckoning." Note that despite obvious similarities, use of Dead Reckoning for the purpose of compression is subtly different from its use for Client-Side extrapolation (see the *Client-Side Extrapolation, a.k.a. Dead Reckoning* section above);[135] in particular, Client-Side Extrapolation is all about purely Client-Side calculations, while Dead Reckoning as a Compression Technique involves the Server reducing the amount of data sent (relying on the Client to use Dead Reckoning to reconstruct the data).

When using Dead Reckoning for Client-Side Extrapolation purposes, we're trying to deal with latency. In other words, we don't have information on the Client-Side (yet), and are instead trying to predict the movement, reducing perceivable latency (i.e., eliminating NPC "teleports" at the moment when we finally get the update from the Server-Side); to do it, no Server-Side processing is required, and there is no precision loss (that is, as soon as the Client gets the data from the Server).

> # Dead Reckoning
>
> In navigation, dead reckoning or dead-reckoning (also ded for deduced reckoning or DR) is the process of calculating one's current position by using a previously determined position, or fix, and advancing that position based upon known or estimated speeds over elapsed time and course.
>
> —Wikipedia

---

[135] In literature, it is usually considered one single "Dead Reckoning" algorithm (part of "DIS," a.k.a. IEEE1278) that reduces both perceivable latency and traffic. However, due to differences in both the effects and implementation, I prefer to consider these two uses of Dead Reckoning separately.

When using Dead Reckoning for compression purposes, we do know exact movement, and also know on the Server-Side exactly how the Client will behave, so we can use this knowledge as a Compression Technique to reduce traffic (normally as a "lossy" compression).

The basic idea with a classical Dead-Reckoning-as-Compression is to use velocities to "predict" the next value of the coordinate, while putting a limit on the maximum deviation of the Client-Side coordinate from the Server-Side coordinate, so from a "Compression" point of view it is a "lossy" technique with a pre-defined limit on data loss.[136]

Let's consider an example. Let's say that we have tuple (x,vx) as a part of our Publishable State, and that at a certain moment the Client has this tuple as (x0,vx0), and that the Server knows this (x0,vx0) for this specific Client.[137] Now, an update comes into the Server-Side that needs to make it (x1,vx1). The server calculates (x0+vx0,vx0) as a "predicted" state, and sees if it is "too different" from (x1,vx1).[138] If it is not too different, the Server can skip sending any update for this coordinate (and, if it is too different, "Incremental Delta Compression" can be used to send a message fixing the difference).

For further discussion of the classical Dead-Reckoning-as-Compression (with a discussion of associated visual effects), see, for example, [Aronson].[139]

Not only coordinates can be compressed using dead reckoning-like compression; actually, pretty much anything that can be predicted with high probability can benefit from it.

One important thing to note about Dead Reckoning is that *not* just coordinates can be compressed using Dead-Reckoning-like compression; pretty much anything that can be predicted with a high probability can benefit from it. One practical example of such non-coordinates compressible by dead reckoning is animation-frame number (that is, if you need to transfer it); most of the time, you'll be able to just say that the "animation frame is incremented as expected," which, in turn, depending on the details of your protocol, can be transferred as one bit (in some cases, even as zero bits).

---

136 While Dead-Reckoning-as-Compression can be made lossless, it won't get much in terms of compression, so the lossless variation is almost-never used.

137 See the discussion about "reference bases" above.

138 "Too different" here is the same as "exceeding pre-defined loss limit."

139 Despite the title, most of the discussion in [Aronson] is not about latency, but about reducing traffic with a pre-defined threshold, which we refer to as one of the "Compression Techniques."

Dead Reckoning As Compression: Variations

Dead Reckoning, as described above, is certainly not the only way to use kinematic equations to optimize traffic. Possible variations include:

1. Using Incremental Delta Compression to encode data when the "loss limit" is exceeded.

2. Using accelerations in addition to velocities (and predicting velocities based on accelerations).

3. Calculating velocities or accelerations (using previous values within the "reference base"[140]) instead of transferring them.

4. Use of smoothing algorithms to avoid sharp change of coordinates when the correction is issued. These are similar to the smoothing algorithms used for Server reconciliation (see the *Running into the Wall, and Server Reconciliation* section above), and the same smoothing algorithm can be used for both purposes. Whether to consider smoothing a part of Compression (or a post-compression handling) is not that important.

5. Using knowledge about the game mechanics to reduce traffic further. As one example, if in OurRPG velocity of PC always grows in a linear manner with fixed acceleration until it reaches a well-defined limit, this can be used to calculate "predicted speed" and to avoid sending updates as long as velocities are changed along this typical pattern (any user actions or collisions will still need to be transferred, but the traffic gain from this class of optimizations can be pretty large).

Such is my tale about Dead Reckoning.

---

140   This assumes that we're keeping more than one snapshot available on both the Server and the Client.

Classical Compression

Just as with any other compression, in the context of games, classical compression algorithms tend to behave very differently depending on the "reference base" they are allowed to use. In this regard, classical compression algorithms can be divided into those working over reliable streams (effectively using a previous part of the stream as a "reference base"), and those working over individual packets (with no "reference base" other than the packet itself).

Compressing Reliable Streams

Quite a few of the classical lossless compression algorithms (such as ZIP, or, more specifically, *deflate*) aim to compress files, or, more generally, reliable streams (such as TCP or ordered reliable UDP streams). Most of such classical-compression-methods-for-reliable-streams[141] are based on two rather basic algorithms. The first usually revolves around LZ77[142] (with the idea being to find similar stuff in the earlier buffer[143] and to transfer a reference to that "earlier buffer" instead of the verbatim portion of the stream). The second algorithm is usually somehow related to so-called Huffman coding,[144] with the idea being to find out which of the symbols occurs in the stream more frequently than the others, and to use less bits to encode these more-frequently-used symbols. Of course, there are lots of further variations around these techniques, but the idea stays pretty much the same. And for the record, ZIP's *deflate* is basically a combination of LZ77 and Huffman coding (and, say, LZ4 can be seen as an incarnation of LZ77 without Huffman).

Unfortunately, classical compression algorithms, such as *deflate*, are not well-suited for compression of the game traffic. One of the reasons is that (as it was shown for *deflate* in [Ignatchenko]), these algorithms are usually not optimized to handle small updates (in other words, "flush" operation,

LZ77

LZ77 is the lossless data compression algorithm published by Abraham Lempel and Jacob Ziv in 1977.

—Wikipedia

---

141   That is, those algorithms that are reasonably fast to be used in games.

142   And/or its close cousins LZ78 and LZW.

143   Effectively using "earlier buffer" as a "reference base."

144   Or a bit more efficient space-wise but significantly slower arithmetic coding; overall, I prefer Huffman but I know a few people who insist on doing arithmetic coding. In any case, the difference between Huffman and arithmetic coding is not that important for the purposes of our current discussion, and you'll be able to decide yourself when playing with them.

which enables sending an update, is expensive for *deflate* and other traditional stream-oriented algorithms).

On the other hand, it *is* possible to have a compression algorithm optimized for small updates; one example of such an algorithm is an "LZHL" algorithm described in the very same [Ignatchenko], designed by my esteemed translator. Like *deflate*, it is a combination of LZ77-like and Huffman-like compression, though unlike *deflate*, it *is* optimized for small updates.

It *is* possible to have a compression algorithm optimized for small updates; one example of such an algorithm is an "LZHL" algorithm."

Compressing Independent Packets

It should be noted that for compressing independent packets, pretty much any algorithm using LZ77-like compression (even optimized-for-small-updates such as LZHL) won't work efficiently. This happens because when trying to compress independent packets, our "reference base" is restricted to one single packet (which is usually less than 1500 bytes), and it happens to be way too small for LZ77 (which tends to start working reasonably well with buffers around 4K-8K bytes, and typical *deflate*-like efficiency reached around 32K bytes or so).

On the other hand, for unreliable UDP packets, you can still try using Huffman coding[145] (albeit without LZ77). I won't go into too much detail on Huffman coding as such here (it is described very well in [Wikipedia, Huffman coding]), however, there is one trick that may help with regard to games.

Usually, implementations of Huffman coding transfer "symbol frequency tables" as a part of compressed data; this leads to complications in the case of lost packets (or, if you transfer the table for each packet, the packets become huge). For games, it is often possible to pre-calculate a symbol frequency table (for example, by gathering statistics in a real game session), and then hard-code this frequency table both into the Server and the Client.[146]

If using Huffman coding (or reasonable facsimiles such as Huffman-like or arithmetic coding) in this manner, lost packets won't affect frequency tables at all, and this variation of Huffman coding will work trivially over both TCP and UDP. Note though that usually gains from Huffman coding (when

---

145   Or a Huffman-like part of LZHL, as described in [Ignatchenko], or arithmetic coding.
146   This is known as "training" compression algorithm to specifics of your data.

It *is* possible to build an algorithm which would work using "reference base" achieved via acknowledged packets from unreliable communications.

taken alone, without LZ77 or other methods) are rather limited; even if your data has lots of redundancies, don't expect to gain more than 20% compression from pure Huffman coding, but it is still usually better than nothing.

Compression Using Acknowledged Packets

In addition to the two scenarios above (i.e., reliable streams and independent packets), it *is* possible to build an algorithm that would work using "reference base" achieved via acknowledged packets from unreliable communications (along the lines described in the *"Reference Base" for Unreliable Communications* section above).

I have to admit that while I built a compression algorithm using an external "reference base" (and it worked like a charm too), I didn't use it for fast-paced game-like communications. Still, it *seems* that such an algorithm could work pretty well for some of the games out there. Very briefly, when applied to packets, such an algorithm would work similar to LZ77 or LZHL, but would issue a reference like "use M bytes from packet T at offset O" (referring *only* to those packets which were already acknowledged) instead of the usual LZ77's "jump N bytes back from current position within the stream, and use M bytes from that point."

Another way to think about it is in terms of "differential update" algorithms (such as *bsdiff*), compressing the *difference* of the upcoming packet to one of the previous packets. Keep in mind though that to be usable in games, existing file-oriented differential algorithms *may* need to be re-optimized for small packets.[147]

Combining Different Compression Mechanisms and the Law of Diminishing Returns

It is perfectly possible to use different Compression Techniques together, combining them in different ways. For example:

► For relatively static data (such as inventory), you may want to use Whole-Field Delta Compression, followed by Classical Compression.

---

[147] Just like *deflate* needed to be re-optimized, as discussed above.

▶ At the same time, for very dynamic coordinate-like data, you may want to use Dead Reckoning (as a lossy compression), with Dead Reckoning using Incremental Delta Compression, and using VLQ to encode differences.

Note that the examples above are just that, examples, and the optimal case for your game may vary greatly.

One further thing to note when combining different compression mechanisms is that all of them are merely reducing redundancy in your data, so even if they're not conflicting directly,[148] traffic reduction from applying two of them simultaneously will almost universally be less than the sum of reductions from each of them separately. In other words, if one compression gives you 20% traffic reduction and another one another 20%, don't expect two of them combined to give you 20%+20%=40% or 1-(0.8*0.8)=36% reduction; most likely, it will be less than that. While there are known synergies between certain compression algorithms, notably for LZ77 followed by Huffman (or for Incremental Delta Compression followed by VLQ), unfortunately they're few and far between.

If one compression gives you 20% traffic reduction and another one another 20%, don't expect two of them combined to give you 1-(0.8*0.8)=36% reduction.

On Using Doubles with Lossless Compression

I've seen quite a few games where developers were thinking along the lines of "hey, we have this data; let's just do Interest Management and Dead Reckoning, and then just feed whatever-we-have (usually expressed in terms of variables having 8-byte *double* type(!)) to *deflate*, which will optimize our data." It is not that this approach won't work *at all*, but it is damn inefficient.

The problem here is—

> *Lossless Compression is extremely inefficient for compressing real-world floating-point numbers.*

---

148 Examples of such direct conflicts are trying to use Dead Reckoning after Classical Compression, or using LZ77 compression after Huffman compression.

The real problem here is that those "noise" bits look like "noise" (usually like "white noise"), and "noise" is not compressible at all.

Let's consider it from the example of the angle field. When we have an angle (out of which we need only about 8-10 bits that have some meaning for rendering) represented as an 8-byte double variable, we essentially have 11 almost-constant bits (exponent), 8-10 meaningful bits (the ones which we really need), and 42-44 "noise" bits (those that we don't really care about, at least for rendering purposes).

From the point of view of compression, the real problem is that those "noise" bits really look like "noise" (usually like "white noise"), and "noise" is not compressible at all.[149]

It means that lossless compression will not be able to compress most of these 42-44 bits; in addition, if the compression is byte-oriented (like *deflate*), it will additionally lose some efficiency because meaningful and meaningless data is not byte-aligned.

Even a simple switch to floats will significantly improve the situation; however, an even better (usually *much* better) approach is:

▶ For transferring purposes, convert your angle to a fixed-point with only those 8-10 meaningful bits.

▶ Treat the value represented by these meaningful bits as one "symbol" and feed this one symbol to Huffman (Huffman-like, arithmetic) coding with frequency tables specific to this field (or to angles in general).

This way, you'll completely eliminate those uncompressible "noise" bits and the rest will have a chance to exhibit some statistical patterns, with Huffman coding being able to compress them a bit further.

On Adaptive Traffic Management

Even if your game is limited to 250kbit/s, there might be players for which the Client channel is too narrow to deal with the data you're sending there. I'd say that in 2017, saturating the Client's bandwidth with 250kbit/s is rather unlikely for home connections,[150] but it *may* still come into play at least in two

---

149 At least if we're speaking about lossless compression such as *deflate*.
150 Though even on home connections it may happen in case of concurrent downloads.

cases: (a) whenever you need to work over a mobile connection, or (b) if you *really* need more that 250kbit/s/player.

In such cases, so-called adaptive traffic management may help; the idea behind it is to (a) detect that the channel to the specific Client is overloaded, and (b) reduce the traffic accordingly.

Adaptive Traffic Management—UDP

One example of what is essentially Adaptive Traffic Management over UDP was described in [Frohnmayer and Gift] as early as 1999—and then a very similar approach was used in *Halo: Reach* (as described in [Aldridge]).

The basic idea is to prioritize all-the-data-of-potential-interest-for-the-specific-Client and push as much as of this data as we can, while avoiding accumulation of the latencies.

Very briefly, Tribes engine (described in [Frohnmayer and Gift]) has a Stream Manager, where the Stream Manager has limited bandwidth, with the bandwidth limit known for each of the Clients. Armed with this information, Stream Manager regularly[151] creates a packet-that-will-be-sent-to-the-Client and then allows different entities to fill this packet with the relevant data (more prioritized data coming first). As soon as the available space in the packet is used, the packet is sent to the Client with all the data that higher-priority data entities managed to fit into it.

As soon as the available space in the packet is over, the packet is sent to the Client with all the data which higher-priority data entities managed to fit into it.

This approach is rather simple in concept (though much more difficult to implement and tune in practice) and allows you to utilize as-much-as-possible-of-the-Client's-channel in a way that makes sense (i.e., providing as much information as possible to the Client, given the limitations on Client bandwidth). Which is exactly what Adaptive Traffic Management is about.

Last, but not least: when speaking about priorities, we may need to make sure that low-priority objects don't stay without updates "forever-and-ever." One way to do it is via a "priority accumulator" as described in [Fiedler, State Synchronization]. Very briefly:

---

151 Normally for each network tick.

▶ In addition to a static object priority, each object has a dynamic "priority accumulator."

▶ On each frame, we're adding object priority to its "priority accumulator."

▶ When deciding what-to-send, we're using "priority accumulators" rather than object priorities.

▶ When we're sending an object, we're resetting its "priority accumulator" to zero.

Adaptive Traffic Management—TCP

In the TCP world, the only real-world system I know that is using some kind of Adaptive Traffic Management is the Lighstreamer server aimed for near-real-time communications [Lightstreamer]. In a manner that is somewhat similar to UDP, TCP-based Adaptive Traffic Management consists of two separate things:

▶ Bandwidth detection (for each Client separately *and* dynamically as a mobile channel's quality can vary *greatly* over time).

▶ Rate limiting based on the detected bandwidth (again, on a per-Client basis). How to implement rate limiting is a different story.

- Unlike *Tribes/Halo* above, to limit or control the bandwidth, instead of prioritization, Lightstreamer uses so-called "conflation." Very briefly, whenever we have a queue mounting on the sending side, we can "conflate" several updates into a single one, saving on traffic while preserving the last value for each field. In other words (and very roughly), if there are two updates of the same field in the queue, we can skip the first one, as it will be overwritten by the second one anyway.

Adaptive Traffic Management in the Context of Authoritative Servers

When looking at those games that are using Adaptive Traffic Management, we can see that they tend to come from P2P architectures (rather than from Authoritative Server architectures). Among other things, it can be attributed to two factors:

1. For a long while, traffic for those games based on Authoritative Servers was bound not by the Client's bandwidth, but by traffic costs on the Server Side.

   a. However, as we have seen (see the *Additional Reasons to Optimize Bandwidth* section above), in 2017 more and more games became bound by Server CPU costs rather than by traffic costs (which can be caused by traffic costs going down faster than Server costs), and this *may* open the door for using all available bandwidth on the Client.

2. Adaptive-Traffic Management causes different Clients to have different visual representations; while from the point of view of "graceful degradation" it is certainly good, from the point of view of the games being *perfectly fair* (as needed for eSports), it is not necessarily so.[152]

> # Graceful degradation
>
> Providing an alternative version of your functionality or making the user aware of shortcomings of a product as a safety measure to ensure that the product is usable.
>
> —W3C

On the other hand, Adaptive-Traffic Management certainly does have its benefits (that is, as soon as you're ready to foot the bill for additional Server traffic beyond "the bare minimum necessary to make the game playable"). In particular, it avoids excessive latencies, while providing as-much-information-as-possible to each of the Clients (sounds pretty much like a Holy Grail, doesn't it?)

Whether Adaptive-Traffic Management is worth the trouble (and downsides listed above) is an open question (and IMO depends on the specifics of your game). However, there is one environment where I'd expect its benefits to clearly outweigh the negatives for quite a few games. In particular, for

Adaptive Traffic Management avoids excessive latencies, while providing as-much-information-as-possible to each of the Clients (sounds pretty much like a Holy Grail, doesn't it?).

---

152 Of course, *any* game will be unfair if played over a bad channel; however, Adaptive-Traffic Management helps to use more bandwidth—effectively making game behavior more dependent on traffic.

mobile games, with mobile games not having that much bandwidth to start with, "graceful degradation" will often be the only viable option.

Traffic and Real-Time Strategies

Real-Time Strategies (RTS) are quite special when it comes to traffic. If your game has a thousand units that will move in a similar, but not identical fashion on one player's click, any naïve implementation of the Publishable State will result in traffic being unacceptable. This problem is actually *that* bad that it has led to widespread use of RTS games based on Deterministic Lockstep; however, Deterministic Lockstep tends to trade off one problem of traffic for a whole bunch of its own very significant problems; in particular, it is inherently wide open to "maphack" ("lifting fog of war") cheating, and also has limitations on the maximum number of players; see Chapter 2 for discussion. As a result, I *strongly* suggest trying to use Authoritative Servers and Publishable States even for RTS—that is, unless it is proven that traffic for a specific RTS cannot be optimized.

When optimizing RTS traffic, there are several things that can and should be used (see also [Amir and Axelrod]; while it overlaps with the list below, there are also significant differences, so make sure to read both):

Interest Management is our friend (at least in larger worlds).

▶ Interest Management is our friend (at least in larger worlds). We don't need to send more than a player is allowed to see (and sending information about only those groups he can see also greatly reduces potential for wallhacks).

▶ The very same observation of "1,000 units moving on one player click" is going to help us with traffic. In particular, almost universally these 1,000 units will be moving according to *similar* (though not identical) patterns. Which means that if we encode these movements not as 1,000 separate movements but along the lines of "this group with 1,000 units moves to (x,y), and they should stand in a well-known formation #N after the movement is complete," we're going to save a damn lot on traffic.

- In some cases it might be necessary to specify deltas (from group position to individual unit position) instead of referring to well-known formations. However, as we're going to use the Client only for rendering, these deltas (and actually group positions) can be approximate; and as soon as they're approximate, they become compressible (in particular, it is very likely that they will have only a few very common values, and then they become ideal candidates for Huffman coding). On the other hand, approximations are inherently imprecise, so we need to be careful to avoid their accumulation (see below).

▶ Most of AI actions can be divided into trivial ones (such as "move along the path…"or "follow…" etc.; see [Amir and Axelrod] for details), and these trivial AI-like actions can be delegated to the Client. In other words, instead of saying "hey, unit has moved" each and every time, we can say to the Client "hey, start moving this group to (x,y) with velocity V with such and such waypoints, also taking into account corrections for individual units within the group too." Note that this, while being a very efficient traffic optimization technique, can easily become another source of imprecision (in particular, due to the lack of 100% determinism between the Client and the Server, or due to different information being available to the Client and the Server at the point of decision making).

- As for delegating pathfinding/A* to the target Client, it might be *partially* possible, but you need to beware of delegating decisions that might cause significantly different movements on the Client and the Server. In particular, if there are two significantly different paths with almost-identical costs, imprecisions and/or not being 100% deterministic can cause these small differences to cause the Client and Server to choose very different paths. To avoid this, make sure that all the stretches you're sending between the Client and Server are small enough so they won't cause any trouble (in other words, split your "move over the whole map" command into

A* Search Algorithm

A* (pronounced as "A star") is a computer algorithm that is widely used in pathfinding and graph traversal… It enjoys widespread use due to its performance and accuracy.

—*Wikipedia*

several smaller ones to make sure that the Clients don't have room to choose a path that is vastly different).

- Note that this is different from performing pathfinding on the *source* Client. Making decisions on the *source* Client is a technique that is not related to traffic optimization but rather to optimizing Server-Side CPU usage. From a cheating point of view, it cannot be used to violate game rules (that is, as long as I'm only making decisions about moving my own units), but can facilitate some helper apps that may be prohibited by T&C (and which may also shift game balance).

▶ If we allow imprecisions (which can arise in several scenarios; see above), we *must* make sure that these imprecisions cannot accumulate. One simple way of doing it is to use commands that specify unit final destinations rather than increments; this way, all imprecisions will automatically become "self-healing."

I have to admit that I didn't see (as in "with my own eyes") an RTS that is built along these lines; however, from what I've *heard* (and trying to extrapolate my experience from different fields), it *seems* perfectly feasible to achieve acceptable traffic levels for an RTS while using an Authoritative Server to run it. Still, no warranties of any kind, and make sure to test your compression before you commit to this model.

Traffic Optimization: TL;DR and Recommendations

It took us a while to get here, but we did it.

It took us a while to get here, but we did it. Now we can summarize my current feelings about optimizing MOG traffic and provide a set of personal recommendations in this regard. As a first approximation, I suggest to optimize things (roughly) in the following order:

▶ First, make sure that you start your analysis in terms of separate Client-Side State, Server-Side State, and Publishable State.

- Even if you find out later that some (or even all) of these States will be the same for your game, it is very important to make this kind of decision with your eyes wide open.

▶ Then, minimize your Server-Side State. It is important not only to minimize traffic, but also to minimize server-side CPU load

▶ Then, minimize your Publishable State. Be aggressive: throw away everything and add fields to your Publishable State only when your Client cannot live without them.

Minimize your Publishable State. Be aggressive: throw away everything, and add fields to your Publishable State only when your Client cannot live without them.

- While you're at it, split your Publishable State into several groups with different timing requirements.

- Make sure to take a close look at the data types you're going to transfer. Try to avoid doubles and even floats; preferable is fixed-point numerics. Make sure also to deal with angles and rotations.

▶ Make sure to implement Interest Management.

▶ For RTS games, take a look at those RTS-specific optimizations discussed above.

▶ Make sure to use "Whole-Field Delta Compression" to allow skipping updates for non-changing objects.

- Treat "non-changing objects" broadly; for example, for many games out there an object that keeps moving with the same speed in the same direction can be treated as "non-changing" (alternatively, you can handle it via "Dead Reckoning").

▶ Think about "Dead Reckoning" compression, keeping adverse visual effects in check (and reducing the threshold if necessary).

- Don't forget about variations of Dead Reckoning; they may make a significant difference depending on specifics of your game.

▶ Think about running Classical Compression on top of the data compressed by previous techniques, but don't hold your breath over it.

- Deflate as such won't work for most games (primarily due to the cost of "flush").

- LZHL works okay for TCP and for reliable-and-ordered UDP, but adapting it for unreliable and/or unordered UDP will require an additional effort.

- Huffman coding (and similar codings such as Huffman-like and arithmetic) with pre-populated frequency tables (see above) will work for UDP, but the gains are limited.

▶ When combining different compression techniques, keep in mind that their order is very important.

▶ I *strongly* suggest separating all types of compression from the rest of your code (including simulation code).

- Moreover, I suggest that compression code should be generated by your IDL compiler based on specifications in IDL, instead of writing compression ad hoc. More on IDL in the *IDL: Encodings, Mappings, and Protocol Changes* section below.

MMOG AND SCALABILITY

If each of your Game Worlds has only up to a dozen players by design (think MOBA), each of them will probably be small enough to be simulated on a single CPU core. In this case, scaling your Game Worlds to serve hundreds of thousands of players (running over tens of thousands of Game Worlds) is trivial.[153]

However, if your game has thousands of players within *one single Game World* (which makes it an MMOG according to the definition in Wikipedia), you won't have the luxury of your whole Game World fitting onto one CPU core. Worse, as soon as your Game World is large enough, you won't even have the luxury of your whole Game World fitting onto one Server box (as

---

153 Scaling your database is a different story, but we're not there yet.

of early 2017, pretty much the largest Server you can get without going into highly specialized hardware is 4 sockets*24 cores/socket=96 cores, which is quite a lot—but is usually still enough to run some kind of simulation for only about 10K players[154]). And as a side note, splitting the same 96 cores onto 4 "workhorse" 2-socket/24-core Servers is going to save you about 2x in Server rental costs.[155]

In other words, when speaking about multiple tens of thousands of simultaneous players within the same Game World, we won't be able to "scale up" and will need to "scale out."

On Shared-Nothing Architecture

As soon as we're into multiple Server boxes, we'll need them to communicate via some kind of message system (and each of the boxes will become a self-contained Shared-Nothing entity).

Usually, I argue for splitting your Game World not into Server-size Shared-Nothing pieces, but into *core-size* Shared-Nothing pieces.

As a side note: usually I argue for going further than that and splitting your Game World not into *Server-size* Shared-Nothing pieces, but into *core-size* Shared-Nothing pieces (i.e., each of the Shared-Nothing pieces will be constrained not to the whole Server, but rather to the single core). This has numerous benefits and we'll discuss them in Vol. II's chapter on (Re)Actors in nauseating detail; for the time being, I'll just say that such core-size pieces:

1. Allow for writing simulation in good ol' game-loop style (which is very straightforward),

2. Allow for significantly better debugging (including such things as production post-factum debugging and replay-based regression testing), and

3. Tend to perform better (due to the lack of inter-thread contention).

Still, for the purpose of this chapter, we can pretty much ignore the size of our Game World pieces and just postulate that:

---

154 Of course, YMMV, but 100 players/core is "kinda-industry-standard" these days.
155 NB: Keep in mind that such a split leads to decreased system MTBF, but for an MMOG handling Game World failures is a necessity anyway and is usually not *that* bad.

> ► Our scalable Server-Side consists of multiple self-contained (="Shared-Nothing") Pieces.

> ► These Pieces are communicating *only* via some kind of messaging. Implementing these messages is a separate task and we'll discuss it in the *Server-to-Server Communications* section below.

And, last but not least: of course, within this chapter we'll just scratch the surface of the topic of MOG scalability (specifically one question of "how to split a large Game World"). Overall scalability is *much* more elaborate than this single topic, and we'll continue to discuss scalability-related issues across pretty much the whole book (in particular, Vol. III, Vol. VI, and Vol. IX have a lot of scalability-related stuff).

The key reason for splitting the Game World is to avoid one single CPU core from being overloaded.

An Obvious One: Separate NPC/AI

As mentioned above, the key reason for splitting the Game World is to avoid one single CPU core (usually the one running the simulation/game loop) from being overloaded. And one obvious solution (mentioned as early as in 2003 in [Beardsley]) is to separate NPCs and their AI onto separate Pieces (with these Pieces able to run on separate cores and separate Servers, it means that scalability has improved).

In this case, from the perspective of our Game World Pieces (those simulating the game), the NPC/AI Pieces act quite similar to usual Clients, communicating via (a) obtaining a more-or-less-up-to-date replica of the current Game World's Publishable State, and (b) sending inputs to the Game World.

As a side benefit, this approach also tends to simplify the code of the Game World Logic significantly as all the characters become handled in pretty much the same manner, regardless of being controlled by players or AI.[156]

---

[156] TBH, you should still expect some differences, in particular, in disconnect handling, but these differences are usually not *that* drastic.

Splitting into Areas

However, while separating AI usually qualifies as a Good Idea™, it is almost-never sufficient to achieve real scalability to hundreds of thousands of players (usually, with such an AI separation, we're speaking about gains in the order of 2-3x, not in the order of 10x-100x).

As a result, most of the time, when your large Game World exceeds a certain size, you'll need to split it into several areas (zones, cells, whatever-other-name-you-want-to-use); then each of your sub-Game-Worlds will be able to run on a separate Piece (which in turn will run on a separate core or Server). This will also mean extremely good scalability: as long as you can split your Game World into as-many-areas-as-you-need, the system will scale in a near-perfect manner.

Within, such a sub-Game-World will work more or less as a usual Game World, however, it will need to pass around your PCs/NPCs to other sub-Game-Worlds.

Implementing sub-Game-Worlds is not *that* difficult if your Large Game World is naturally split into zones (rooms, etc.) that do *not* interact with one another directly and if *each* is small enough to be run on a single CPU core. However, if you happen to have a large Game World without such obvious boundaries, we're speaking about a so-called "seamless Game World," where things tend to become difficult.

Seamless Worlds: Overlap!

One common technique to enable splitting of the seamless Game World can be described as "split-with-an-overlap." It is described in detail in [Beardsley] and is still actively used these days; see, for example, [Baryshnikov].

The basic idea is to have the large seamless Game World split into several sub-Game-Worlds, with objects close to the border (i.e., within a pre-defined "shared area") present on *both* sub-Game-World Pieces at the same time. "Shared area" is usually defined as the one that is visible from both sub-Game-Worlds (or, more precisely, the area that guarantees that the "area of interest" for each player always fits into one single sub-Game-World).

The basic idea is to have the large seamless Game World split into several sub-Game-Worlds, with objects close to the border present on *both* sub-Game-World Pieces at the same time.

Then, we need to have all the objects within our "shared area" to be present within *both* our sub-Game-World Pieces. Here, there is one usual implementation, though it can be seen from two slightly different angles.

As a first option, we can say that we're simulating the same "shared" object in *both* sub-Game-Worlds (though only one remains authoritative at any given point in time, so we always know how to reconcile). Information from the "authoritative" sub-Game-World is pushed to the non-authoritative one(s), and they adjust their positions to bring their objects in sync with the authoritative representation (using reconciliation if necessary).

The second way to see pretty much the same thing is that for those objects that are non-authoritative in our sub-Game-World, we're obtaining information from the other sub-Game-World, which is currently-authoritative-for-that-object (in the same manner as Clients do), and then we also are running Client-Side Prediction for such non-authoritative-in-our-sub-Game-World objects (once again, using reconciliation if necessary). It is interesting to note that regardless of how we see it (as the first option or the second), the end result will be pretty much the same.

Note that in any case we'll need to take care of transferring object ownership from one sub-Game-World to another; this is usually not that difficult. With only one of the sub-Game-Worlds being authoritative, it is the one that will make the decision to pass the object around when the object crosses the sub-Game-World boundary.

The more complicated question with regard to sub-Game-Worlds is the one of "how exactly our Game World should be split?" Quite often, you'll need to resort to the model with the Pieces and sub-Game-Worlds based on the current load of each Piece, which leads to moving sub-Game-World boundaries. While handling these moving boundaries is possible (in particular, as described in [Beardsley] and [Baryshnikov]), it is highly game-dependent and is often not trivial (and *don't* forget to build some kind of hysteresis into your moving-sub-Game-World-boundaries algorithms, or you'll end up with completely unnecessary oscillating boundaries trying to chase the ever-changing optimum).

On Server-Side Uncertainty

One issue that often arises within the context of sub-Game-Worlds is the question of time synchronization between them, and the related question of uncertainty. As noted above, when having those objects-shared-between-sub-Game-Worlds, we cannot always guarantee that the copy of the object on the non-authoritative sub-Game-World is exactly the same as the original object on the authoritative server.

This is similar to the situation with the Client, which often has almost-but-not-exactly-the-same data as the Server (see, for example, the *Running into the Wall, and Server Reconciliation* section above). However, for Servers (and sub-Game-Worlds), the situation is actually even worse, because—

> *These non-authoritative and non-exact objects can interact with authoritative ones and potentially can cause differences in behavior of authoritative objects.*

Practically in the context of games (i.e., unless you're running a scientific simulation), most of the time such uncertainty is not a problem. While having certainty and determinism is a Good Thing™ in general, for practical purposes we can live with a component-level determinism (such as the one discussed in Vol. II's chapter on (Re)Actors), and not aim for determinism of the system as a whole.

Practically in the context of games (i.e., unless you're running a scientific simulation), most of the time such uncertainty is not a problem.

However, you may still need to keep this Server-Side uncertainty in mind, as depending on the specifics of your game (and on implementation details), it *might* cause rather unpleasant macroscopic effects. For example, in some implementations your player *might* escape an otherwise inevitable death just because the packet that transferred the authority about him between sub-Game-Worlds was delayed compared to the packet that transferred the bullet (and there was a moment when the player didn't exist in either of the sub-Game-Worlds and it was exactly the moment when the bullet should have hit him). Whether it will be a substantial problem you never know, but in certain cases it *might*.

Eliminating Uncertainty Completely: Time Sync

Speaking of uncertainty, there actually exists a strict way (actually, more than one such way) to eliminate Server-to-Server uncertainties altogether (which is equivalent to making the Server-Side, taken as a whole, deterministic).

Before we go into detail, let's note that eliminating uncertainty is equivalent to establishing one uniform time covering all the sub-Game-World, effectively performing time sync between different sub-Game-Worlds (and performing all the calculations according to this synchronized time). On the other hand, the mechanics of this inter-sub-Game-World time sync is substantially different from time sync between the Client and the Server (the one we've discussed in the *Time Synchronization* section above): in particular, for inter-sub-Game-World time sync, there is usually no single authority for time (in spite of each object having its own authority at each given moment, sub-Game-Worlds themselves are usually not subordinate to one another), which in turn causes quite a few complications.

Synchronization without Rewind: CMS/LBTS. Lockstep

One class of approaches to eliminating-uncertainty and time-sync revolves around academy-developed algorithms such as CMS and LBTS. I don't want to discuss them too much (for further discussion, please refer to [Smith and Stoner]), but, in a nutshell, the idea of these algorithms is to delay simulation on all the nodes until the Server receives calculations of the previous "network tick" from all the relevant Servers. In other words, it is a very close cousin of "Lockstep" algorithms. While Lockstep algorithms are known to be very fragile when Clients are involved, in the Server world (and Servers within the same Datacenter), it might fly.

I would still be quite reluctant to use any kind of blocking synchronization.

However, I would still be quite reluctant to use any kind of blocking synchronization. First, the risks of stopping the whole thing just because one of the Servers slowed down is rarely a good thing if you have a dozen Servers, and for a hundred it is usually catastrophic. In addition, I don't like the idea of running at the speed of the slowest guy in the Server crowd (and at every moment too). Still, if nothing else does the trick, these approaches have been reported to work.

Synchronization via Server Rewind: "Value Date"

The second wide class of approaches to time-sync and eliminating uncertainty is based on the same Server Rewind that (with respect to Lag Compensation) we were discussing in the *Server Rewind* section above.

Let's consider an example when both sub-Game-World A and sub-Game-World B simulate their own parts of the Game World, and there is a need to apply changes calculated by sub-Game-World A to sub-Game-World B. In this case, all that is necessary on the side of sub-Game-World A is to send a message to sub-Game-World B adding a timestamp with the semantics of "when it is supposed to happen" to the message; that's it.

On receiving such a message, sub-Game-World B would see how the current time within its own simulation compares to the timestamp specified in the message and, depending on the result, will do one of the following: (a) wait until its own "current time" reaches the timestamp, (b) apply the message immediately, or (c) "rewind" its own Game World back in time to apply the message "as if" it happened at whatever-time-is-specified-in-the-timestamp.

Logically, this "when it is supposed to happen" timestamp field is conceptually identical to the "value date" field that is associated with SWIFT banking transfers. As a SWIFT transfer takes time (even in 2016, it can easily take 3-5 business days(!)) and we as customers certainly don't want our money "hanging" somewhere without generating any interest,[157] each SWIFT transfer carries a "value date" field. It means "whenever you, as the receiving bank, get this transfer, you make sure to enter it into the target account 'as if' the transfer has happened on the 'value date'; this includes calculating all relevant interest, etc. To implement it, at this point, the recipient bank effectively "rewinds" time to the date specified in the "value date" field (due to banking accounts being mostly independent, it is not *that* difficult for a bank), then applies the transfer, and then re-calculates all the interest and whatever-other calculations since that point.

This analogy becomes even more obvious when a "value date"-like timestamp is used in conjunction with Inter-DB Asynchronous Transfer

SWIFT

The Society for Worldwide Interbank Financial Telecommunication (SWIFT) provides a network that enables financial institutions worldwide to send and receive information about financial transactions in a secure, standardized and reliable environment.. The majority of international interbank messages use the SWIFT network.

—Wikipedia

---

157   Well, these days banking interest is more of a theoretical point but, OTOH, it still
          needs to be accounted for.

(described in the *Going Further: Inter-DB Async Transfer with Transactional Integrity* section below).

Regardless of the "value date" analogy, "Server Rewind" effectively achieves perfect eventual synchronization regardless of the relative order of packets and calculations, and without additional latencies. Also let's note that for Server-to-Server communications (assuming that you control all the Servers, so they can be equally trusted), the issue of cheating (which is inherent when Server Rewind is done according to timestamps coming from the Client) doesn't apply, so this downside of "Server Rewind" doesn't apply to Server-to-Server Rewinds.

"Server Rewind" effectively achieves perfect eventual synchronization regardless of the relative order of packets and calculations—and without additional latencies.

On the other hand, for most of the games out there, I'd say that making the system "strict" and making special efforts to eliminate uncertainty is overkill. OTOH, *if* aiming for a perfectly correct Game World, I would probably try going the way of "Server Rewinds" (that is, applying them to communications between sub-Game-Worlds).

TRANSIENT EVENTS, FORWARDED INPUTS, AND (KINDA-) BROADCASTED MESSAGES

After we've spent that much time discussing state synchronization and replication, we need to think about other types of Server-2-Client communication.

Transient Events

> Should anyone here present know of any reason
> that this couple should not be joined in holy matrimony,
> speak now or forever hold your peace.
>
> —*Traditional phrase used during a marriage ceremony*

Of the remaining types of Server-2-Client communication, let's briefly discuss "Transient Events" first (they are usually used to implement explosions, bullet hits, and so on).

As was noted in the beginning of this chapter, Transient Events have an important property that they don't make much sense if delivered late; so, from our perspective, we should either deliver them "right now" or "never." In addition, Transient Events tend to go at the same time to all interested players, though they *may* be subject to Interest Management.

Forwarded Inputs

Transient Events mentioned above are very common in games (more often than not, explosions, bullet hits, etc. are implemented on top of them). In contrast, another type of Server-2-Client communication, the one that effectively forwards inputs from other Clients to our Client, and which we're going to discuss now, is not common at all; on the other hand, it was successfully used in at least one AAA game (see [Aldridge]).

The idea behind forwarding inputs goes as follows: we're considering a situation where some other player has already pressed a button to move left, and the Server already knows it. However (for example, due to inertia) it may take a while[158] until this movement manifests itself in the Publishable State—*and then* this manifestation will be further delayed by the lag between the Server and the Client. Therefore, if we pass this "other Client pressed a button to move left" information to our Client, we can improve precision of our Client-Side Prediction (and effectively reduce the lag between other-PC-movements and show these movements on the screen of our Client).

Potential for Information Leaks

While all the logic above holds, there is a Big Fat Problem™ with such Forwarded Inputs—and the problem is once again related to cheating (more specifically Information Leak attacks). If the cheater's Client has information that the opponent presses "left" but the movement to the left is not really visible yet, then a cheat that extracts this information from the cheater's Client, and shows an arrow pointing to the left as an overlay for the game (effectively

---

158   Yes, 20ms qualifies as "a while" for fast-paced games.

If you come to a situation where you need Forwarded Inputs, make sure to think about whether they are indeed *really* necessary for your game.

predicting where the opponent is *going* to move), could change the whole game balance drastically in favor of the cheater.

That being said, as discussed above, making players happy is usually *much* more important than preventing more subtle varieties of cheating, so I can think about a game or three (all FPS) where you *might* need to use Forwarded Inputs. On the other hand, if you come to a situation where you need Forwarded Inputs, make sure to think about whether they are indeed *really* necessary for your game (or maybe you can remove the need for it just by changing gameplay just a little).

Overall, exactly the same logic as discussed in the *OTOH, Player Happiness Is Much More Important* section above also applies to Forwarded Inputs. Let's just note that the impact of cheats enabled by Forwarded Inputs may be significantly higher than that of Lag Compensation and therefore Forwarded Inputs should be subject to even more scrutiny that Lag Compensation before you decide to use them.

Implementation

Implementation-wise, Forwarded Inputs exhibit pretty much the same properties as Transient Events. They also need to be transferred ASAP or never at all, and they also tend to be intended for all players (subject to Interest Management).

(Kinda-)Broadcasted Messages (Broadcast with Interest Management)

As we just observed above, both Transient Events and Forwarded Inputs have very similar requirements, so no wonder they can be implemented on top of the same mechanism. I'm speaking about (kinda-)Broadcasted Messages.

The idea behind (kinda-)Broadcasted Messages is pretty simple—we're just sending something to everybody in sight, and don't care whether our message has made it or not (because if the message didn't make it, re-sending the message will be a waste of resources by definition, as it will be late to the party anyway).

As a rule of thumb, unreliable UDP packets are the best fit for implementing (kinda-)Broadcasted Messages. Let's note though that they need to be implemented as multiple *unicast* UDP packets (i.e., via one packet going to each of the players) rather than a single *multicast* UDP packet.[159]

POINT-TO-POINT COMMUNICATIONS AND NON-BLOCKING RPCS

As a rule of thumb, unreliable UDP packets are the best fit for implementing (kinda-) Broadcasted Messages.

After we've discussed the Publishable State and communications on top of (kinda-)Broadcast Messages, the next (and actually last) thing we'll need for our MOG communication-wise is Point-to-Point communications. While Publishable State and (kinda-)Broadcast is all about Servers communicating with Clients, Point-to-Point communications can happen either between the Client and the Server or between two Servers. These two types of Point-to-Point communications have quite a bit in common, but there are also substantial differences.

In the context of Client-2-Server point-to-point communications, most of the time we're speaking about Clients sending their inputs (and other requests such as commands) to the Server-Side. And in the context of Server-2-Server communications, there are *lots* of different things that may require being communicated (more on it below).

Note that the differences between TCP and UDP are still beyond the scope until Vol. IV; we're still (mostly) speaking of *what* we need and not about *how* to implement it.

---

159 There are two reasons for it: first (as discussed in Vol. IV's chapter on Network Programming), multicast UDP doesn't work over the Internet. Second (as if the first one is not enough) is that Interest Management implies that different Clients should receive different information

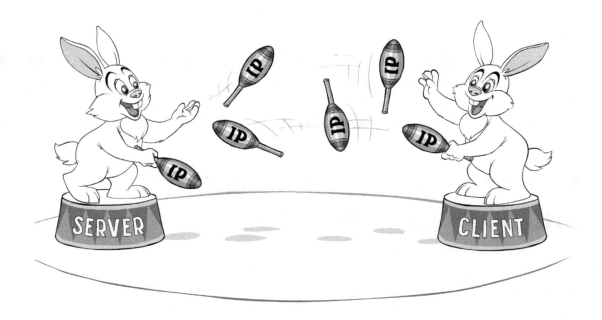

RPCs

Regardless of the parties involved in a Point-to-Point communication (whether it's between Client and Server or between two Servers), all Point-to-Point communications share certain common properties.

In particular, it is common for games to implement Point-to-Point communications as non-blocking Remote Procedure Calls (RPCs). While this is not required (and you can use a simple message exchange instead, with either handwritten or IDL-based marshalling), non-blocking RPCs tend to be convenient and straightforward.

It should be noted, however, that while non-blocking RPCs are perfectly viable for games, you really *should* stay away from blocking RPCs (such as those used by DCE RPC/COM/CORBA/ICE); at the very least, as long as we're speaking about WAN.[160] We'll discuss the reasoning behind the inapplicability of blocking RPCs to Internet apps in Vol. II's chapter on (Re)Actors.

It should be noted, however, that while non-blocking RPC are perfectly viable for games, you really *should* stay away from blocking RPC—at the very least as long as we're speaking about WAN.

---

160   This covers both communications between Servers and Clients, and Server-2-Server communications that go beyond one single Datacenter.

Implementing Non-Blocking RPCs

To implement non-blocking RPCs, you need a way to specify signatures of your remotely callable functions; such specification defines the interface (and often protocol, though see more on encodings in the *Example: Encoding* section below) between RPC caller and RPC callee.

Sometimes such specification is done by adding certain attributes to existing functions and methods in your usual programming language. For example, in *Unity* it is done by adding *[RPC]/[ClientRpc]/[Command]* C# method attributes, and in *UE4* it is done via *UFUNCTION()* C++ macros.

However, I usually prefer to define such signatures in a separate Interface Definition Language (IDL) instead, and to process it with my own separate IDL compiler to generate stubs (with the stubs used by application-level code on both sides of communication).

We'll discuss IDLs in detail (including intra-language vs standalone IDLs too) in the *IDL: Encodings, Mappings, and Protocol Changes* section below; for the time being, it is sufficient for our purposes to realize that we'll be specifying function signatures *somewhere* and will be able to implement these functions on one side of communication—and to call them on the other side.

> ## IDL
>
> An interface description language or interface definition language (IDL), is a specification language used to describe a software component's application programming interface (API).
>
> —*Wikipedia*

Void vs Non-Void Non-Blocking RPCs

When speaking about non-blocking RPCs, we need to realize that, in general, there are two cases for non-blocking RPCs.

The first case is a non-blocking RPC that returns *void* (and can't throw any exceptions). For such *void* RPCs, everything is simple—the caller just marshals RPC parameters and sends a message to the callee, and the callee unmarshals it and executes the RPC call. That's it. From all points of view (except for pure syntax), calling such an RPC is exactly the same as sending a message. In other words, such a *void* non-blocking RPC is merely a way to marshal its parameters.

An example of an IDL defining void RPC (Client-to-Server one) can look along the following lines:[161]

```
STRUCT Input {
  //DIRECTIONS
  bool left;
  bool top;
  bool right;
  bool bottom;

  //MODIFIERS
  bool shift;
  bool ctrl;
};

void moveMe(Input in);
```

Non-Void RPCs

The second (and much more complicated) case is an RPC that either returns a value or is allowed to throw an exception (often both). An example IDL for such a non-void RPC is a rather common Server-to-Server RPC along the lines of:

```
STRUCT PLAYERDATA {
  int level;
  int xp;

  INVENTORY inv;
  RELATIONS rel;
  ETC etc;
};

PLAYERDATA dbGetPlayer(int user_id);
```

The point here is as simple: to provide a way for a Game World Server to request a DB Server for data about a specific player (with *PLAYERDATA* being

The second (and much more complicated) case is an RPC that either returns a value, or is allowed to throw an exception (often both).

---

161 Note that all IDL examples in this chapter do not imply any existing IDL, but rather an example IDL (which you can implement yourself along the lines discussed in Vol. IV's chapter on Marshalling and Encodings).

sufficient to instantiate the player in this Game World). Note that this RPC (unlike *moveMe()* example above) is inherently non-void: we *do* need a reply from the other side of the conversation (DB Server), and we cannot really proceed with other related tasks (such as player instantiation) before we get the result back.

Such non-blocking non-void RPCs are significantly more complicated to implement, and most of the popular game engines out there do *not* support them (see Vol. II's chapter on 3rd-party Game Engines for more information on Unity/Photon/UE4/Lumberyard).

The main issue with implementing non-void non-blocking RPCs is for the caller to specify what to do when the function returns (or throws an exception). In the context of event-driven programming, there are several ways of implementing this logic (from plain message processing to co-routines, with callback hell, lambda pyramids, futures and promises, and "code builder" in-between), and we'll discuss all of them in detail in Vol. II's chapter on (Re)Actors. For now, let's just note that all these methods are strictly equivalent in what they're doing, so that the choice is not about "whether it will work," but about "which way is the most convenient to use." At the moment, I personally prefer "code builder" and/or co-routines,[162] with a distinct advantage over futures and promises (and a whole world of advantage over other stuff such as lambda pyramids).

Non-blocking non-void RPCs are significantly more complicated to implement, and most of the popular game engines out there do *not* support them.

Whenever your engine does *not* support non-void-RPCs, you can implement it on top of a void RPC function call with another void RPC function call in the opposite direction to return the result. In such a case, our last example will need to be rewritten along the following lines:

```
//Game World Server to DB Server:
void dbRequestPlayer(SERVERID where_to_reply, int user_id);
    //implementation of dbRequestPlayer()
    // calls gameWorldPCData() from within

//Game World Server to DB Server:
void gameWorldPlayerData(PLAYERDATA data);
```

---

162   That is, if they can be implemented within a given environment; see Vol. II's chapter on (Re)Actors for details.

or in a more generic manner (to allow multiple outstanding requests from the same Game World, which is almost-always a good idea to support):

```
//Game World Server to DB Server:
void dbRequestPlayer(SERVERID where_to_reply,
                     int request_id, int user_id);
  //implementation of dbRequestPlayer()
  // still calls gameWorldPCData() from within

//Game World Server to DB Server:
void gameWorldPlayerData(int request_id, PLAYERDATA data);
```

While this will work (and again, is strictly equivalent to the other alternatives discussed in Vol. II's chapter on (Re)Actors), implementing matching between calls and replies (which, in turn, requires storing a map of currently outstanding calls) is quite cumbersome and inconvenient; for more details and alternatives, see Vol. II.

Client-to-Server and Server-to-Client Point-to-Point Communications

Now, as we've discussed the similarities between different flavors of point-to-point communications, let's start describing the differences between them. And arguably, the most important difference between Client-to-Server and Server-to-Server communications is related to disconnects.

As a rule of thumb, for Server-to-Server communications the disconnects are extremely rare, and all the disconnects are transient.

As a rule of thumb, for Server-to-Server communications disconnects are extremely rare, and all the disconnects are transient (that is, unless your whole site is down). It means that we can expect that they are restored quickly, which in turn means that we can (and *should*) try to hide a temporary loss of connectivity from the application layer (i.e., "as if" it has never happened). On the other hand, for Client-to-Server (and Server-to-Client) communications, this "restored really quickly" observation doesn't stand, and dealing with disconnects becomes a very important part of application logic.

Let's speak about Client-to-Server and Server-to-Client communications first.

Inputs

One thing that you'll inevitably need to transfer from the Client to the Server is Player Inputs. For a non-simulation game (think blackjack, a stock exchange, or a social game), everything is simple: you've got an input and you're sending it to the Server right away.

For simulation games, however, it is not that trivial. Traditionally, simulation-based games operate in terms of "simulation ticks" (a.k.a. "network ticks"), and usually single-player games are just polling the state of the keyboard, mouse, and controller on each tick. As a result, when moving from a single-player simulation game to a network one, it is rather common to mimic this behavior just by the Client sending the state of the (keyboard+mouse+controller) to the Server on each tick. An alternative (and also pretty common) approach would be to send only changes to this (keyboard+mouse+controller) state; this can be done either as soon as the state is changed,[163] or again on each "tick."

As long as there are no disconnects (nor packet loss), there is no that much difference between these approaches. However, as soon as we realize that packets can be lost (and, as a result, disconnects can happen), handling Player Inputs becomes quite different.

If we're transferring the state of players' input devices on each tick, then in case of a lost packet[164] the PC will effectively stop on the Server-Side; moreover, at the same time, if we implement Client-Side Prediction (as described in the *Client-Side Prediction* section above), the very same PC will still be running on the Client Side.

On the other hand, if we're transferring only changes to the keyboard or mouse controller state, then in case of packets being lost, our PC will keep running for some time (until we detect a disconnect) even if the player has already released the button; this may potentially lead to the PC running off the cliff even if the player's actions didn't cause it (just because the disconnect happened at an unfortunate time).

As soon as we realize that packets can be lost, handling Player Inputs becomes quite different.

---

163 Though this option is rarely, if ever, used.
164 That is, beyond the capabilities of the input buffer.

A kind of "hybrid" approach is possible if we're using Client-to-Server acknowledgment packets (which will arise anyway in pretty much any Game World State Sync schema; see, for example, the *"Reference Base" for Unreliable Communications* section above) to distinguish between "player is still keeping the button pressed" and "we have no idea, as the packet got lost" situations. In other words, if an acknowledgment arrived but without any information about the keyboard state change, then we know for sure what is going on on the Client Side.[165] And if there is no acknowledgment, then something is wrong with connectivity, so our Server can stop the PC before he runs off the cliff.

Overall, there is no one universally "better" approach, so you'll basically need to pick one schema, try it, and test if it works and feels fine for your purposes in case of the-worst-connections-you-need-to-handle. We'll have an in-depth discussion on testing (including finding and simulating bad connections) in Vol. VI.

Input Timestamping

One issue that is often associated with inputs is the Client-Side input timestamp (in practice, usually it will be a tick-stamp).

Timestamps are indeed necessary to facilitate things such as Lag Compensation described in the *Lag Compensation* subsection above. On the other hand, as soon as the Server starts to trust this timestamp, this trust (just as about any kind of trust) can be abused.

For example, if within your game you have a Good-Bad-Ugly-style shootout and compensate for the lag, then the Bad guy, while having worse reflexes, could compensate for it by sending a "shoot" input packet with an input timestamp that is 50ms earlier than the packet is actually sent, essentially gaining an unfair advantage for these 50ms. In general, such cheating (regardless of the way we're implementing our Lag Compensation[166]) is a

For example, if you have a Good-Bad-Ugly-style shootout, and compensate for the lag, then the Bad guy, while having worse reflexes, could compensate for it by sending a "shoot" input packet with an input timestamp that is 50ms earlier than the real time, essentially gaining an unfair advantage for these 50ms.

---

165 And if keyboard state change has happened, it can and *should* be combined with the acknowledgment IP packet to save on bandwidth, but this is a different story, which will be discussed in Vol. IV.

166 BTW, measuring pings instead of relying on input timestamps doesn't prevent the cheat; it just makes the cheat a bit more complicated.

fundamental problem of any kind of Lag Compensation, so you should be really sure what you're going to do with various abuse scenarios before you introduce it. For more discussion on Lag Compensation-related cheating and dealing with it, see the *Lag Compensation* section above.

"Macroscopic" Client Actions

In addition to sending bare input to the server, quite a few games out there need to implement some Client actions that go beyond it. Examples of such actions (let's name them "macroscopic" actions) usually result from such sequences of inputs (eventually leading to an RPC call) as:

- ▶ Player looking at object (processed purely on Client-Side).

- ▶ Client showing HUD saying that "Open" operation is available because the object under the cursor is a container (again, processed purely on the Client-Side).

- ▶ Player pressing "Action" button (which means "Open" in this context).

- ▶ Client showing a container inventory (obtained via an RPC call, or taken from the Publishable State).

- ▶ Player choosing what to take out.

- ▶ Only then, Client invoking a Client-to-Server RPC such as *takeFromContainer(item_id, container_id)*.

For such "macroscopic" RPC calls as *takeFromContainer()*, in most cases disconnect during the call can be simply ignored (so that the player will need to press a button again when or if the connection is restored).

Another set of "macroscopic" actions (usually having even longer chain of events before an RPC call can be issued) is related to dialog-based Client-Side interactions such as in-game purchases. In these cases, all the interactions (except, maybe, for some requests for information from the Server) usually stay on the Client-Side until the player decides to proceed with the purchase; when this happens, the Client-to-Server RPC call containing all the information necessary to perform the purchase is issued.

For such RPC calls, the handling of a disconnect during an RPC call is not that obvious. If you want to be really player-friendly (and usually you should be), you need to consider two scenarios. The first is when the disconnect is transient and the Client is able to reconnect quickly; then, you need a mechanism to detect whether your RPC call has reached the Server, to get the result if it did, and to re-issue the call if it didn't; this would allow you to make the disconnect look really transient for the player and to show the result of the purchase as if the disconnect never occurred. To implement it, you'll need to implement both the re-sending of the RPC call on the Client Side and deal with duplicates on the Server-Side in a manner similar to the one described in the *Seamless Handling of Transient Disconnects* section below.

The second scenario occurs when the RPC call is interrupted by a disconnect before obtaining the reply, and the disconnect takes that long that Client gets closed (or the Server gets restarted).

The second scenario occurs when the RPC call is interrupted by the disconnect before obtaining the reply, and the disconnect takes that long that the Client gets closed (or the Server gets restarted). In this case, the only things we can practically do for the player are not directly related to the communication protocols (but they still need to be done). The two most common features that help make the player not that unhappy in this second scenario, are (a) to send her an e-mail if the "purchase" RPC call has reached the Server (unfortunately, it doesn't help to vent frustration if the call didn't reach the Server), and (b) to provide her with a way to see the list of all her purchases from the Client when she's back online (which we need to do anyway if we want to be player-friendly).

Server-to-Client

While the Server normally sends a lot of information to the Client (both as a part of the Publishable State and as replies to Client-to-Server RPC calls), it is not too common to *initiate* an RPC call[167] from the Server-Side (to be executed on the Client Side).

On the other hand, in some cases, such RPC calls (especially *void* RPC calls without the need to process the reply on the Server side) are helpful. One such example is passing pocket cards to the Client in a poker game.

---

167   Here, we're speaking about "making a decision to call RPC from the Client"; this doesn't include technicalities such as the "Server calling void RPC in response to void Client RPC call to pass back requested data."

Using Point-to-Point Server-2-Client communication will allow you to exclude pocket cards from the Publishable State, and this generally qualifies as a Good Idea™. If keeping pocket cards within the Publishable State, we'll need to rely on Interest Management to prevent leaking them to other players; as not doing it properly will allow for game-killing cheating (see the discussion in the *Interest Management: Traffic Optimization and Preventing Cheating* section above), I prefer to have a more obvious separation between public and private data than merely a filter within the Interest Management code.

In other words, IMO, while using Interest Management to filter *semi-public data* is perfectly fine, using it to filter *strictly private data*, while possible, can be too dangerous, so for strictly private data I would seriously consider using Point-to-Point Server-2-Client communications to reduce the chance of potentially-extremely-expensive mishaps.

Server-to-Server Communications

Seamless Handling of Transient Disconnects

As noted above, from the point of view of the application layer, Server-to-Server communications can (and *should*) be made seamless (i.e., hiding disconnects, which are inherently transient for Server-2-Server, from the application layer). This is necessary not only to deal with inter-server disconnects at the TCP level (which are extremely rare in practice, but do happen once in a while), but is also one of the prerequisites to deal with scenarios when we're restoring or moving our Game Worlds or other Server-Side entities (as discussed in Vol. II's chapter on (Re)Actors and Vol. III's chapter on Server-Side Architecture).

From the point of view of the application layer, Server-to-Server communications can (and *should*) be made seamless.

It simplifies the job of the Server app-level developers a *lot*; however, this simplicity comes at the cost of the infrastructure level doing this work behind the scenes. Let's discuss two ways of implementing such a "seamless transient disconnect handling" protocol.

First, let's note that for the purpose of this chapter, we'll use the term "Server-Side entity" to describe some large-scale entity, one of those discussed in Chapter 1 (such as "Game World" or a "Split-part of the Game World" or "Lobby" or "Cashier," etc.), and not a smaller entity such as "PC" or "NPC."

Option 1. Separate Caller/Callee Handling

One fairly common protocol that does achieve seamless handling of transient point-to-point disconnects implements two related but distinct parts. It can be described as follows:

▶ Part I. Ensuring "at least once" delivery.

■ Each RPC call has its ID, and each of its replies has *matching* IDs.

■ Caller keeps a list of outstanding RPC calls with their IDs (and removes items from the list on receiving the matching reply).

■ If disconnect-and-reconnect happens, all the outstanding RPC calls are re-issued.

▶ Part II. Ensuring "at most once" delivery.

■ Callee keeps a list of "recently processed IDs" (and associated replies that were sent back).

■ If a duplicate RPC call arrives (i.e., the one with the ID from the "recently processed" list), an associated reply is sent back without any processing (as the processing was already done before).

That's pretty much it. Part I of the algorithm above is closely related to common implementation of "non-blocking non-void RPC calls" (which we'll most likely need anyway). To support some kind of callback (whether being OO-style callback, lambda, or future, more on them in Vol. II's chapter on (Re)Actors), we'll need to keep a list of "outstanding RPC requests" (with their respective IDs) on the caller side anyway. And as soon as we have this list of "outstanding RPC calls," we have sufficient information to re-send the RPC request in case of a lost packet or disconnect.[168]

---

168 As noted in the *Server-Side: TCP often wins over the UDP* section below; we'll probably use TCP for inter-server communications anyway, so such a re-send will need to happen only on a TCP disconnect and reconnect.

On the other hand, Part I by itself, while guaranteeing that we will get *at least one* RPC request on the callee side for each RPC call on the caller side, doesn't guarantee that it will be *the only one*. In other words, if implementing only Part I above, in case of disconnects, duplicate RPC calls on the callee side can happen for a single RPC call on the caller side. While making all the RPC calls idempotent would solve this problem, in practice making sure that each and every call is idempotent at the application layer is usually too much of a burden (making it not exactly realistic).

That's why Part II of processing (this time on the callee side) needs to be added. If some request with an ID from a "recently processed" list comes in to the callee side, we should just provide the associated reply without really doing anything else. This scenario may legitimately happen if the connection was lost-and-restored after the request was received, but before the reply was acknowledged.

As soon as we have these two parts of processing (in practice, it will be a bit more complicated, as information on "which replies can be dropped from the 'recently processed list'" will also need to be communicated, plus, most likely, we'll need to implement handshakes to distinguish between a new connection and the broken one), we can say that our Server-to-Server communication is tolerant of all kinds of transient inter-Server disconnects.

Option 2. Two Guaranteed Delivery Streams

An alternative way of dealing with such transient-disconnect issues is to create two "guaranteed delivery" message streams (going in opposite directions).

Each of these streams will keep its own list of "unacknowledged messages" and will re-send them on the loss-and-restore of the underlying connection; on the receiving side, a simple "last ID processed" field is sufficient to filter out all the duplicates.[169]

Once again, some additional logic of handshaking to "match" new transport-level TCP connection to an existing "guaranteed message delivery stream," and to communicate acknowledgments (so that the sending side can

Idempotence

Idempotence is the property of certain operations in mathematics and computer science, that can be applied multiple times without changing the result beyond the initial application.

—*Wikipedia*

As soon as we have these two parts of processing, we can say that our Server-to-Server communication is tolerant of all kinds of transient inter-Server disconnects.

---

169 This is assuming that message IDs are guaranteed to be monotonous, but this is trivial to achieve.

drop the messages from the "unacknowledged" list) will be necessary; overall this schema might be a bit simpler than Option 1 (while providing exactly the same guarantees of *each RPC call initiated on the caller side, being called once and only once on the callee side*).

Going Further: Inter-DB Async Transfer with Transactional Integrity

There are only two hard problems in distributed systems:

2. Exactly-once delivery
1. Guaranteed order of messages
2. Exactly-once delivery

—Mathias Verraes

One thing that should be noted about the algorithms above is that delivery guarantee they provide stands only if we're assuming that apps on both sides of the communication do not crash.

One thing that should be noted about the algorithms above is that the delivery guarantees they provide stand only if we're assuming that apps on both sides of the communication do not crash; in other words, with the algorithms above, we're only handling transient failures of the communication layer.

While these guarantees certainly have their value, in quite a few contexts (in particular, Shared-Nothing distributed databases, see detailed discussion of it in Vol. VI's chapter on Databases), consistency guarantees should stand even if one (or both) apps performing communications crash themselves. In such cases, we'll be relying on *databases* of each of the apps to keep the-state-necessary-for-recovery.

For this subsection, we'll be considering a system with two Server-Side Entities (A and B), each having its own (and separate from everything else) database. We'll consider a scenario when Server-Side Entity A wants to transfer something (like "an artifact") to Server-Side Entity B.

To be sure that the artifact (which may cost thousands of real-world dollars) is neither lost in transit nor is duplicated because of retransmits, and that's *even if any or both Entities themselves can crash*, we need a higher level of guarantee (in fact, implementing an inter-DB distributed transaction).

In addition, to make sure that the Server-Side Entity B cannot possibly block the Server-Side Entity A, we want our transfer to be *asynchronous*. In other words, we do *not* want to stop processing by Server-Side Entity A while the request is going to Server-Side Entity B and the reply goes back. This requirement automatically rules out using a two-phase commit protocol (this includes XA protocol, and at least those federated databases that are based on XA and/or two-phase commit).

Essentially, as the whole transaction is essentially *asynchronous*, we'll be speaking about providing so-called *eventual consistency guarantees*. In other words, we'll be implementing so-called BASE (Basically Available, Soft State, Eventually Consistent) guarantees, as opposed to an ACID transaction involving multiple databases (the latter is impossible to achieve without blocking). Note, however, that we'll still use ACID-transactions-within-one-single-DB to implement our logic.

Apparently, there *is* an algorithm that satisfies all the requirements above. The protocol that guarantees inter-DB eventual consistency in an asynchronous manner (i.e., without any inter-DB locks whatsoever), while providing strict eventual-consistency guarantees even if any or all Server-Side Entities crash[170] can be implemented as follows:

Apparently, there *is* an algorithm that satisfies all the requirements above.

▶ Server-Side Entity A decides to transfer *something* to Server-Side Entity B.

▶ Entity A makes an ACID transaction over its own DB, taking this *something* out of a regular table and putting it to a special *outgoing-transfer* table (all within the same ACID transaction!).

▶ *Outgoing-transfer* table stores (transfer-ID,transfer-data), with transfer-ID always being incremented for each new record.

▶ Entity A sends a message with (transfer-ID,transfer-data) to Entity B. How exactly the message is delivered doesn't matter much (simple TLS-over-TCP will do the trick).

▶ Entity B receives the message, checks that the transfer-ID came in the order compared to the previous transfers coming from Entity A

---

170   What we need is a guarantee that Entity databases should still recover from the crash, complying with all the ACID properties after recovery. However, this is rarely a problem for serious modern databases.

(otherwise the re-initialization procedure described below applies), and makes its own ACID transaction (over its own DB), writing the transfer-ID into the *incoming-transfers* table, *and* adding the artifact-that-was-transferred to a regular table (again, both things *must* be within the same ACID transaction).

▶ Entity B sends an 'ACK' back to Entity A, informing it that "all transfer-IDs up to and including transfer-ID=X are processed."

▶ Entity A removes all the rows with transfer-ID <= X.

Let's name this protocol an "Inter-DB Async Transfer Protocol," and we'll refer to it quite a lot in subsequent volumes.

On first glance, our Inter-DB Async Transfer Protocol may look over-engineered, but only until we take into consideration that our Server-Side Entities can fail. If they fail, with Inter-DB Async Transfer Protocol, after we get our Entities back up, we can apply the following re-initialization procedure:

▶ On restart, Server-Side Entity A can see that its *outgoing-transfers* table has some unacknowledged transfers.

▶ It sends all these unacknowledged transfers to Entity B (using the same means as during usual communication).

▶ Entity B skips all the transfer-IDs that are lower than the last transfer-ID in its own *incoming-transfers* table and processes the rest.

▶ Entity B issues an 'ACK,' which is then processed by Entity A as usual.

The key point here is that—

> *Inter-DB Async Transfer Protocol guarantees transactional integrity not only if communication is broken, but also if any of the Entities crashes (and DBs can crash too, as long as the ACID properties in Entity databases are guaranteed to stand after DB recovery).*

Formal proof of this statement goes beyond this book, but it should be relatively easy to understand the idea behind it. The idea revolves around an observation that at each and every point in time there is exactly one "active" copy of the *something* being transferred. While *something* is moved within the boundaries of one single Entity, this is guaranteed by ACID transactional properties over the DB of the respective Entity (specifically by letter 'A' and 'D' in 'ACID,' which stand for Atomicity and Durability; more on it in Vol. VI's chapter on Databases); and while our *something* is moved between the Entities, this "exactly one active copy" is guaranteed by the way transfer-IDs are handled.

At each and every point in time, there is exactly one "active" copy of the *something* that is being transferred.

Whenever you need to transfer something-of-real-world-value between DBs (or more generally, to perform any kind of inter-DB transaction), I *strongly* suggest that you use the algorithm above. While there are other ways of providing inter-DB transactional integrity (notably two-phase commit and XA/federated DBs), they usually have a blocking nature and, in general, "blocking" is a foul word when we speak about scalability (more on it in Vol. III).

Server-Side Entity Addressing

The next set of issues in the context of Server-2-Server communications is related to how Server-Side Entities address one another. And as your Server-Side grows, this question will become more important. If your game has thousands of Server-Side Entities, spread over hundreds of Servers (and moving around to ensure load balancing and/or fault tolerance) it *may* become a significant problem.

As a rule of thumb, I usually suggest the following approach:

▶ First, make sure from the very beginning that your Server-Side Entities do *not* address one another by IP and/or port. Use meaningful string-based entity identifiers instead (like "GameWorld-CityX-Instance23"), or anything else to the same effect (tuples of strings, or whatever-else, but *without* IPs and ports).

First, make sure from the very beginning that your Server-Side Entities do *not* address each other by IP and/or port.

▶ At the first stage, while your number of Servers is low (I'd say "up to 10 or so," though I've seen up to 50 working this way without much problem), conversion from entity identifiers to the IP:port format can usually be done via a simple config file sitting on each of your Servers.[171]

▶ Then, as the number of your Servers grows, you *may* need to implement some kind of directory where to look for your Server entities. This directory can be implemented in quite a few ways (either centralized or decentralized), but it is important to remember that with a centralized directory you create a single-point-of-failure, so it *should* use some of the fault-tolerance techniques described in Vol. III.

▶ The most important thing here, however, is to avoid changes to your Server-Side Entities (you may have a *lot* of them by this point). That's why Entity identifiers were so important from the beginning: as soon as your Entities are using entity identifiers, you can change the way Entity identifiers are mapped into IP:port pairs, without any changes to your Server-Side Entities at all (only changing infrastructure-level code outside of your entities, which is usually *much* easier to change).

Server-Side: TCP Often Wins Over UDP

One of the questions you will face when designing your Server-Side is about the underlying protocol used for inter-server communications, whether it should be TCP or UDP. While overall discussion of "TCP vs. UDP" won't happen until Vol. IV's chapter on Network Programming, for Server-2-Server communication it is simple enough to mention right here.

My take is simple—

> *Even if you're using UDP for Client-to-Server communications, **do** seriously consider using TCP for Server-to-Server communications.*

---

171 Yes, I know it is a fallacy, but you can (and probably will) get away with it as long as the number of Servers is relatively small.

Detailed discussion on TCP's (lack of) interactivity is coming in Vol. IV's chapter on Network Programming, but, for now, let's just say that poor interactivity of TCP becomes observable only when you have packet loss,[172] and if you have non-zero packet loss within the LAN that connects your Servers, you need to fire your admins.[173]

On the positive side, TCP has three significant benefits. First, *if* you can get acceptable latencies without disabling Nagle algorithm, TCP is likely to produce much fewer hardware interrupts (and overall context switches) on the receiving Server's side, which in turn is likely to reduce the overall load of your Game Servers and, even more importantly, the DB Server. Second, TCP is usually much easier to deal with than UDP (on the other hand, this may be offset if you have already implemented UDP support to handle Client-to-Server communications). Third, if you need to transfer large amounts of data, TCP plays its home game, where it is extremely difficult to beat.

Overall, while TCP has a bad name for interactivity, I didn't see any problems when using it *specifically for inter-Server communications within a single Datacenter.* When inter-Server communications go across different Datacenters, in theory, things may become worse for TCP (as packet losses can go higher), though if your Datacenter providers do a decent job (which they usually do), this packet loss shouldn't go high enough to also cause any realistically observable latencies. On the other hand, for inter-Datacenter communications YMMV, so make sure to test your communications under real-world conditions before starting to rely on it.

I didn't see any problems when using TCP *specifically for inter-Server communications within a single Datacenter.*

Of course, if your communication library (such as ZeroMQ) already provides support for UDP, feel free to try it, but don't assume UDP will be necessarily better for Server-to-Server: with packet loss being next-to-zero, the whole game becomes very different (with most of the differences between TCP and UDP disappearing).

---

172   That is, if you have Nagle algorithm disabled, but this capability is provided by all the sane TCP stacks out there.

173   There is a valid question of "if it is zero packet loss, why would we need to use TCP at all?"; in this regard, I'll note that when I'm speaking about "zero packet loss," I can't rule out two packets lost in a day, which can happen even if your system is *really* well-built. And while a-few-dozen-microseconds additional delay twice a day won't be noticeable, crashing twice a day won't be good.

Using Message Queues
for Server-to-Server Communications

By this point, we've discussed quite a few complications related to Server-to-Server communications. When speaking about implementing all of them, a question of "hey, somebody should have already implemented all of this stuff, and there should be a library doing it for us" naturally arises.

In particular, it is rather common to use Message Queue (MQ) products for communications between MOG servers (for example, WoT uses Rabbit-MQ [Baryshnikov]). Overall, I don't see anything bad with it, *as long you're using MQ as a mere transport (essentially as a kind of "improved TCP")*.

MQs and Transactional Integrity

One of the common issues with common MQ products is that they're often used while *assuming* a level of guarantee they don't really provide.

One of the common issues with common MQ products is that they're often used while *assuming* a level of guarantee they don't really provide.

In particular, whenever you're using an MQ product, extreme care should be exercised whenever your communications require inter-DB transactional integrity (similar to the one described above). More specifically—

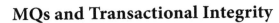

Even when your MQ product supports something named "transactional queues," to have transactional integrity even when Entities crash,[174] *you need to make sure that transactions over these queues* ***involve transactions with your Entity's DB****!*

In other words, to ensure transactional integrity, your MQ should allow for some kind of transaction (for example, an XA transaction) that involves *both* placing the message into the outgoing queue *and* making the transaction in your Entity's DBMS.[175] Unfortunately, MQs that support this are not

---

174   And believe me, they can crash at any moment—though they usually prefer crashing at *the worst possible moment.*

175   Note that as long as XA transaction is *completely* on one side of communication, it doesn't normally cause any blocking, so using XA is usually okay in such cases.

common,[176] so even if your MQ supports "transactional queues," which do guarantee all-or-nothing behavior *between different messages within the queue,* usually nobody guarantees all-or-nothing behavior while you're transferring your valuable stuff from your RDBMS to your MQ product.

For example, let's consider that you have your usual MQ product, and processing within the Server-Side Entity goes as follows:

1. Take out *something* from your regular RDBMS table.

2. Write it to the "transactional queue" of your MQ.

The problem with this process is that if your Server-Side Entity crashes between step (a) and step (b) above, you've lost your valuable *something* without any way to recover it[177] after you restart your Server-Side Entity.

In contrast, our Inter-DB Async Transfer Protocol described above *does* guarantee that *something* is never lost even in such scenarios (this is guaranteed because taking-out-*something* and putting it into the *outgoing-transfer* table is made within the same RDBMS transaction, which guarantees ACID properties, most importantly Atomicity and Durability).

On the other hand, you *may* run our Inter-DB Async Transfer Algorithm (as described in the *Going Further: Inter-DB Async Transfer with Transactional Integrity* section above) *on top* of MQ, essentially using MQ as a replacement for TCP. This will provide all the guarantees we need, and without also placing the burden of implementing XA transactions on MQ software.

On the other hand, you *may* run our Inter-DB Async Transfer Algorithm *on top* of MQ, essentially using MQ as a replacement for TCP.

---

176 Except for enterprise-level MQ products, which are rarely used for games. To see whether your product of choice does it, you generally should look for "XA transaction support" in it and, more often than not, there won't be such a thing; and even if your MQ does support XA transactions, you'll need to check that your DBMS supports XA too.

177 Well, except for support going through all the relevant logs and figuring it out.

On Transactions in AMQP

Advanced Message Queueing Protocol (AMQP) is an MQ protocol (with AMQP v0.9.1 implemented, in particular, by RabbitMQ[178]), which provides support for transactions. However, *AMQP transactions do not aim to address inter-DB transactional integrity*; instead, they are more like batching several messages, buffering them on the receiving side, and committing (or rolling back) all of them at once (see, for example, [Rabbit MQ]).

As a result, AMQP doesn't seem to provide any support for inter-DB transactional integrity. While it is still possible to use AMQP as a replacement for TCP, relying on AMQP for inter-DB transactional integrity will be a Big Mistake™.

Brokered vs Brokerless MQ

Whenever you're using an MQ product, there can be several different models of its operation.[179] In the first model, all the MQ entities are connected to a "broker," and each entity sends all the messages addressed to all the other entities to the broker (of course, each message is accompanied by the address of the target entity). This way, the "broker" has knowledge about all the entities and can easily forward messages where applicable. This is known as "brokered" MQ architecture. And of course, the "broker" in such an architecture can easily become a bottleneck (and avoiding it to become a Single Point of Failure, a.k.a. SPOF, will also be quite a challenge).

SPOF

A single point of failure (SPOF) is a part of a system that, if it fails, will stop the entire system from working

—Wikipedia

A second model is that there is no broker, and entities interact directly. In this case, in complicated deployments, distributing all the addresses to all the entities that need it will become quite a problem.

Broker as Directory Service

That's why there is an "in-between" model, which uses the "broker" only as a kind of directory service. With such a model, each entity still connects to the "broker," but only to publish its name and current address (usually IP:port).

---

178   No relation to 'No Bugs' Hare or ITHare.com.

179   While some MQs are limited to a single model, this is just their design decision rather than a fundamental restriction.

Then, when any entity needs to connect to another, it can go to the "broker," request current IP:port of the entity by the entity's name, and connect to that current IP:port. For further discussion see, for example, [ZeroMQ]. With this model, the broker becomes a kinda-DNS service, and you can actually use a good old DNS server (such as *bind*) to implement it without any specialized MQ products.

However you implement this "broker as a directory service" model, it is going to be more complicated than both previous ones, but it solves both the "broker overload" problem[180] and the "how to find addresses" problem. On the other hand, in dynamic environments it introduces a new problem: the problem of "stale addresses" (which, in turn, can be solved, but solving it will require further efforts).

However you implement this "broker as a directory service" model, it is going to be more complicated than both previous ones, but it solves both the "broker overload" problem and the "how to find addresses" problem. On the other hand, it introduces a new problem: the problem of "stale addresses."

In the MQ world, a question of "brokered vs brokerless" MQ architectures is traditionally quite a hot one. However, I personally don't see it as too important compared to the other concepts described above. Even more importantly, with quite a few products (such as ZeroMQ), it is a deployment-time decision so you can change your architecture later if necessary. Such an ability to change from brokered to brokerless (or vice versa) is IMO much more important than choosing a specific model during development—just because during development any guesswork on "how we might want to deploy it six months from now" is pretty much hopeless.

Brokers and Transactional Integrity

One important thing to keep in mind in this "brokered vs. brokerless" debate is that (as discussed above)—

> *For most of the implementations out there,*
> *brokers have nothing to do*
> *with Inter-DB transactional integrity.*

---

180 And while SPOF is still an issue, it is *much* easier—and *much* cheaper—to implement redundancy for a not-so-loaded directory service than for a system pumping through billions of messages per day.

It is often argued that brokered systems provide better delivery guarantees. However, if considering the whole path from one DB to another (and this is the case that really matters in practice), to achieve better guarantees, MQ would need to integrate very closely with RDBMS (see above about XA transactions or the equivalent), which is rarely the case. In practice, some of the brokered architectures may reduce the "vulnerability window" (i.e., reducing chances for data loss), but this is still very far from providing any kind of *guarantee* (and the lack of a guarantee will hit you as soon as your game grows large enough; from what I've seen, chances of such things hitting you grow in a heavily non-linear manner with the growth of your game).

Using MQ on the Server-Side: Summary

As you've probably noticed, for Server-to-Server communications using MQ—

> *I am arguing for using MQ merely as a replacement of a TCP-like transport.*

(that is, unless your MQ product supports transactions-integrated-with-your-DB, which is possible but unlikely).

On the other hand, even in this case, MQ products might have value for MOGs. In particular, they *may* work pretty well to deal with the addressing issues discussed above. In this case, we'll be using MQ as a "TCP that provides meaningful addressing rather than IP:port addressing" (for discussion on the importance of meaningful addressing, see the *Server-Side Entity Addressing* section above).

As for the "brokered" vs. "brokerless" MQs, my *very* rough suggestion[181] would go along the following lines:

▶ Within the same Datacenter: you *may* use brokerless MQ (such as ZeroMQ in brokerless configuration) for all the intra-Datacenter communication.

---

181 ="bring even more salt than usual."

- At the same time, you *may* want to use a centralized broker (with fault tolerance(!)) as a directory service for your Datacenter.

▶ On the other hand, whenever your messages need to go across Datacenter boundaries, I would suggest that you have a broker on each side of the inter-Datacenter link. It can be either one-broker-per-inter-datacenter-link or one-broker-per-Datacenter, depending on your specifics.

Whenever your messages need to go across Datacenter boundaries, I would suggest that you have a broker on each side of the inter-Datacenter link.

However,

> the most important part in this regard is to stay flexible, and to be able to change your deployment configuration without changing your Server-Side code.

As noted above, an important part of it is using logical entity names (opposed to IP:port kind of addresses) from the very beginning of your Server-Side development.

ON PROTOCOL CHANGES

When developing our MOG, we *must* realize that—

> our protocols will change.

As our game becomes successful, we'll need to adjust certain things, will need to add features, and will need to fix cheating loopholes, et cetera, et cetera. Quite of few of these changes will require changes to our protocols. Which, in turn, means that—

> we need to have a strategy for dealing with protocol changes.

It is Client-2-Server (and Server-2-Client) protocols which tend to cause most of the trouble with regards to protocol changes

In this regard, there are a few very practical observations to be made:

▶ For Server-2-Server communications, protocol changes are rarely a problem (most of the time, we can just recompile all-our-Servers to the new protocol and restart them simultaneously).

▶ It is Client-2-Server (and Server-2-Client) protocols that tend to cause most of the trouble in this regard.

▶ For Client-Server protocols, due to Client update mechanics (in particular, as we usually do *not* want to stop gameplay while Clients are updated, more on it in Vol. V) we will likely need to support more than one version of the protocol on the Server Side at the same time. Usually it is better to think about it in terms of the "window" of protocols and/or Clients that our Server can support.

▶ In the real world, most of the protocol changes are about adding and extending fields. Removing fields is rare (and leaving an unused field is rarely a big problem).

▶ In general, I've seen three different approaches to the handling of Client-Server protocol changes:

  ▪ Version numbers. In this case, the Client has a protocol version number (and advertises it to the Server during the very first handshake). The Server "knows" a list of protocol versions it supports (and refuses to work with unsupported ones).

    • One of the big problems with version numbers is that it is quite difficult to guarantee consistency between the Server's-understanding-of-the-version-N and the Client's-understanding-of-the-version-N.

      ▷ This, however, can be at least partially alleviated by using per-message (or per-RPC-call) version numbers (opposed to per-Client version numbers). If your IDL compiler supports these per-message version numbers (more on it in the *Versioning* section below), it will certainly provide further help in this regard (and it might even work this way <wink />).

  ▷ In theory, it *might* be possible to generate a mapping of "whichever-message-versions-correspond-to-the-Client-protocol-version" during build time. However, it would lead to several significant complications, which IMVHO[182] are likely to cause more trouble than it is worth.

- Named (or otherwise identified) fields. The idea is to identify each of the fields so that we can always tell which fields were transferred and which weren't. This approach works well for XML (but XML is really wasteful in the context of Client-Server communication for games) and works a bit worse for binary protocols with field IDs (such as *protocol buffers*, which, while beating XML size-wise hands down, is still rather wasteful compared to alternatives).

- Growing messages. The very basic idea about this approach goes as follows: if we have a message that consists of some fields, *and* we know the total length of the message, then when updating our protocol we can just add fields to the end of the message for the "newer" message format (specifying default for all such added fields). For such optional fields, the parser will simply check whether the message has already ended (and fill them with defaults in this case). For an example of this approach, see the *Growing Messages. Fences* section below.

- As for choosing the best model, I've seen growing-message-based-formats to be quite robust in the real world.[183] On the other hand, it *seems* that per-message version numbers are likely to work pretty well too (especially if version support is

I've seen growing-message-based-formats to be quite robust in the real world.

---

182 I didn't try it myself.

183 i.e., "it was not-so-easy to make a stupid mistake which would break it."

provided by the IDL compiler); on the plus side, versioning can also allow obfuscation generators (more on them in Vol. VIII's chapter on Bot Fighting), and IMNSHO they're very important in the never-ending battle with cheaters. However, I am still quite reluctant about per-Client protocol version numbers (not that they cannot work in theory, but organizing your code to make them work is IMO going to be rather ugly). As for identified fields, they tend to take quite a bit of space for per-field(!) IDs (and need to reserve space for future IDs too), so I don't really like them for game-oriented Client-Server communications either (NB: they're usually perfectly fine for Server-2-Server communications).

- What's more important though is to allow ourselves more flexibility in this regard (so we could change the-way-we're-dealing-with-versions later without rewriting the whole thing). This is where IDL comes into play, effectively isolating our APIs from our on-the-wire formats and protocols.

IDL: ENCODINGS, MAPPINGS, AND PROTOCOL CHANGES

Marshalling

is the process of transforming the memory representation of an object to a data format suitable for storage or transmission, and it is typically used when data must be moved between different parts of a computer program or from one program to another.

—*Wikipedia*

While we were discussing the various MOG communications, I mentioned Interface Definition Language (IDL) quite a few times. Now it is time to take a closer look at it.

Motivation for having an IDL is simple. While manual marshalling of your data is possible, it is damn error-prone (you *manually* need to keep in sync at least two different pieces of code—the marshalling one and the un-marshalling one), not to mention being inconvenient and limiting for further optimizations. In fact, the benefits of IDL for communication were realized at least thirty years ago, which has led to the development of ASN.1 in 1984 (and in 1993, to DCE RPC).

IMO the best way to think about IDL is as a *contract* between the communicating parties. Among other things, it helps to enforce a clean separation between parts of your program (and clean separation is a Good Thing™).

Intra-Language vs Standalone

These days in game engines, quite often a (kinda) IDL is part of the language and the engine itself; examples include *[RPC]/[Command]/[SyncVar]* tags in *Unity 5*, or *UFUNCTION(Server)/UFUNCTION(Client)* declarations in *Unreal Engine 4*.

However, in most cases I still prefer to have my own IDL, and standalone (i.e., not-being-a-part-of-my-normal-program) too. The reason to have standalone IDL is that it is inherently better suited for cross-language use.

The reason to have my own IDL is that none of the IDLs I know are flexible enough to provide reasonably efficient compression for games; for example, the per-field Encoding specifications described below are not possible.

For in-language RPC declarations, we'll need to at least specify them once again in the second language (what makes code maintenance very error-prone, especially when extensions to existing RPCs are involved).[184]

The reason to have my own IDL is that none of the IDLs I know are flexible enough to provide reasonably efficient compression for games; for example, the per-field Encoding specifications described below are not possible;[185] also such features as the flexibility of having different Encodings and Mappings, the ability to map into existing structures, and support for protocol changes are either non-existent, or are present only in a very limited subset of existing IDL compilers. We'll discuss "how to implement your own IDL compiler" in Vol. IV's chapter on Marshalling and Encodings.

Still, neither having standalone IDL nor having your own IDL is a hard requirement, and you can get away with *Unity*-style or *UE4*-style RPC declarations (especially if you don't need cross-language capabilities, *and* do not care too much about compression); however, bear in mind that keeping up with protocol changes is going to be pretty ugly <sad-face />.

IDL Development Flow

With a standalone IDL (i.e., IDL that is not a part of your programming language), development flow (almost?) universally goes as follows:

1. You write your interface specification in your IDL.

    a. This IDL does *not* contain any implementation, just function and structure declarations.

2. You compile this IDL (using IDL compiler) into stub functions and structures in your programming language (or languages).

3. For the callee, you implement callee-side functions in your programming language (they will be called by IDL-compiler-generated stubs).

---

184 In theory, you could use one language as an IDL for another one, but I haven't seen such things (yet?).

185 And even if Encodings (along the lines described below) are implemented as a part of your programming language, they would make it way too cumbersome to read and maintain.

4. For the caller, you call the caller-side stub functions (again in your programming language). Note that the programming language for the caller may differ from the programming language for the callee.

One important rule to remember when using IDLs (as well as any other code generator) is:

> ***Never ever*** *make manual modifications* *to the code generated by the IDL compiler.*

Modifying generated code will prevent you from modifying the IDL itself (ouch), may violate the contract specified in IDL, and usually qualifies as a Really Bad Idea™. If you feel the need to modify your generated code, it means one of two things. Either your IDL declarations are not as you want them (then you should modify your IDL and re-compile it), or your IDL compiler doesn't do what you want (then you need to modify your IDL compiler, which is easily doable as long as you have your own IDL compiler, as suggested above).

Modifying generated code usually qualifies as a Really Bad Idea™.

IDL + Encoding + Mapping

Now, let's take a look at the features we want our IDL to have. First, we want our IDL to specify protocol that goes over the network. Second, we want to have our IDL compiler generate code in our programming language, so we can use those generated functions and structures in our code, with marshalling for them already generated by our IDL compiler.

When looking at the existing IDLs, we'll see that there is usually one single IDL that defines both these things. However, for a complicated distributed system such as an MOG, I suggest having it separated into three different files to have a clean separation of concerns, which tends to simplify things in the long run.

The first file I'm speaking about is the IDL itself. This is the only file that is strictly required. The other two files (Encoding and Mapping) should be optional on a per-struct-or-function basis, with the IDL compiler using reasonable defaults if they're not specified. The idea here is to specify only IDL to

ASN.1

Abstract Syntax Notation One (ASN.1) is a standard and notation that describes rules and structures for representing, encoding, transmitting, and decoding data in telecommunications and computer networking.

—*Wikipedia*

start working, but to have the ability to specify better-than-default encodings and mappings if or when they become necessary. We'll see an example of it a bit later.

The second file ("Encoding") is a set of additional declarations for the IDL, which allows it to define Encoding (and IDL+Encodings effectively define over-the-wire protocol). In some sense, IDL itself is similar to ASN.1 definition as such, and IDL encodings are similar to ASN.1 "Encoding Rules." In other words, IDL defines *what* we're going to communicate, and Encoding defines *how* we're going to communicate this data. On the other hand, unlike ASN.1 "Encoding Rules," our Encoding should be more flexible and allow us to specify per-field encoding if necessary.

Among other things, having Encoding separate from IDL allows us to have different encodings for the same IDL; this may be handy when, for example, the same structure is sent to both the Client and between the Servers (as optimal encodings may easily differ for Server-to-Client and Server-to-Server communications; the former is usually all about bandwidth, but for the latter CPU costs may play a significant role, as intra-Datacenter bandwidth usually comes for free until you're overloading the Ethernet port, which is not that easy these days).

The third file ("Mapping") is another set of additional declarations that define what kind of code we want to generate for our programming language. The thing here is that the same on-the-wire data can be "mapped" into different data types; moreover, there is no one single "best mapping," so it all depends on your needs at the point where you're going to use it (we'll see examples of it below). Changing "Mapping" does *not* change the on-the-wire protocol, so it can be safely changed without affecting anybody else.

In an extreme case, the "Mapping" file can be a file in your target programming language.

In an extreme case, the "Mapping" file can be a file in your target programming language.

Example: IDL

While all that theoretical discussion about IDL, Encodings, and Mapping is interesting, let's bring it a bit closer to Earth.

Let's consider a rather simple IDL example. Note that this is just an example structure in the very example IDL; the syntax of your IDL may vary very significantly (and in fact, as argued in the *Intra-Language vs. Standalone* section above, you generally *should* develop your own IDL compiler—that is, at least until somebody makes an effort and does a good job in this regard for you):

```
PUBLISHABLE_STRUCT Character {
  UINT16 character_id;

  //COORDINATES
  NUMERIC[-10000,10000] x;//for our example IDL compiler,
              // notation [a,b] means
              // "from a to b inclusive"
              //our Game World has size of
              // 20000x20000m
  NUMERIC[-10000,10000] y;
  NUMERIC[-100.,100.] z;//Z coordinate is within +- 100m

  //VELOCITIES
  NUMERIC[-10.,10.] vx;
  NUMERIC[-10.,10.] vy;
  NUMERIC[-10.,10.] vz;

  NUMERIC[0,360) angle;//where our Character is facing
              //notation [a,b) means
              // "from a inclusive to b exclusive"

  //ANIMATION
  enum Animation {Standing=0,Walking=1, Running=2} anim;
  INT[0,120) animation_frame;//120 is 2 seconds
              // of animation at 60fps

  SEQUENCE<Item> inventory;//Item is another
              // PUBLISHABLE_STRUCT
              // defined elsewhere
};
```

This IDL declares *what* we're going to communicate: a structure with the current state of our Character.[186]

On Sanitizing Input Data

For want of a nail the shoe was lost,
for want of a shoe the horse was lost;
and for want of a horse the rider was lost;
being overtaken and slain by the enemy,
all for want of care about a horse-shoe nail.

— Benjamin Franklin, *The Way to Wealth*

One important feature that IDL can (and IMO *should*) provide is data sanitizing. This is especially important when speaking about untrusted data sources, and in our context it happens whenever the data is coming from Client to Server. We'll discuss the concept of data sanitizing in more detail in Vol. IV's chapter on Basic Security, but very briefly it is related to protecting your Server-Side code from unexpected data coming from the Client. Roughly the same thing stated from a slightly different perspective is that IDL represents a contract between communicating parties, and—

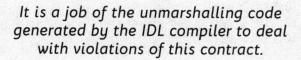

> *It is a job of the unmarshalling code generated by the IDL compiler to deal with violations of this contract.*

One further thing in this regard is that to perform sanitization efficiently, IDL should be specific enough.

One further thing in this regard is that to perform sanitization (and enforce the contract) efficiently, IDL should be specific enough. For example, if you don't have a concept of *enum* in your IDL, then you'll encode *enums* with integers. This would mean that on the receiving side, *any* integer will be seen as a valid one (while there will obviously be some invalid values). This, in turn, will lead to a lack of checks on the receiving side, allowing unexpected values to slip in and to cause all kinds of trouble on the Server-Side code; in extreme cases, it can even allow the attacker to take over your Server.

---

186   Yes, I remember that I've advised to separate inventory from frequently updated data in the *Publishable State* section, but for the purpose of this example, let's keep them together.

To avoid these things,

> *Your IDL SHOULD be as specific as possible.*

Examples of things that your IDL *should* allow in this regard include (but is not limited to):

▶ Support for *enums*.

▶ Allowing to specify whether special values (such as NaN for floats) are allowed.

▶ Support for allowed ranges for integers and floats.

▶ Support for allowed ranges of characters within strings (such as "this is a string consisting of printable-ASCII-symbols only.")

Test Case Generation

One more thing that we will be able to (and *should*) do with our IDL is to implement IDL-based test-case generation. If we know that our field is *float*, we know that there are certain special values (like *NaN*) that do qualify as test cases. If we know that our field I is an unsigned integer which should be from X to Y, we can easily generate a few test cases of interest, including such values as 0, X-1, X, X+1, Y-1, Y, Y+1, and UINT_MAX.

These test cases may be used in at least two different ways. In the first scenario, we can just run these tests and look at the results to see that the system behaves as expected. In the second scenario, we can feed these tests as "initial test cases" to a fuzz testing tool such as *afl* (see Vol. II's chapter on (Re) Actors for more on Fuzz Testing).

Fuzz Testing

Fuzz testing or fuzzing is a software testing technique, often automated or semi-automated, that involves providing invalid, unexpected, or random data to the inputs of a computer program. The program is then monitored for exceptions such as crashes, or failing built-in code assertions or for finding potential memory leaks.

—Wikipedia

Example: Mapping

Now let's see how we want to map our IDL to our programming language. Let's note that mappings of the same IDL *may* differ for different communication parties (such as Client and Server). For example, Mapping for our data above *may* look as follows for the Client:

```
MAPPING("CPP","Client") PUBLISHABLE_STRUCT Character {
  UINT16 character_id;//can be omitted, as default mapping
                    // for UINT16 is UINT16

  double x;//all 'double' declarations can be omitted too
  double y;
  double z;

  double vx;
  double vy;
  double vz;

  float angle;

  enum Animation {Standing=0,Walking=1, Running=2} anim;
      //can be omitted too
  UINT8 animation_frame;

  vector<Item> inventory;
};
```

For the Mapping specified above, the IDL-compiler-generated C++ struct may look as follows:

```
struct Character {
  UINT16 character_id;

  double x;
  double y;
  double z;

  double vx;
  double vy;
  double vz;

  float angle;

  enum Animation {Standing=0, Walking=1, Running=2} anim;
  UINT8 animation_frame;

  vector<Item> inventory;

  void idl_serialize(int serialization_type, OurOutStream& os);
    //implementation is generated separately
```

```
    void idl_deserialize(int serialization_type,
                         OurInStream& is);
       //implementation is generated separately
};
```

On the other hand, for our Server, we might want to have inventory implemented as a special class Inventory, optimized for fast handling of specific Server-Side use cases. In this case, we *may* want to define our Server-Side Mapping as follows:

```
MAPPING("CPP","Server") PUBLISHABLE_STRUCT Character {
  // here we're omitting all the default mappings
  float angle;

  class MyInventory inventory;
    //class MyInventory will be used as a type for generated
    //  Character.inventory
    //
    //To enable serialization/deserialization,
    //  MyInventory MUST implement the following
    //  member functions:
    //
    //  size_t idl_serialize_collection_get_size(),
    //  const Item& idl_serialize_collection_get_item(
    //              size_t idx),
    //  void idl_deserialize_collection_reserve_size(size_t),
    //  void idl_deserialize_collection_add_item(const Item&)
};
```

As we see, even when we're using the same programming language for both Client-Side and Server-Side, we *may* need different Mappings for different sides. One classical (though rarely occurring in practice) example is that IDL's *SEQUENCE<Item>* can be mapped either to C++'s *vector<Item>* or to *list<Item>*, depending on the specifics of your code; and as the specifics can be different on the different sides of communication, you may need to specify Mapping.

Even when we're using the same programming language for both Client-Side and Server-Side, we *may* need different Mappings for different sides.

   Moreover, in the case of different programming languages, such situations will become more frequent (in particular, collection types are usually rather different between different languages, in spite of providing similar functionality—and looking *exactly the same* on the wire).

In addition, as we can see from our example above, there is another case for non-default Mappings, which is related to making IDL-generated code to use custom classes (in our example, *MyInventory*) for generated structs (which generally helps make our generated *struct Character* more easily usable).

Mapping to Existing Classes

One thing that is commonly missing from existing IDL compilers is an ability to "map" an IDL into existing classes. As soon as you have your own IDL compiler, this can be handled in the following way:

▶ You do have your IDL and your IDL compiler.

▶ You make your IDL compiler parse your class definition in your target language (this is going to be the most difficult part, especially if parsing C++).

▶ You do specify a match between IDL fields and class fields (usually by name).

▶ Your IDL generates serialization and deserialization functions for your class.

▶ To avoid modifying your existing classes, usually, such functions won't be class members, but rather will be freestanding serialization functions (within their own class if necessary), taking the object of the needed class as a parameter.

  ▪ In programming languages such as C++, you'll need to specify these serialization and deserialization functions as *friends* of the class-you're-serializing (or to provide a macro that will do essentially the same thing). For other languages, different trickery may be needed (such as *internal* modifier for C#).

Example: Encoding

We've already discussed IDL and Mapping (and can now use our generated stubs and specify how we want them to look). Now let's see what Encoding is all about. First, let's see what will happen if we use "naïve" encoding for our C++ *struct Character*, and transfer it as a C *struct* (except for inventory field, which we'll delta-compress to avoid transferring too much of it). In this case, we'll get about 60bytes/Character/network-tick (with 6 doubles responsible for 48 bytes out of it).

Now let's consider the following Encoding:

```
ENCODING(MYENCODING1) PUBLISHABLE_STRUCT Character {
  VLQ character_id;

  DELTA {
    FIXED_POINT(0.01) x;//for rendering purposes,
                // we need our coordinates
                // only with precision of 1cm
                //validity range is already de ned
                // in IDL
                //NB: given the range and precision,
                // 'x' has 20'000'000 possible values,
                // so it can be encoded with 21 bits
    FIXED_POINT(0.01) y;
    FIXED_POINT(0.01) z;

    FIXED_POINT(0.01) vx;
    FIXED_POINT(0.01) vy;
    FIXED_POINT(0.01) vz;
  }

  DELTA FIXED_POINT(0.01) angle;//given the range
                // specified in IDL,
                // FIXED_POINT(0.01)
                // can be encoded
                // with 16 bits

  DELTA BIT(2) Animation;//can be omitted, as 2-bit is default
                        // for 3-value enum in MYENCODING1
  DELTA VLQ animation_frame;

  DELTA SEQUENCE<Item> inventory;
```

```
};
```

VLQ

A variable-length quantity (VLQ) is a universal code that uses an arbitrary number of binary octets (eight-bit bytes) to represent an arbitrarily large integer.

—*Wikipedia*

Here we're heavily relying on the properties of MYENCODING1, which is used to marshal our *struct Character*. For the purposes of our example above, let's assume that MYENCODING1 is a quite simple bit-oriented encoding that supports delta-compression (using 1 bit from bit stream to specify whether the field has been changed), and also supports VLQ-style encoding; also, let's assume that it is allowed to use rounding for FIXED_POINT fields.

As soon as we make these assumptions, specification of our example Encoding above should become rather obvious; one thing that needs to be clarified in this regard is that DELTA {} implies that we're saying that the whole block of data within brackets is likely to change together, so that our encoding will be using only a single bit to indicate that the whole block didn't change.

Now let's compare this encoding (which BTW is not necessarily the best possible one) to our original naïve encoding. Statistically, even if the Character is moving, we're looking at about 20 bytes/Character/network-tick, which is 3x better than naïve encoding.

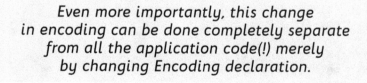

Even more importantly, this change in encoding can be done completely separate from all the application code(!) merely by changing Encoding declaration.

Such separation between the code and Encodings is in fact very useful; in particular, it allows us to use lots of optimizations that are too cumbersome to think of when you're developing application-level code.

This independence is the whole point of having Encoding separate from our IDL. It means that we can develop our code without caring about specific encodings and then, even as late as during "closed beta" stages, discover optimal encoding and get that 3x improvement by changing only the Encoding declaration.

Such separation between the code and Encodings is in fact very useful; in particular, it allows us to use lots of optimizations that are too cumbersome to think of when you're developing application-level code.

To continue our example and as a further optimization, we can add Dead Reckoning, and (as usual for this line of examples, assuming that we have our own IDL compiler) can be as simple as rewriting the Encoding above into:

```
ENCODING(MYENCODING2) PUBLISHABLE_STRUCT Character {
  VLQ character_id;

  DELTA {
    DEAD_RECKONING(x, vx, 0.02) {
              //0.02 is maximum acceptable
              // coordinate deviation
              // due to dead reckoning
      FIXED_POINT(0.01) x;
      FIXED_POINT(0.01) vx;
    }

    DEAD_RECKONING(y, vy, 0.02) {
      FIXED_POINT(0.01) y;
      FIXED_POINT(0.01) vy;
    }

    DEAD_RECKONING(z, vz) {
              //by default, maximum
              // acceptable deviation
              //  due to dead reckoning
              // is the same as for coordinate
              //  (0.01 in this case)
      FIXED_POINT(0.01) z;
      FIXED_POINT(0.01) vz;
    }
  }//DELTA

  DELTA FIXED_POINT(0.01) angle;

  DELTA BIT(2) Animation;
  DELTA VLQ animation_frame;

  DELTA SEQUENCE<Item> inventory;
};
```

When manipulating encodings is *this* simple, then experimenting with encodings to find a reasonably optimal one becomes a breeze. How much can be gained by such specialized encoding still depends on the game, but if you can

How much can be gained by each such specialized encoding still depends on the game, but if you can try-and-test a dozen different encodings within a few hours, it will usually allow you to learn quite a few things about your traffic (and also optimize things both visually and traffic-wise).

try-and-test a dozen different encodings within a few hours, it will usually allow you to learn quite a few things about your traffic (and to optimize things both visually and traffic-wise).

Protocol Changes and Backward Compatibility

One very important (and way-too-often-ignored) feature of IDLs is support for protocol changes. As discussed above, when our game becomes successful, features are added all the time, and adding a feature often implies a protocol change. With Continuous Deployment, it can happen several times a day.

As discussed above:

▶ One of the requirements in this process is that the new Server always remains backward-compatible with at least some of old Clients.

▶ The two most common changes of the protocols are (a) adding a new field, and (b) extending an existing field. These are the changes that we'll concentrate on.

▶ Adding/extending fields can be achieved by different means. So, let's take a look at our options in more detail.

Field Identifiers

The first way to allow adding/removing fields is to have field names (or other kinds of IDs) transferred alongside the fields themselves. This is the approach taken by XML, as well as by Google Protocol Buffers, where everything is always transferred as a key-value pair (with keys depending on field IDs, which can be explicitly written to the Protocol Buffer's IDL).

Therefore, to add a field, you just add in a field with a new field-ID. That's it. To be able to extend fields (and also to skip those optional-fields-you-don't-know-about), you need to have a size for each of the fields, and Google Protocol Buffers have it too (usually implicitly, via field type).

Overall, this approach works pretty well,[187] but has a cost: those 8-additional-bits-per-field[188] (to transfer the field ID+type) are not free.

Growing Messages. Fences

The second way to allow adding fields into encoded data is a bit more complicated, but allows us to deal with not-explicitly-separated (and therefore not incurring the 8-bits-per-field cost) data streams, including bitstreams. To add or extend fields to such non-discriminated streams, we may implement the following approach:

Let's introduce a concept of "fence" into our Encodings.

▶ Introduce the concept of "fence" into our Encodings. There can be "fences" within structs and/or within RPC calls.

  ▪ One possible implementation for "fences" is assuming an implicit "fence" after each field; while this approach rules out certain encodings, it does guarantee correctness.

  ▪ Between "fences," an IDL compiler is allowed to reorder and combine fields as it wishes (though any such combining and reordering *must* be strictly deterministic; i.e., defined only by input IDL+Encoding).

  ▪ Across "fences," no such reordering and combining is allowed.

▶ Then, adding a field immediately after the "fence" is guaranteed to be backward-compatible as soon as we define it with a default value.

  ▪ Within a single protocol extension, several fields can be added and extended simultaneously only after a single "fence."

  ▪ To add another field in a separate protocol update, another "fence" will be necessary.

▶ Extending a field can be implemented as adding a (sub-)field, with a special interpretation of this (sub-)field, as described in the example below.

---

187   Well, as long as you're careful with field-IDs.
188   Google Protocol Buffers use an overhead of 8 bits per field; in theory, you may use something different while using key-value encodings, but the end result won't be that much different.

Let's see how it may work if we want to extend the following Encoding:

```
ENCODING(MYENCODINGA) PUBLISHABLE_STRUCT Character {
  UINT16 character_id;

  DELTA {
    FIXED_POINT(0.01) x;
    FIXED_POINT(0.01) y;
    FIXED_POINT(0.01) z;

    FIXED_POINT(0.01) vx;
    FIXED_POINT(0.01) vy;
    FIXED_POINT(0.01) vz;
  }
};
//MYENCODINGA is a stream-based encoding
//  and simply serializes all the fields
//  in the specified order
```

Let's assume that we want to extend our *UINT16 character_id* field into *UINT32* and add another field *UINT32 some_data*. Then, after making appropriate changes to the IDL, our extended-but-backward-compatible Encoding may look as follows:

```
ENCODING(MYENCODINGA) PUBLISHABLE_STRUCT Character {
  UINT16 character_id;

  DELTA {
    FIXED_POINT(0.01) x;
    FIXED_POINT(0.01) y;
    FIXED_POINT(0.01) z;

    FIXED_POINT(0.01) vx;
    FIXED_POINT(0.01) vy;
    FIXED_POINT(0.01) vz;
  }


  //Up to this point, the bit- or byte-stream
  //  is exactly the same
  //  as for "old" encoding

  FENCE
```

```
EXTEND character_id TO UINT32;
   //at this point in the stream, there will be
   //   additional 2 bytes placed
   //   with high-bytes of character_id
   //   if after-FENCE portion is not present — character_id
   //   will use only lower-bytes from pre-FENCE portion
   UINT32 some_data DEFAULT=23;
   //if the marshalled data doesn't have
   //   after-FENCE portion,
   //   application code will get 23
};
```

As we can see, for the two most common changes of the protocols (adding a field and extending a field), making a compatible IDL is simple. Moreover, after introducing the concept of "FENCE" into IDL, making the IDL compiler compare these two IDLs to figure out that they're backward-compatible is trivial. Formally, IDL B qualifies as a backward-compatible version of IDL A, if and only if all of the following stands:

▶ IDL B starts with full IDL A.

▶ After IDL A, in IDL B there is a FENCE declaration.

▶ After the FENCE declaration, all the declarations are either EXTEND declarations or new declarations with a specified DEFAULT.

Last but not least: when implementing encoding for growing messages, we need to make sure that every independently extendable entity (such as a *PUBLISHABLE_STRUCT*) has a clear boundary in our encoding (otherwise the parser won't be able to distinguish between fields before and after the fence). One way to do it is to have such independently extendable entities first marshalled to buffer, and then further encoded as blocks of bytes; while it is certainly not the most efficient way of marking these boundaries, it should give an idea of what I am speaking about.

Versioning

The third approach to handling protocol changes is by supporting several different versions of the protocol within our Server (so that it can handle both "old" and "new" Clients).[189]

Let's note that versioning is subtly different from the two methods described above. With both field identifiers and growing messages, we were speaking about protocols that are themselves backward compatible (i.e., without any external "glue"—and forever-and-ever). In case of versioning (and as we need to support multiple protocol versions at the same time), we're speaking about *different* on-the-wire protocols that are "glued" together to support more than one such protocol.

Also, let's note that here we'll be speaking only about *per-message*[190] versioning (as opposed to per-Client versioning); as discussed above, I don't like per-Client versioning too much (and also it is less useful for obfuscation purposes, which, as discussed below, are IMO one of the biggest reasons to use versioning in the first place).

One way to deal with per-message versioning is to realize that it is only on-the-wire format that changes (while describing essentially the same data, and being mapped into the same structures); in other words, we are speaking about the same IDL and Mapping, but about different Encodings for this IDL.

With this in mind, an Encoding-with-versioning may look as follows:

```
ENCODING(MYENCODING1) PUBLISHABLE_STRUCT Character {
  VERSION 456;

  //...
};
```

Another (updated) version of the same *PUBLISHABLE_STRUCT Character* would look almost exactly the same, just adding a *some_data* field:

In the case of versioning, we're speaking about *different* on-the-wire protocols that are "glued" together to support more than one such protocol.

---

189 In general, we *may* also have the Client supporting several versions of our Server; however, to make our discussion more specific, let's center on the "single-Server-supporting-multiple-Clients" model.

190 Or *per-RPC-call.*

```
ENCODING(MYENCODING2) PUBLISHABLE_STRUCT Character {
  VERSION 457;

  //...
  UINT32 some_data;
};
```

Note that unlike with fences and field IDs, these two encodings do *not* need to be related in any way and can be *completely* different (except that they need to start with *version_number* field, which always uses the same encoding). As a result, in general these encodings are not compatible; to make an encoding that is able to accept *both* versions, we may create another "glue" Encoding:

```
ENCODING(VERSION-GLUE) PUBLISHABLE_STRUCT Character {
  SUPPORT VERSION 456 DEFAULT some_data=23;
  SUPPORT VERSION 457;
  //...
};
```

This information is sufficient to generate a parser-which-can-handle-either-version-456-or-version-457 (and if version 456 arrives, it will populate *some_data* field with the default value 23 as specified above).

Versions for Replies

By this point, we have solved the problem of dealing with multiple versions of the sender in one single receiver. However, this alone is not sufficient to handle different versions of the Client on our Server. Namely, in addition to *receiving* different versions of our message, we also need to *send* different versions of the message from our Server to our Client—moreover, these messages-being-sent-by-the-Server *must* match the version supported by our Client.

In addition to *receiving* different versions of our message, we also need to *send* different versions of the message from our Server to our Client. moreover, these messages-being-sent-by-Server, *must* match the version supported by our Client

There is more than one way to handle it, but at the moment I tend to prefer to rely on the following observation: *on the Server-Side, the vast majority of packets*[191] *sent to the Client are sent in the context of some previous request coming from the Client.* This stands regardless of whether we're working in

---

191   Usually, it is *all* the packets.

a simple HTTP-style request-response model or are dealing with state sync stuff (which amounts to the Client coming and requesting "gimme the state of Game World X, including all the future updates").

This observation, in turn, means that we can say that *whenever we send something to the Client, we must compose it using the same version number as was used by the Client's request-in-the-context-of-which-we're-sending-the-packet.* It means that we'll need to care about matching version numbers in our protocols, but, on the other hand, they still need to match only within one context (and contexts are usually relatively limited—or at least rarely changed).

To support this concept, we *should* add support for such matching version numbers into our IDL; for example, it can be done as follows:

```
MATCHING-VERSIONS {
  SUBSCRIPTION_REQUEST GameWorld_Request;
  PUBLISHABLE_STRUCT Character;

  //...
};
```

Whenever we have such specification (which BTW can often be made implicit, especially if we're speaking about RPCs and generic implementations of *state sync*), the IDL compiler can enforce that versions for all the items listed within the *MATCHING-VERSIONS* clause always match when we're compiling Client stubs. This way, we have a guarantee that as long as our Server always uses the version-number-from-corresponding-Client-request to compose its reply, the Client will get exactly the version it needs.

Let's also note that in extreme cases we can say that our *context* is just the context of the Client's connection, so *all* version numbers must be the same. This would essentially lead us to a per-Client protocol version; however, I would advise against such per-Client versions (it is significantly simpler to keep things coherent within one single context, where changes are tightly related to one another anyway).

Merits of Versioning

For a long while, I wasn't a fan of versioning (preferring growing-message approaches). However, versioning has two advantages: (a) it allows us to drop fields[192] (and, more generally, change protocol in *any* way); (b) much more importantly, it allows to use obfuscation generators; this, in turn, can provide substantial benefits against bot writers (more on it in Vol. VIII's chapter on Bot Fighting).

Much more importantly, versioning allows us to use obfuscation generators.

Which One to Choose?

After describing the three ways of making your Clients backward-compatible with your Servers, a natural question of "which one is better?" arises. As noted above, I had good experiences with growing-messages, and I see significant merits for per-message versioning too (you just cannot have too many obstacles for bot writers, so each and every improvement is a Good Thing™).

However, what IMNSHO is most important is to

> *hide all these details behind the IDL compiler, separating our code from these complexities as much as possible.*

If it is just an implementation detail of our IDL compiler, and we don't need to change our code (well, except for specifying defaults for missing fields in encodings), we can change our encodings (as well as the-way-we-handle-protocol-changes) pretty much overnight.[193] And, from what I have seen, such flexibility is usually a Very Good Thing™.

192　And unlike Field Identifiers, it allows us to drop them without polluting Field-ID space.

193　Note that for matching versions, we *may* need to add a bit of app-level code to the Server-Side, so the process will take longer; still, most of the time it won't be *too* bad.

Implementing IDL and Specific Encodings

In this chapter, we've discussed quite a lot about the *principles* behind IDL and encodings. However, at this point we won't go into any discussion about *implementing* an IDL compiler or specific encodings (neither tailored to your specific games nor existing ones such as Google Protocol Buffers). Implementing IDL compiler (including encodings and marshalling) is a separate subject that deserves a separate and rather lengthy discussion, and it belongs to the implementation realm rather than to the architecture one, so we'll come back to it in Vol. IV's chapter on Marshalling and Encodings.

SUMMARY FOR CHAPTER 3

We've spent quite a bit of time discussing MOG protocols in Chapter 3. Trying to squeeze it into a one-page summary, I think the most important things we've discussed are as follows:

▶ Simple "Client-to-Server-and-back" flow (shown on Fig. 3.1) often works well for {asynchronous|social|casino|other-slow-paced} games, but is usually not good enough for fast-paced games.

  ▪ Client-Side Interpolation, Client-Side Extrapolation, and Client-Side Prediction are your friends in this regard.

  ▪ Lag Compensation (with Server Rewind or not) and Forwarded Inputs *might* help too, but they're inherently vulnerable to cheating, so avoid them *until you're 100% sure that they're the only way to keep players happy*.

▶ You *should* start your analysis from Client-Side State, Server-Side State, and Publishable State being different.

  ▪ You *may* end up with some of them (or all of them) being the same, but it is not *that* common.

  ▪ *Don't even think* of transferring movements of all your meshes and vertexes from the Server to Clients.

    • Instead, the Publishable State *should* describe scenes in terms of macroscopic objects (and/or whole characters).

  ▪ The Server-Side State *may* be a low-poly version of the Client-Side State.

▶ Interest Management can become *the absolute must* for at least two separate reasons:

  ▪ Reducing traffic (in particular, avoiding traffic growing as $O(N^2)$), *or*

  ▪ Preventing Information Leak attacks.

▶ Minimizing data is important even before you start compression.

  ▪ Quite a few important minimizing techniques are related to fixed-point lossy representations.

▶ Compression goes well beyond traditional Delta Compression and Dead Reckoning.

  ▪ Classical algorithms such as *deflate* don't work well for games; however, some parts of them (in particular, Huffman coding and its cousins), can be used.

▶ We should start thinking about the scalability of our MOG as early as possible. Scaling to many small Game Worlds is easy,[194] but scaling to one single large (and especially seamless) Game World can be a challenge.

▶ Blocking RPCs are bad; non-blocking RPCs are good.

▶ For Server-2-Server communications, TCP is usually okay.

▶ Guarantees for reliability of Server-2-Server communications are not as easy as they may look.

  ▪ In particular, ensuring inter-database consistency guarantees is not trivial.

    • We described an Inter-DB Async Transfer protocol, which provides very strict eventual-consistency guarantees without blocking.

▶ Using MQ for Server-2-Server communications is okay, *as long as we're essentially using it as a replacement for TCP.*

▶ You *should* use IDL, one way or another.

  ▪ Standalone DIY IDL is usually preferred over an in-language and/or third-party one.

  ▪ In different contexts, the same IDL can be used more efficiently with different Encodings and/or Mappings.

---

194   Except for scaling DB, which is beyond the scope of this chapter.

- There are at least three different approaches to providing IDL with strict guarantees on backward compatibility. Among them, versioning *may* help with obfuscation, which is in turn important for Bot Fighting.

Bibliography

Aldridge, David. 2011. *I Shot You First: Networking the Gameplay of HALO: REACH.* http://www.gdcvault.com/play/1014345/I-Shot-You-First-Networking.

Amir, Gideon, and Ramon Axelrod. 2005. "2.8 Architecture and Techniques for an MMORTS." In *Massively Multiplayer Game Development 2.*

Aronson, Jesse. 1997. *"Dead Reckoning: Latency Hiding for Networked Games".* http://www.gamasutra.com/view/feature/131638/dead_reckoning_latency_hiding_for_.php.

Baryshnikov, Maksim. 2016. "Engineering Decisions behind World of Tanks Game Cluster." http://www.gdcvault.com/play/1022945/Engineering-Decisions-Behind-World-of.

Beardsley, Jason. 2003. "Seamless Servers: The Case For and Against." In *Massively Multiplayer Game Development.*

Boulanger, Jean-Sébastien, Jörg Kienzle, and Clark Verbrugge. 2006. "Comparing Interest Management Algorithms for Massively Multiplayer Games." http://gram.cs.mcgill.ca/papers/boulanger-06-comparing.pdf.

DisplayLag.com. 2017. *"Display Input Lag Database".* http://www.displaylag.com/display-database/.

Fiedler, Glenn. 2015. *Snapshot Compression.* http://gafferongames.com/networked-physics/snapshot-compression/.

—. 2015. *State Synchronization.* http://gafferongames.com/networked-physics/state-synchronization/.

Frohnmayer, Mark, and Tim Gift. 1999. *The TRIBES Engine Networking Model.* http://gamedevs.org/uploads/tribes-networking-model.pdf.

Gambetta, Gabriel. 2013. *"Fast-Paced Multiplayer (Part II): Client-Side Prediction and Server Reconciliation".* http://www.gabrielgambetta.com/fpm2.html.

—. 2013. *"Fast-Paced Multiplayer (Part IV): Headshot! (AKA Lag Compensation)"*. http://www.gabrielgambetta.com/fpm4.html.

—. 2013. *"Fast-Paced Multiplayer"*. http://www.gabrielgambetta.com/fpm1.html.

Glazer, Joshua, and Sanjay Madhav. 2016. "Multiplayer Game Programming."

Grigorik, Ilya. n.d. *"High Performance Browser Networking"*. http://chimera.labs.oreilly.com/books/1230000000545/ch01.html.

Human Benchmark. 2017. *Reaction Time Statistics*. http://www.humanbenchmark.com/tests/reactiontime/statistics.

Ignatchenko, Sergey. 1998. *"An Algorithm for Online Data Compression"*. http://www.drdobbs.com/an-algorithm-for-online-data-compression/184403560.

Leadbetter, Richard. 2009. *"Console Gaming: The Lag Factor"*. http://www.eurogamer.net/articles/digitalfoundry-lag-factor-article.

Lightstreamer. 2006. *lightstreamer white paper*. http://www.lightstreamer.com/docs/Lightstreamer_WhitePaper.pdf.

Lipps, David B., Andrzej T. Galecki, and James A. Ashton-Miller. 2011. *"On the Implications of a Sex Difference in the Reaction Times of Sprinters at the Beijing Olympics"*. http://journals.plos.org/plosone/article?id=10.1371/journal.pone.0026141.

McShaffry, Mke, and David "Rez" Graham. 2012. "Game Coding Complete 4th Edition."

Murphy, Curtiss. 2011. "Believable Dead Reckoning for Networked Games." In *Game Engine Gems 2*.

Pasini, Filippo L. Scognamiglio. 2014. *"The Myths Of Graphics Card Performance: Debunked"*. http://www.tomshardware.com/reviews/graphics-card-myths,3694-4.html.

Rabbit MQ. 2011. *AMQP 0-9-1 Complete Reference Guide*. https://www.rabbitmq.com/amqp-0-9-1-reference.html.

Simpson, Zachary Booth. 2000. *A Stream-based Time Synchronization Technique For Networked Computer Games*. http://www.mine-control.com/zack/timesync/timesync.html.

Smith, Roger, and Don Stoner. 2005. "2.11 Time and Event Synchronization Across an MMP Server Farm." In *Massively Multiplayer Game Development 2*.

West, Mick. 2008. *Measuring Responsiveness in Video Games.* http://www.
gamasutra.com/view/feature/3725/measuring_responsiveness_in_
video_.php.

Wikipedia. 2017. *Huffman coding.*
https://en.wikipedia.org/wiki/Huffman_coding.

—. 2017. *Input Lag.* https://en.wikipedia.org/wiki/Input_lag.

—. 2017. *Internet Exchanges.* https://en.wikipedia.org/wiki/List_of_
Internet_exchange_points_by_size.

Zarb-Adami, Mark. 2002. "2.4 Quaternion Compression." In *Game
Programming Gems 3.*

ZeroMQ. 2012. *Broker vs. Brokerless.*
http://zeromq.org/whitepapers:brokerless.

VOLUME I
SUMMARY

In this volume, we started at the very beginning—and, for games, the "very beginning" is the Game Design Document also known as the GDD (discussed in Chapter 1); most importantly, we concentrated on those GDD issues that are *specific for multiplayer games* (and, evidently, there are quite a few).

Then, in Chapter 2, we proceeded to the all-important argument of "should our game be P2P or Server-based, or Deterministic Lockstep-based," and found that, considering the risks coming from cheaters (and them attacking *all* successful games), our only viable option for a multiplayer-game-with-thousands-of-simultaneous-players is Authoritative Servers.

In Chapter 3, we ended preliminaries and got to the real stuff—specifically, to communications and communication flows. First, we briefly examined[195] different communication flows between the Client and the Server from the viewpoint of latencies, input lag, and RTTs. We started from simplistic Server->Client->Server communication (which works only for slower games), and went all the way to Client-Side Prediction, Lag Compensation, and Forwarded Inputs (eventually reaching the state-of-the-art latency-wise).

Then, we arrived at the all-important question of reducing traffic. This discussion included varied topics such as having the Client State different from the Server State and also different from the Publishable State, Interest Management (which also has very important implications in reducing the potential for cheating), and then we tried to systematize different flavors of Compression.

Afterward, we briefly mentioned Scalability (it was just a small part of the overall discussion on Scalability; more to follow in Vol. III, Vol. VI, and Vol.

---

195   Yes, thirty pages is a very brief discussion for this kind of thing.

IX), and examined Server-2-Server communications (including the all-important Async Inter-DB Transfer protocol; we'll need it desperately later to achieve DB scalability). And, last but not least, we discussed an Interface Definition Language; while it is possible to do without IDL, it provides *so* many advantages that I certainly advise *not* to do any serious new development without one.

WHAT'S NEXT

Now, we're prepared to start discussing the building blocks of our system—and Client-Side architecture.

Development and Deployment of

MULTIPLAYER ONLINE GAMES

Volume II: DIY, (Re)Actors, Client Arch, Unity/UE4/Lumberyard

In Vol. II, we'll start with Chapter 4, briefly arguing what-we-should-do-ourselves and what-we-should-reuse.

Then, in Chapter 5, we'll get to presenting my favorite way of implementing distributed systems—(Re)Actors (a.k.a. event-driven programs, a.k.a. Game Loops, a.k.a. ad-hoc Finite State Machines, et cetera, et cetera). While (Re)Actors are not *strictly* required to get your game flying, for medium- and larger-sized games, they tend to get you there *much* faster (and tend to result in *much* more reliable programs). When speaking about (Re)Actors, we'll discuss quite a few related issues, from handling RPC returns in a non-blocking manner (with a whopping *eight* different ways to do it(!)) to determinism (which tends to help a lot with debugging and testing, including such things as replay-based testing and production post-factum debugging), as well as various ways to scale and organize (Re)Actors.

Chapter 6 will be dedicated to Client-Side Architecture; we'll examine both generic architecture and a (Re)Actor-based one (as a specialization of the former). In addition, we'll also address the questions of choosing a programming language for the Client-Side (including ways to use C++ for browser) and integrating web-based stuff with downloadable Clients.

Last but not least, in Chapter 7, there will be an examination of the different ways of "how 3rd-party game engines can be used to build your MOG." In particular, special attention will be paid to comparing several popular game engines (specifically, Unity, UE, Lumberyard, and Urho3D) and also the associated network technologies and libraries (including Photon and RUDP libraries).

This will conclude Vol. II.

INDEX

LETTER FROM THE AUTHOR

Hello, fellow game developer!

I hope you've found something of interest (and maybe even useful) within all my barely coherent blabbering. And I hope that you're going to get your hands on Vol. II of this epic work.

For the time being, chapters of 1st beta of Vol. II-VI are available on ithare.com/category/dnd-of-mogs-vol1-1st-beta/ and ithare.com/category/dnd-of-mogs-vol2-1st-beta/, with more content added every week. If you have any comments or criticism, please e-mail me at nobugs@ithare.com, or comment right on the site. For this volume, Vol. I, comments from website readers (and on Reddit) have helped add a lot of previously missing things, and have fixed quite a few mistakes of varying severity. THANKS A LOT to everybody who pointed out omissions and mistakes (and I hope for further comments to also make future volumes better)!

Last but not least:

Please consider
reviewing this book on Amazon

(or Goodreads, if you already have an account). It will help both me (the author) and others who could benefit from reading this book. The landscape of even-somewhat-useful books on multiplayer game programming is IMO really barren these days, so letting others know that there is something worth reading is really important.

Best regards (and thanks for reading this far <smile />),

No Bugs Hare

Printed in the USA
CPSIA information can be obtained
at www.ICGtesting.com
LVHW010232101123
763580LV00004B/15

9 783903 213067